Palgrave Macmillan Studies in Family and Intimate L

Titles include:

Graham Allan, Graham Crow and Sheila Hawker
STEPFAMILIES

Harriet Becher
FAMILY PRACTICES IN SOUTH ASIAN MUSLIM FAMILIES
Parenting in a Multi-Faith Britain

Elisa Rose Birch, Anh T. Le and Paul W. Miller
HOUSEHOLD DIVISIONS OF LABOUR
Teamwork, Gender and Time

Deborah Chambers
SOCIAL MEDIA AND PERSONAL RELATIONSHIPS
Online Intimacies and Networked Friendship

Robbie Duschinsky and Leon Antonio Rocha (*editors*)
FOUCAULT, THE FAMILY AND POLITICS

Jacqui Gabb
RESEARCHING INTIMACY IN FAMILIES

Stephen Hicks
LESBIAN, GAY AND QUEER PARENTING
Families, Intimacies, Genealogies

Clare Holdsworth
FAMILY AND INTIMATE MOBILITIES

Peter Jackson (*editor*)
CHANGING FAMILIES, CHANGING FOOD

Riitta Jallinoja and Eric Widmer (*editors*)
FAMILIES AND KINSHIP IN CONTEMPORARY EUROPE
Rules and Practices of Relatedness

Lynn Jamieson, Ruth Lewis and Roona Simpson (*editors*)
RESEARCHING FAMILIES AND RELATIONSHIPS
Reflections on Process

David Morgan
RETHINKING FAMILY PRACTICES

Eriikka Oinonen
FAMILIES IN CONVERGING EUROPE
A Comparison of Forms, Structures and Ideals

Róisín Ryan-Flood
LESBIAN MOTHERHOOD
Gender, Families and Sexual Citizenship

Sally Sales
ADOPTION, FAMILY AND THE PARADOX OF ORIGINS
A Foucauldian History

Tam Sanger
TRANS PEOPLE'S PARTNERSHIPS
Towards an Ethics of Intimacy

Elizabeth B. Silva
TECHNOLOGY, CULTURE, FAMILY
Influences on Home Life

Lisa Smyth
THE DEMANDS OF MOTHERHOOD
Agents, Roles and Recognitions

Palgrave Macmillan Studies in Family and Intimate Life
Series Standing Order ISBN 978–0–230–51748–6 hardback
978–0–230–24924–0 paperback
(*outside North America only*)

You can receive future titles in this series as they are published by placing a standing order. Please contact your bookseller or, in case of difficulty, write to us at the address below with your name and address, the title of the series and the ISBN quoted above.

Customer Services Department, Macmillan Distribution Ltd, Houndmills, Basingstoke, Hampshire RG21 6XS, England

Stepfamilies

Graham Allan
Keele University, UK

Graham Crow
University of Edinburgh, UK

and

Sheila Hawker
C&S Academic Services

First published 2011
Published in paperback 2013 by
PALGRAVE MACMILLAN

Palgrave Macmillan in the UK is an imprint of Macmillan Publishers Limited, registered in England, company number 785998, of Houndmills, Basingstoke, Hampshire RG21 6XS.

Palgrave Macmillan in the US is a division of St Martin's Press LLC, 175 Fifth Avenue, New York, NY 10010.

Palgrave Macmillan is the global academic imprint of the above companies and has companies and representatives throughout the world.

Palgrave® and Macmillan® are registered trademarks in the United States, the United Kingdom, Europe and other countries.

ISBN 978–1–403–90492–8   hardback
ISBN 978–1–137–32408–5   paperback

This book is printed on paper suitable for recycling and made from fully managed and sustained forest sources. Logging, pulping and manufacturing processes are expected to conform to the environmental regulations of the country of origin.

A catalogue record for this book is available from the British Library.

A catalog record for this book is available from the Library of Congress.

10   9   8   7   6   5   4   3   2   1
22   21   20   19   18   17   16   15   14   13

Printed and bound in Great Britain by
CPI Antony Rowe, Chippenham and Eastbourne

For Charlotte, Dan, Mia, Katie, Belle, Maddie, Ed, Isabelle and Caspar, each one both a grandchild and a step-grandchild

Contents

List of Diagrams and Tables

Diagrams

Tables

Series Editors' Preface

The remit of the *Palgrave Macmillan Studies in Family and Intimate Life* series is to publish major texts, monographs and edited collections focusing broadly on the sociological exploration of intimate relationships and family organization. As editors we think such a series is timely. Expectations, commitments and practices have changed significantly in intimate relationship and family life in recent decades. This is very apparent in patterns of family formation and dissolution, demonstrated by trends in cohabitation, marriage and divorce. Changes in household living patterns over the last twenty years have also been marked, with more people living alone, adult children living longer in the parental home and more 'non-family' households being formed. Furthermore, there have been important shifts in the ways people construct intimate relationships. There are few comfortable certainties about the best ways of being a family man or woman, with once conventional gender roles no longer being widely accepted. The normative connection between sexual relationships and marriage or marriage-like relationships is also less powerful than it once was. Not only is greater sexual experimentation accepted, but it is now accepted at an earlier age. Moreover heterosexuality is no longer the only mode of sexual relationship given legitimacy. In Britain as elsewhere, gay male and lesbian partnerships are now socially and legally endorsed to a degree hardly imaginable in the mid-twentieth century. Increases in lone-parent families, the rapid growth of different types of stepfamily, the de-stigmatization of births outside marriage and the rise in couples 'living-apart-together' (LATs) all provide further examples of the ways that 'being a couple', 'being a parent' and 'being a family' have diversified in recent years.

The fact that change in family life and intimate relationships has been so pervasive has resulted in renewed research interest from sociologists and other scholars. Increasing amounts of public funding have been directed to family research in recent years, in terms of both individual projects and the creation of family research centres of different hues. This research activity has been accompanied by the publication of some very important and influential books exploring different aspects of shifting family experience, in Britain and elsewhere. The *Palgrave Macmillan Studies in Family and Intimate Life* series hopes to add to this list of influential research-based texts, thereby contributing to existing knowledge and informing current debates. Our main audience consists of academics and advanced students, though we intend that the books in the series will be accessible to a more general readership who wish to understand better the changing nature of contemporary family life and personal relationships.

We see the remit of the series as wide. The concept of 'family and inti-mate life' will be interpreted in a broad fashion. While the focus of the series will clearly be sociological, we take family and intimacy as being inclusive rather than exclusive. The series will cover a range of topics concerned with family practices and experiences, including, for exam-ple, partnership; marriage; parenting; domestic arrangements; kinship; demographic change; intergenerational ties; life course transitions; step-families; gay and lesbian relationships; lone-parent households; and also non-familial intimate relationships such as friendships. We also wish to foster comparative research, as well as research on under-studied populations. The series will include different forms of book. Most will be theoretical or empirical monographs on particular substantive topics, though some may also have a strong methodological focus. In addition, we see edited collections as also falling within the series' remit, as well as translations of significant publications in other languages. Finally we intend that the series has an international appeal, in terms of both top-ics covered and authorship. Our goal is for the series to provide a forum for family sociologists conducting research in various societies, and not solely in Britain.

Graham Allan, Lynn Jamieson and David Morgan

Acknowledgements

We would like to thank the people who took part in this study. We very much appreciate the time they gave us and their willingness to discuss in detail their family relationships and experiences. We would also like to thank our colleagues at Keele University and the University of Southampton for providing us with supportive environments in which to work. We are especially grateful to David Morgan who read through an earlier draft of this book and to Philippa Grand, Jill Lake and Olivia Middleton at Palgrave Macmillan for their help and patience. Finally we would also like to acknowledge the support we received from the Economic and Social Research Council to undertake the research on which this book is based (Grant number R000237504: Step-Families and the Construction of Kinship).

1
Introduction

It is common for people to claim that family life is altering. In every era, pundits of different types, as well as those with a professional interest in the subject, assert that families are not what they were, sometimes tinged with regret for a more wholesome past. Leaving aside the normative evaluation, such a perspective on change is not mistaken. Families are never static; modification and change are not only entirely normal, they are built into the very nature of family life. Indeed, as Hareven (1982) argued, conceptually family change can be understood as having three distinct dimensions: historical, cohort and life course. Life course change reflects the changes that individuals experience as they age, as their different relationships develop, mature and end, in whatever patterns emerge as they construct their biographies. Cohort change refers not solely to individual experience but to change that impinges on those who are born at a particular time and age together. The contingencies of their lives are patterned by wider social and economic events – war, recession, political upheaval, technological developments, etc – which shape and structure their lives, including their familial relationships, in ways which render them different from the experiences of previous and future cohorts. Finally, historical change refers to longer-term changes in family organisation and patterning, often consequent on structural transformations in a society's social and economic formation. Importantly what starts as a cohort change may, over time, be understood as a more permanent and fundamental historical shift.

There is no doubt that currently Britain, like other western, industrial countries, is experiencing significant shifts in many aspects of family life (Allan and Crow, 2001; González-López, 2002; Williams, 2004; Widmer and Jallinoja, 2008). Moreover it seems likely that these changes are historical rather than cohort changes. That is, the ways in which family life is currently altering represents a restructuring of family relationships that is likely to result in a long-term modification to family patterns. While explaining the changes there have been is complex, it is relatively easy to describe them. Most evidently, over the last 40 years, demographic patterns of family and household formation and dissolution have changed dramatically (Cherlin, 2004). In particular, since the 1970s, there have been large increases in births outside marriage, in cohabitation, in divorce, in lone-parent households, in second and subsequent marriages, in lone-person and non-family households and in gay and lesbian families. In essence, whereas once the majority of people's family lives followed a more or less standard pattern, this is no longer the case to anything like the same degree. The notion of a 'family cycle' in which people passed through a standard series of stages in their family life – from, quite typically, living in the parental home, to marriage, to child-rearing, to 'empty nest', to death of one of the partners – no longer equates with the experiences people have. Now it is more sensible to conceptualise phases in family experience in terms of 'family course', involving different commitments and responsibilities at different times, but lacking the standard ordering inherent in a 'family cycle' perspective.

Within this, two overarching issues are paramount. First, there has been a very clear separation of sex, birth and marriage, a point emphasised by Lewis and Kiernan, (1996; see also Lewis, 2001). Whereas once these three were understood as a 'package', with sex and childbirth accepted as only legitimate within the regulation of marriage, this is no longer so. The rise of cohabitation as an accepted form of union and the growth in the numbers of births to single and cohabiting women clearly reflects shifts in normative understandings of the trilogy which 'sex-childbirth-marriage' previously formed. Second, and a little more contentiously, the changes there have been signify a shift in cultural assumptions about the character of commitment, intimacy and love. Whereas for much of the twentieth century, the dominant form of partnership – marriage – was taken to entail a lifelong commitment, this no longer holds to anything like the same extent. Those who marry certainly still hope and desire that their union lasts their lifetime, but there is now a far greater acceptance that it might not. Moreover, those in other committed 'partnerships' – typically cohabitation, though the number of 'LAT' couples, (couples 'living apart together') has also grown – do not necessarily define their commitment to their relationships as lifelong. Increasingly, intimate relationships are understood to be contingent on their providing continuing satisfactions. Once it is recognised that they no longer do provide this, the moral position is not simply to accept this 'for better or for worse', but to end the relationship and 'move on' to other relationships or forms of living. Here, despite the criticisms that can be made of them (see, in particular, Jamieson, 1998, 1999; Smart, 2007), the arguments of Giddens (1992) and Beck and Beck-Gernsheim (1995) have a clear resonance with the spirit of the changes occurring, as indeed does the increasing dominance of the term 'partnership' to describe committed, intimate relationships.

As its title indicates, this book focusses on one aspect of these changes: the emergence and growth of stepfamilies as an increasingly common familial/household form over the last 30 years. While in the past, death – and especially maternal death – and remarriage generated numerous stepfamilies, in recent years the numbers of such families have grown rapidly as a consequence of the types of change discussed above, particularly increases in non-marital births, cohabitation, divorce, remarriage and other forms of serial partnership. The 2001 census revealed that stepfamilies comprised 10 per cent of all households with dependent children in them (ONS, 2005) and the proportion is likely to have increased since then. There are many more children in lone-parent households whose other parent is married or cohabiting and who are consequently involved in (partly or wholly) non-resident stepfamilies. Many other people are also party to (non-resident) stepfamilies as adults, through parents' or children's new unions. It seems highly probable that these trends will continue in the medium term resulting in increasing numbers of stepfamilies being formed (and dissolved). Moreover as these patterns become more common and result in greater numbers of serial partnerships across the generations, the familial and household experiences of those in stepfamilies are likely to become increasingly complex.

Rather surprisingly, there remains little public focus on stepfamilies. Other alternative forms of family, in particular, lone-parent families, have received a great deal more public attention, both from official agencies and within the media. Indeed, to some degree, stepfamilies seem to have been regarded as the 'solution' to the problems of lone-parent families. They appear to represent a reconstituted form of the so-called natural nuclear family, and thus do not warrant specific interest in their own right. As discussed further in Chapter 2, one clear indicator of this is the limited attention family law has given to the legal implications and consequences of stepfamily relationships, despite their increasing numbers, in Britain as well as in other jurisdictions (Edwards, Gillies and Ribbens McCarthy, 1999; Malia, 2005; Atkin, 2008).

There are also notably few voluntary agencies which seek to cater for any specific concerns of stepfamilies, and those there have been often struggle to survive. The National Stepfamily Association – which was Britain's main agency concerned with stepfamily issues – for example, merged into Parentline Plus, a government-sponsored association, in 2000, as a consequence diluting, if not altogether losing, its special identity as a forum for stepfamily debate. In many ways, the relative paucity of interest in stepfamilies reflects the ways in which stepfamilies themselves seek to be portrayed. Although in 'private' contexts people involved in stepfamilies regularly recognise the particular issues this form of family generates, in more 'public' settings they are often at pains to present themselves simply as ordinary families (Ganong and Coleman, 2004). As writers like Burgoyne and Clark (1984) and Ribbens McCarthy, Edwards and Gillies (2003) have pointed out, this also influences the extent to which people choose to use the term 'stepfamily' as a descriptor of their family situation. This is an important issue. Contemporarily, given the changes there have been in family demography, stepfamilies are at one and the same time 'ordinary families', yet ordinary families in which particular, shared issues, tensions and dilemmas can arise. In part, this book is concerned with analysing and understanding this duality.

Stepfamilies

Overall, the book seeks to provide a quite broad-ranging sociological analysis of some of the main characteristics of stepfamily life and to examine the particular issues and challenges which often confront people in stepfamilies. In part, it will focus on the internal dynamics of stepfamily households. However, it will also be concerned with the relationships that people in stepfamilies sustain with those outside the household. Indeed, one of the key features of stepfamilies reflects precisely this issue. Relationships within the stepfamily household are affected in numerous ways by other individuals and relationships outside of it. This, of course, is generally true of all family relationships. Family relationships do not exist in isolation; by the very nature of family connection, they are part of a wider kinship network in which any particular relationship, or set of relationships, is liable to be influenced by other relationships in that network. However, this issue tends to be more acute in stepfamilies because of the genealogical significance of those outside the household. As Walker and Messinger (1979) argued some years ago, the boundaries around stepfamilies are more permeable than the boundaries around 'natural' families (see Chapter 4).

We will follow some of our respondents' lead here and use the term 'natural' families in this book to refer to families in which a married or cohabiting couple are the biological parents of all their children. Among the other terms sometimes used to describe these families are 'first-time' (or 'first'), 'biological', 'blood', 'reconstituted' and 'real'. There is little agreement among either researchers or the general public about the most appropriate term. However in using the term 'natural' we are not suggesting that such families are more 'natural' in any other sense. For ease of flow, we will not place the term 'natural' in quotation marks in the rest of the book.

The book is also going to focus on a wide range of different types of stepfamily (Coleman, Troilo and Jamison, 2008; Teachman and Tedrow, 2008). Frequently when people think of stepfamilies, they think of a household in which two married adults are living with dependent children who are biologically related to only one of the adults. Even this incorporates diverse patterns. In many instances, children will be living with their mother and a stepfather, but they may also be living with stepsiblings – their stepfather's natural children – and more commonly half-siblings – children born to their mother and stepfather. So too, some children live with their father and a stepmother, and some of these also live with stepsiblings or half-siblings. In many other cases, stepsiblings may live with their other parent, but play some part in the stepfamily household. Obviously too, increasingly complex patterns are being forged as the developing emphasis on continuing parental responsibility encourages the maintenance of relationships between non-resident parents and their children. In addition though, some stepfamilies are more fluid in their domestic arrangements with children living with one parent for some of the time and the other parent at other times. This may be for regular days each week, for alternate weeks or occasionally for longer periods at particular parts of the year, summer holidays for example. And again one or both parents may now be living with a new partner, with or without step or half-siblings present when the children are there (Stewart, 2007).

One issue here is that stepfamilies are not the same as households (see Chapter 2). Within everyday thought – and much social science – the terms 'family' and 'household' have been treated as though they were synonymous. But, of course, they are not, an issue that has become particularly clear with the growth of demographic diversity in recent years. Essentially 'family' refers to genealogical connection, while 'household' refers to co-residence and common domestic economies (see Allan and Crow, 2001). In analysing stepfamilies, we will at times be concerned with domestic arrangements and the dynamics of household living. However at other times we will be focussing on ties of kinship – or its absence – as effectively it is this which defines a stepfamily as a stepfamily. And within this, we will not only be concerned with family or kin relationships within a household. We will also be examining stepfamily relationships outside of households. As implied above, this involves repartnered parents with dependent children who are living with their other parent rather than the repartnered one. However it also involves stepfamilies with non-dependent children, that is, children who are adult and living with neither parent. These people also belong to stepfamilies, though the issues they face at a day-to-day level are different from those in a stepfamily household.

Further factors add to the diversity of stepfamilies. There is, for example, the age of the children when their parent or parents repartner. In some instances, this happens at a very early age, with the step-parent taking on a primary 'parenting' role. Other children will have lived with both parents before their separation, and then spent some time in a lone-parent family before the stepfamily was formed. And for some, the new partnership will have been formed after they became socially and economically independent of their parents. Furthermore, in some cases, children will have had a period to develop a relationship with their step-parent prior to any co-residence; in others, there will be less time to adjust to the new stepfamily. So too, there may be a wide or narrow age difference between stepsiblings and half-siblings; some children will have experienced serial stepfamilies as their parents become involved in different relationships; and some will be part of a stepfamily household for only a short period. Moreover, as noted above, there will be differences in their involvement with their non-resident parent which is likely to depend on, as well as influence, the way the stepfamily operates.

These and other such related matters all generate wide diversity in the circumstances of stepfamilies and in the experiences which their members have. No two families are ever entirely the same, and this applies to stepfamilies as much as any other type of family (Cheal, 2002). Equally though, there are certainly commonalities in the issues which arise in stepfamilies and correspondences in the responses which emerge. Nonetheless recognising diversity *within* stepfamilies is as important as recognising diversity *between* them. In many regards, families are culturally understood as social and economic groupings with a shared identity and a collective experience. To talk of 'the family' is to emphasise its unity and similarity. Yet different family members experience their family in quite distinct ways. Children do not 'live' family life the same way as parents, nor do mothers and fathers, husbands and wives, brothers and sisters or older and younger siblings. Experientially, each individual is embedded in a different set of relationships with different constraints, responsibilities, freedoms and futures.

This most certainly applies to stepfamilies. As we will develop in later chapters, the sense of unity which 'family' represents is frequently less evident in stepfamilies than natural families. Its members do not always see themselves as having evidently shared commitments and common interests in the way natural families often do. For example, while the children may share solidarity with their natural parent in the household, they may not feel any loyalty or commitment to their step-parent. In turn, the step-parent may define his or her participation in the family as essentially dependent on the relationship with the natural parent, and understand their involvement with the stepchildren in household rather than familial terms. So too, the members of a step-family may not yet have forged the shared history which serves to unite natural families. Their different pasts may contain elements which serve to separate rather than generate a common identity. As importantly, within stepfamilies there are differing loyalties, both within the house-hold and outside it as a consequence of the different kinship histories and family relationships different members have. While there is always differentiation as well as identification within natural families, at issue here is the extent to which these are liable to be more marked within stepfamilies.

In other ways too stepfamilies can be recognised as both complex and diverse. While facing the same issues as natural families, the way these are resolved often differ in significant ways. To pick an obvious example, modes of household order and the disciplining of children vary across families. However, in stepfamilies there are added compli-cations because of the more complex considerations which influence the development of step-parental relationships. Thus, depending on their age, children may be less liable to accept control and discipline in whatever form from step-parents than from natural parents. Some of the natural parents in these households may also have reservations about the degree to which a step-parent should be involved in disci-plining and in other aspects of day-to-day childcare. So too step-parents may want to impose a different order within the household to the one already established. Within natural families, these same issues of how the family/household is to be ordered inevitably arise, with the two parents sometimes taking different stances. Yet within such families, the right of both parents to be involved in such matters is rarely questioned – it is part of their joint, established parenting role. Within stepfamilies, parental rights and responsibilities are far less clear-cut. The issues are more contentious than they usually are in natural families, generating more diversity (and less certainty) in how parenting is managed.

In turn, the parenting role adapted over time by the non-resident natural parent is also likely to impact at some level on the management of childcare within the household. Again here, recognising that there is no standard pattern within this is important. Over time, different families, different parents, establish different arrangements for their parenting. Expressed simply, some non-resident parents continue to play a very active part in their children's lives, while others become distant or even absent figures (Bradshaw et al., 1999). The relative involvement of the non-resident parent is likely to be one – but only one – of the factors which influence the parenting role the step-parent adopts. And, importantly, the patterns of non-resident parents' involvement with their children has been altering. As Burgoyne and Clark (1984), for example, indicate, a little over a generation ago there was a tendency to believe that children benefited most from a 'clean break'. Non-resident fathers especially often tended to have rather little to do with their children, in part presuming that an absence of contact led to a more rapid adjustment. Recently policy, research and common practice have fostered different responses. Now the emphasis is far more on parents having a continuing relationship with their children, irrespective of their partnership circumstances. As would be expected, this has again generated more complexity and more diversity in the arrangements which stepfamilies negotiate and establish.

The involvement of other non-household family members will also vary depending on a range of circumstances. An obvious issue, though one which relates more to divorce than to stepfamilies *per se*, is the relationship maintained between the grandparents on the non-resident parent's side and their grandchildren. Often this is mediated by the relationship the non-resident parent has with his or her children, though this is not always so in a direct sense. In some cases, these relationships may be shaped more by the relationship these grandparents sustain with their ex-daughter-in-law or ex-son-in-law. Stepfamily formation may also have a consequence for the development of these relationships, though inevitably there is diversity in the specific outcomes which follow in individual cases. So too other ties with the non-resident parent's kin may be affected through the creation of a stepfamily. In some instances, little may change, particularly if the separation or divorce had already led to reduced involvement in these relationships or if the relationship is routinely mediated through the non-resident parent. In other cases, the existence of a stepfamily may generate additional practical or symbolic dynamics that pattern the negotiation of kinship ties.

The complexity of stepfamilies is also evident in the relationships different stepfamily members develop with the step-parent's kin. In particular, the existence of stepsiblings from a previous partnership that the step-parent had is likely to impact on the stepfamily household in numerous and diverse ways. This will be most evident when the stepsiblings are themselves members of the household, either regularly or periodically. Even when they are not, the character of the relationships maintained between the various members of the wider stepfamily will be diverse, sometimes reflecting a degree of cohesion and solidarity, and in other cases generating a sense of separateness and difference which itself may or may not be experienced as problematic. Equally, the involvement of the step-parent's own parents with the stepfamily will be varied. This may range from an active, 'grandparent-appropriate' participation in their stepgrandchildren's lives to an absence of any significant involvement at all beyond cordiality when they meet. So too, other members of the step-parent's kin may have little involvement with the stepfamily or alternatively construct familial relationships with them. Collectively there are few normative understandings about these matters, and consequently a good deal of variation in their practical enactment.

Outline of the book

This book is concerned with exploring and understanding these types of issue. It seeks to provide a sociological portrayal of contemporary stepfamily life, but one which recognises the diversity there is in different people's experiences of this family form. It focusses on a broad range of matters which impinge on stepfamily living, but does not seek to 'problematise' these issues or suggest solutions to any of the various dilemmas particular stepfamilies face. Rather, it is concerned with the different ways in which members of stepfamilies construct their family lives, the various complexities and dilemmas they face in doing this, the patterns of negotiation and response involved and the consequences these have for the routine operation of family life – or in Morgan's (1996, 2011) useful term, 'family practices'.

As noted above, the book's focus is both on 'family as kinship' and on 'family as household'. In stepfamilies, as in other forms of family, the management of relationships within the household lies at the heart of much family life. It is within the relationships occurring here that 'family' is lived out; it is within this arena of daily living that the joys and tensions, conflicts and rewards of the institution we know as 'family' most commonly occur. Certainly it would be impossible to analyse stepfamilies adequately without recognising the centrality of a shared household to the dynamics which arise. It is within the household that many key aspects of family order, family resources and family member-ship are played out.

Yet as we will develop in Chapter 2, 'family' is more than just 'house-holds'. Our understandings of 'family' are also patterned by ideas we have about belonging, commitment and solidarity. In this sense, family is about kinship – about our relationships with those others who, conven-tionally or otherwise, we come to see as sharing a common bond, a degree of unity and membership of a broader collective. Who is included within this broader collective is neither uniform nor static. Membership changes over time, as do the relationships we have with those who are members. Nor are relationships with those who we define as 'family' necessarily positive or supportive. Moreover, as noted above, different members of what at an everyday level is commonly referred to and regarded as the 'same' family have different kinships and different solidarities with those who are members, notwithstanding a high degree of overlap.

The concerns of this book are as much on issues to do with 'family as kinship' as they are on 'family as household'. While it would be wrong to overplay the distinction between them, equally both need to be incor-porated into any analysis of the ways in which stepfamily members construct and experience their family lives (Coleman and Ganong, 1990). To do this, the book relies heavily on material from a study of stepfamily kinship undertaken in England by the authors and funded by the ESRC. However the book is not designed simply as a report on this research. Rather it seeks to integrate material from this study with ideas and infor-mation from a range of other research in order to produce a volume in which key aspects of stepfamily life can be more fully interrogated and better understood. In the process we also hope that the book will con-tribute to knowledge about broader family and kinship practices and to debates on how 'families' are constructed in late modernity, a period in which there have been major transformations in the demographic and social ordering of family life.

The research study

The empirical study on which this book draws was designed to examine the complexity of family and kin relationships in stepfamilies. More specifically, it sought to analyse the patterns of kinship identification and solidarity within stepfamilies, how different family loyalties were negotiated and managed and how kin-based dilemmas and difficulties were resolved. It was a qualitative study in which a total of 80 respondents were interviewed in depth about their different kinship ties. Of these 80, 30 were with respondents who were related to at least one of the other respondents participating in the study, thus allowing for different accounts to be generated of relationships in their kinship network. The respondents were selected through a combined process of writing to and telephoning people living in particular neighbourhoods in a town in southern England – given the pseudonym of Middleston here – and through snowballing techniques. The respondents varied on a number of key dimensions including age, class and gender. They also had diverse experiences of stepfamilies, a factor which itself attests to the complexity of contemporary family life. Some respondents could be identified clearly as, say, a stepmother, a stepson or a stepgrandparent, but many had multiple 'step' roles. They were, for example, not just a stepfather, but also a stepchild and a stepuncle. This had the advantage of facilitating comparative reflection by these respondents in discussing their different relationships in the interviews.

Each respondent in the study was interviewed once, with the interviews typically taking between 60 and 90 minutes each. Interviews began with the collection of genealogical data through means of genogram techniques (McGoldrick and Gerson, 1985; McGoldrick, Gerson and Petry, 2008). The genogram was mapped as the respondents discussed their kin relationships, and used to structure the rest of the interview. This interviewing technique provided an active visual focus for the interview which, as well as capturing the respondents' interest, encouraged detailed discussion and comparison of different relationships within their family networks. It also made the interview more manageable by enabling its focus to move between the different segments of the kinship network. As well as discussing their own relationships and how they had changed over time, the respondents provided information about relationships between others in their networks. This was useful both in locating their own relationships within a wider framework and in providing us with pertinent data on an extended range of kin relationships. While the accounts given reflect the perspective of the interviewee, respondents routinely had a well-grounded knowledge of the dynamics of other relationships in their networks. For example, a mother is in a privileged position to describe her children's relationships with their grandparents, as is a wife with regard her husband's relationships with his children and parents. (Fuller details of the research methods used in the study and of the characteristics of the sample are provided in Appendix.)

Outline of chapters

The next chapter, Chapter 2, is concerned with examining some key issues which shape the rest of this book. We start by developing the discussion of family and household further, focussing particularly on the linked themes of 'family as household' and 'family as kinship'. We then turn to consider the different research perspectives that have informed the sociological analysis of stepfamilies. Although we pay heed to early US work on stepfamilies, in this chapter we focus more on British family research. Our aim here is to indicate how major developments in sociological analyses of family processes over the last 20 years have influenced our own approach to studying stepfamilies. In particular, we show how our study has been influenced by approaches which explore fluidity and diversity within contemporary family – and stepfamily – relationships.

Chapter 3 has a quite different focus. In this, we present four case illustrations drawn from our own study of stepfamily relationships. In doing this, our aim is to provide accounts of stepfamily matters as they were experienced by our respondents. We do not provide an explicit analysis of the material included in the chapter, though clearly the process of selecting the cases necessarily involves an element of analytical judgement. We have tried to select four cases that highlight some of the core issues we explore in later chapters while also reflecting the diversity of experience that people in stepfamilies have. Chapter 4 is concerned with aspects of family boundaries. This is a topic that has framed much research on stepfamily relationships and one which remains crucial for understanding similarities and differences in the social organisation of stepfamilies and of other modes of family living such as lone-parent or nuclear families. In this chapter we draw heavily on the material presented in Chapter 3. While that chapter is essentially descriptive, this chapter takes a more analytical stance and explores the different boundary issues that were evident in the descriptions respondents provided of their different family experiences.

Chapters 5 and 6 examine stepmothering and stepfathering respectively. Again we draw on some of the material from Chapter 3, but also on the accounts a number of our other respondents provided, to highlight core issues that pattern step-parent/stepchild relationships. Chapter 5 is mainly concerned with the relationships resident stepmothers have with their stepchildren. The analysis is framed around the consequences of the routine division of domestic labour within these households and the patterns of stepmother/stepchild involvement which are consequent on them. However the chapter also explores how differently non-resident stepmother/stepchild relationships are patterned. In Chapter 6 the focus turns to stepfathering, again with a concentration on resident stepfathering. We start by exploring the experiences of resident step-fathers, but also draw on the accounts we obtained from respondents who lived in stepfather households as stepchildren. In both chapters we are concerned not just with the relationships that developed when the stepchildren were children, but also with how the relationships were constructed once the children had themselves become adult.

The focus of Chapter 7 turns to an examination of stepfamily kinship. The core question here concerns the degree to which different stepkin are defined by those involved as 'family'. Focussing principally on step-grandparents and stepsiblings, the chapter explores the diversity there is in people's involvement with these stepkin. Building on the analysis of the earlier chapters and again using the material our respondents provided, we assess the different conditions that generate family solidarity or, in turn, restrict a sense of family connection from developing. Our main argument is that while the routine social organisation of family life frequently results in the limited involvement of stepkin in people's family networks, this is not always the case. As with so many aspects of family life, there is a good deal of diversity in the structuring of stepkin relationships.

The final chapter, Chapter 8, concludes the book by considering issues of time, change and continuity in stepfamily relationships. In line with other research into contemporary family change, it argues that expecta-tions around stepfamily organisation have been altering so that now there is a greater acceptance that stepfamilies typically involve more complex and fluid relationship networks. Not only do people expect stepfamilies to have more complex household dynamics, but they also recognise the need for flexibility and continuing negotiation around the management of different individuals' different family commitments. Equally though, there is continuity across time in the ways that individual relationships, both inside and outside the household, are structured. There are certainly common patterns in stepfamily networks, but so too, as with other family forms, there is diversity and fluidity. In this, continuity and change operate in tandem.

2
Analysing Stepfamilies

As we have noted, the ways that stepfamilies are created and the different pathways they can take are complex. Historically the available pathways were relatively clear, at least for the great majority. Because divorce was less frequent and early death more common than now, stepfamilies were formed when a widow or widower with children remarried. Whether or not the family was recognised as a stepfamily possibly depended on the residential position of the children involved; if they were no longer living in the household, then the remarriage may not have been defined as resulting in a stepfamily. In some ways contemporary ideas about step-families mirror this. The 'standard' notion of a stepfamily is of a natural parent and a step-parent cohabiting together in a household in which there are dependent children. This narrow conception could be charac-terised as a 'stepfamily household', as the key criteria are the presence of dependent children in the household together with a committed couple who are not both the natural parents of the child.

But if 'family' is conceived as 'kinship' rather than 'household', then clearly the idea of stepfamilies is rather wider than this (Cherlin and Furstenberg, 1994). One can, for example, consider whether a stepfamily ceases once there are no longer dependent children in the household. Even leaving aside issues of youth dependence and independence (Holdsworth and Morgan, 2005; Jones, 2009), it would seem rather curious to assert that the stepfamily no longer exists as such if there are no dependent children living in it. The child's relationships with the natural parent and with their partner, the step-parent, are likely to continue, just as they do in other forms of family. But equally, of course, step relationships can be formed and sustained without the need for residence. With separation and divorce rather than death, children can have a continuing relationship with their non-resident (or in some cases partially resident) natural parent. Where this parent re-partners, that partner can be regarded within the family genealogy as a step-parent. They may not live for much of the time, or at all, in the same household, but in terms of 'family as kinship' they are in a stepfamily relationship. If there is no continuing relationship with the natural parent, it is unlikely that any new partner that parent has would become incorporated in any way into the child's family networks. As we shall discuss later, the discontinuation of parental relationships following divorce or separation is becoming rarer, no longer being seen as a reasonable 'solution' to the dilemmas of divorce either culturally or in policy terms.

Similarly, in principle, a stepfamily is not bounded in other ways by residential criteria, just as natural families are not. In other words, family networks are not limited by household criteria. Culturally, we define 'family' in a variety of ways and include a variety of people within the term, albeit depending somewhat on context. Put simply, many people would regard grandparents, aunts, uncles, cousins, grand-children and the like as part of their family. Here 'family as kinship' involves family networks which spread well outside the household. So too, one can argue stepfamily members are not inevitably restricted to individuals who share household membership. There can be stepgrand-parents, stepaunts and stepuncles, as well as stepbrothers and stepsisters. Whether these individuals are in fact regarded as part of one's 'family' or part of one's 'kinship' is a moot point that needs addressing empirically rather than simply conceptually; the answer will vary depending on the quality of the relationship (if any) sustained between those involved, just as issues of where natural kinship ends depend on actual relational criteria rather than just genealogical connection. Further complications arise, of course, because of the relative instability of contemporary patterns of partnership. Put simply, if a relationship between a parent and a step-parent ends, does that of itself mean that any 'kinship' connection between the child and the step-parent also ends? Similarly does it also spell the end for any 'kinship' with the step-parent's kin? These too are issues for empirical investigation, with answers likely to vary somewhat depending on the nature of the relationships sustained and the reasons for the parent's and step-parent's separation.

Families: Households and kinship

In order to understand the nature of contemporary stepfamilies, it is necessary to consider in more detail some of the key issues and distinctions involved here. In particular, some of the different elements entailed in the concept of 'family' need to be examined in greater depth. As we have seen, the comparative separation of marriage, sex and childbirth as a strongly linked trinity, together with changed patterns of family and household formation and dissolution, has generated a range of family-relevant ties which fit somewhat imperfectly into traditionally conventional conceptions of kinship. Included among these, of course, are step relationships. This has presented a challenge to sociologists and others concerned with family matters, as the very subject of their analysis appears to be shifting. At the least, it has required more careful conceptualisation of the construct 'family' than was previously the case (Morgan, 1996, 2011; Silva and Smart, 1999a; Cheal, 2002).

In everyday discourses, the idea of 'family' carries various meanings. For the purposes of this chapter, we are going to focus on two of the more important, each of which itself entails a further range of related dimensions. These two, which have already been introduced, are 'family as kinship' and 'family as household'. Until quite recently these two components of family tended to be treated as largely synonymous. Especially perhaps in American family sociology with its strong roots in Parsonian functionalism, 'family' meant those family members living together within the same household. There tended to be rather less focus on kinship as such or even on ideas of overlapping and interlocking related family households.

More recently, largely because of changing family and household demography, there has been an increased emphasis on the analytical separation of 'family' and 'household' (Allan and Crow, 2001; Allan, Hawker and Crow, 2003). Importantly, increasing numbers of people are living in households which are not based on or comprise family relationships, or at least not solely so. For example, the number of single person households has increased quite dramatically over the last generation, reaching approximately 1 in 3 of all households by 2006 (Chandler et al., 2004; ONS, 2009). In significant part, this is the result of increasing numbers of elderly people, especially widows, living alone, but it is also consequent on increased levels of divorce. Equally, there has been a rise in the numbers of young adults who are sharing housing with unrelated others, not on a short-term basis as in the past but as an integral element of their housing 'careers' (Heath and Cleaver, 2001; Berrington, Stone and Falkingham, 2009). Importantly, of course, as discussed earlier, there are also many individuals now living in partnerships outside marriage. Some of these are taken to be 'marriage-like', though precisely if and when these partners come to be understood as 'family' is uncertain, as indeed is the issue of when others in the kinship network treat them as such. Others are not seen as marriage-like, being understood as temporary cohabitations that do not involve a longer-term commitment (Jamieson et al., 2002).

As a result of shifts like these in people's living arrangements, the inadequacy of any implicit convergence between 'family' and 'household' in analyses of family patterns became quite apparent. Just as the term 'family cycle' – sensible in its mid-twentieth century manifestation – was necessarily replaced by 'family course' as the family stages that individuals experienced became more diverse and less orderly, so there was a need for aspects of *household* organisation and practice to be distinguished analytically from specifically *family* organisation and practice. This is not always easy, because for many people what occurs within the domestic sphere of the household is very much wrapped up with gendered and generational familial processes and relationships. Nonetheless it became clear that, despite many people's lived experience, as analytical categories 'household' and 'family' could not be treated as synonymous.

In many ways cohabitation provides the most interesting illustration of the need for this division. From being a stigmatised, minority mode of living, cohabitation is now generally understood to be a routine phase of relationship building, whether or not those involved define their relationship as a committed one. Language change reflects this shift in normative understandings, with the popularity of the term 'partner' for both heterosexual and gay/lesbian relationships, as well as for married and unmarried ones, being indicative of the ways in which cultural understandings of the appropriate ordering of intimate relationships have altered. In the case of heterosexual relationships, marriage served not only to legitimate the partnerships but also to integrate the spouse into the family 'realm'. With cohabitation the position is less certain. Even if we take partnership to always involve cohabitation – in other words a domestic as well as a sexual relationship – it does not follow that those involved see each other as 'family'. Certainly there is no ceremonial 'moment' in which family ties are created, as there is with marriage. The trajectory into 'family', if it occurs, is an individual one in which issues of commitment and projected futures are significant. Clearly if children are born into the partnership this is likely to cement notions of family, as is the acceptance of the partner by other kin, especially perhaps with regard to participation in formal and informal family events and rituals.

Issues of 'family' are also complex in gay and lesbian partnerships, notwithstanding the establishment of gay marriage/civil registration in

Britain and other countries. In part, this is because of the degree to which such relationships lie outside the historically heterosexual construction of marriage as the accepted form of partnership, but also because these relationships are sometimes still kept separate, if not hidden, from other kin. Thus while now far more accepted than previously, there may be relatively little overlap between the gay and straight segments of social networks and little celebration, or even recognition, by other family members of the gay partnership (Weeks, Heaphy and Donovan, 2002). Rather than being embedded into kinship activity in the way heterosexual partnerships routinely are, gay partnerships tend to operate more on the fringes of kinship. Somewhat ironically, the whole idea of 'families of choice' (Weston, 1991; Weeks, Heaphy and Donovan, 2002), whereby gay couples construct 'family-like' networks with people who are not conventionally seen as kin, highlights the extent to which these partnerships are at times seen as lying outside the normal realm of 'family' relations.

At the same time the idea of 'families of choice', along with other similar constructs like 'voluntary kin' (Braithwaite et al., 2010), highlights the difficulties of specifying what 'family' actually signifies. In particular, in thinking about partnership and cohabitation the distinction between 'household' and 'family' begins to seem less fruitful than it initially appeared. In other words, while it can be recognised that households can exist without any sense of family, and that family does not necessarily entail any form of domestic sharing or co-operation, in practice constructing and sharing a home together generally involves a degree of commitment and intimacy that effectively locates the relationships within the 'family' realm, even though they lie outside standard cultural criteria of family membership – 'blood' and marriage. For this reason, it is more helpful for our purposes to think of household and kinship as analytically distinct realms, with the notion of 'family' overlying them both. This returns us to the notions of 'family as household' and 'family as kinship' we introduced earlier. Yet what becomes crucial is that the sense of 'family' in either formulation depends to quite a large degree on the construction of commitment and solidarity within these relationships.

To explore this further, it is helpful to consider David Schneider's (1968) classic analysis of American kinship. In this influential work, Schneider argues that American kinship is clearly understood as being about 'blood' and 'marriage'. These are the two criteria that frame people's understandings of the kinship system. They do, however, constitute distinct realms. 'Blood' is understood to be given by nature and so is unalterable, even though, at least prior to DNA testing, paternity especially was always contestable in principle. Marriage, on the other hand, was recognised as a social phenomenon and so could be terminated, with clear consequences for kinship connection. Yet culturally kinship is more than just 'blood' or 'marriage' which at one level are just the criteria used for kinship allocation. According to Schneider, what is also crucial is the cultural link that exists between on the one hand, 'blood' and 'marriage', and, on the other, 'love'. It is love, itself evidently a cultural construct, which acts as the core component of 'family as kinship'.

For Schneider, love within the kinship realm can be understood as 'diffuse, enduring solidarity'. This phrase thus captures what it is that differentiates the realm of kinship from other social realms. This does not mean that such love does not occur in other relationships; nor that all those recognised as connected by 'blood' or marriage will necessarily feel love for one other. Clearly this is not so. What it means is that culturally this is what 'family as kinship' represents and signifies. When people talk of 'family', the dominant discourse is one in which diffuse, enduring solidarity is integral. While Schneider was specifically concerned with American culture and while he was writing in the 1960s – a period when divorce and cohabitation were not as prevalent as they are now – his idea of diffuse, enduring solidarity still captures the essence of 'family' connection as it is conventionally understood in contemporary Britain. Taken with notions of 'blood' and marriage/partnership as the principles of genealogical connection, it conveys what most people think 'family as kinship' represents.

Of course, the idea of 'diffuse, enduring solidarity' is itself rather a vague one – deliberately and necessarily so if it is to capture conceptions of 'family'. But it encapsulates a framework against which the 'family as kinship' characteristics of different relationships can be assessed. All three elements here are of consequence, though it is the existence – and nature – of the solidarity that is most significant. Without a sense of solidarity – a degree of commitment and a sense of shared identity – the idea of a relationship being within the orbit of 'family as kinship' becomes just a matter of genealogical connection, and thus effectively not 'family'. Importantly, that sense of commitment and solidarity experienced is not narrow, limited or specific – hence the relevance of Schneider's 'diffuse' and 'enduring' qualifiers. It is not readily characterised in terms of particular actions or responsibilities. Instead it represents a commitment which is both multifaceted and long-lasting, in principle enduring over time and potentially encompassing a wide range of diverse activities.

As noted, marriage was one of the two central planks of Schneider's analysis. The changes in partnership formation and dissolution, whether or not particular partnerships result in the birth of children and therefore connections of 'blood', have consequences for people's understandings of whom they are kin with. They also have consequences for the degree to which members of your family also recognise others whom you may consider to be part of your family to be part of theirs. There have always been issues around the extent to which 'in-laws' are incorporated into each other's kinship (see, for example, Firth, Hubert and Forge, 1970). These issues though have become more uncertain with the rise of new modes of cohabitation and partnership. When do such relationships become conceived of as 'family' by those in the partnership? When do other family members inside and outside the household regard the partner as part of their kinship? Is it a question of time – how long they have been together? Is it a question of commitment? To what extent is it influenced by whether they have children between them, creating a 'blood' connection?

It would seem that all these factors matter, though not in a straightforward or simplistic fashion. To draw on Schneider again, the key issue is the degree to which the relationships involved – especially but not only the partnership – are understood to be characterised by 'enduring, diffuse solidarity'. The more they are, the more likely they will be thought of as part of the 'family as kinship' domain. If on the other hand, they are not seen as enduring, into the future as well as from the past, and if they are not seen as entailing diffuse solidarity, then they are likely to be defined as lying outside this family realm, even though the relationship involves substantial domestic and sexual exchanges.

A proportion of cohabiting partnerships never do involve a marked degree of diffuse and enduring solidarity. Commitment within them is limited and they do not last beyond the relatively short term (Sassler, 2004; Manning and Smock, 2005). As such, they never really enter the 'family as kinship' realm. They are a personal and largely private arrangement, perhaps representing little more than a mode of what used to be termed 'going steady'. Even if they do become more established, they are unlikely to be recognised as 'kinship' until they are accepted as being enduring – as in this sense becoming 'marriage-like' – especially by other family members. Although there is little research on this, having children within a continuing cohabiting partnership is also likely to place the relationship more firmly in the kinship realm. In part this is because it signifies a continuing commitment, but also because the couple now have an indirect 'blood' link through the child

(Berrington, 2001). For their kin too, the child will be taken to represent a level of diffuse, enduring commitment between the partners as well as a 'blood' connection, even if the possibility of future separation may be recognised. The 'unrelated' partner is thus liable to be drawn into their kinship realm.

Divorce also often entails new dilemmas within the family and kinship realm. Where there are no children, there are normally few issues. As the marriage ends, so too does the 'family as kinship' connection, both for the couple and their wider kin groups. However it is different when there are children, of whatever age. Here the 'family as kinship' connection between the couple will almost certainly change. Generally, the ex-spouses will not feel the same degree of enduring commitment to one another as they once did, though in some cases a modified sense of 'family as kinship' will continue, perhaps expressed principally through their shared parenting (Fischer, De Graaf and Kalmijn, 2005). More importantly, the family connection between the children and both of their now-separated parents commonly continues. Both are likely to remain significant within the child/ren's 'family as kinship', as will members of each parent's kinship network – the children's grandparents, aunts and uncles. As a consequence of the divorce, however, some of these figures may over time become more peripheral to the child's life – and involve a reduced level of commitment – than would have been the case otherwise.

Stepfamilies: Research perspectives

With the changes there have been in the demography of households and families, and especially the construction and endings of married and unmarried partnerships, it is evident that the distinction between 'family as kinship' and 'family as household' has become both more complex and more pertinent in people's family experiences. This distinction is also important for understanding processes of domestic and kinship organisation within stepfamilies. In particular issues of family commitment and solidarity internal and external to the household are central for understanding the dynamics and ordering of stepfamily practices. The chapters that follow this one will explore these issues in greater detail. First though it is necessary to set the scene for the analyses that follow by discussing some key research studies of stepfamilies, as well as recent theoretical developments that have shaped the focus and concerns of contemporary family sociology more broadly. We are not here trying to provide a comprehensive review of research on stepfamilies.

Rather we want to highlight themes from a select number of studies that have proved particularly influential, both generally and more specifically for the focus of this book. We will begin by considering two papers on stepfamilies which reflect the early research agenda created around stepfamily relationships.

Undoubtedly the most important early article written on stepfamilies was Andrew Cherlin's 'Remarriage as an incomplete institution' published in 1978. With hindsight, this article can be seen to have encapsulated many of the key research questions which framed consequent debates around this family form within family studies. In it, Cherlin argues that in the US, and by implication elsewhere, there are few established normative guidelines available to families created through remarriage, few culturally validated ways of handling the different problems they face and little institutionalised social support for them. Instead each stepfamily has to construct its own ways of ordering relationships within the new family, based principally on normative understandings which have developed in the context of first-time families. The lack of institutionalisation of the stepfamily form was particularly apparent, according to Cherlin, in the confusion existing over relationship terminology and the absence of any significant legal or policy concerns explicitly focussed on issues of remarriage and stepfamily living.

The issue of language and terminology in stepfamilies is a perennial one. As Cherlin (1978, p. 643) notes, the absence of agreed terminology for the different relationships involved is, *prima facie*, indicative of an absence of social recognition and regulation. There are two elements to this. First while the term stepfamily is well-established, it is evident that people in stepfamilies often dislike the use of the term. Partly as a consequence of the negative ways stepfamilies are generally portrayed in popular culture (Hughes, 1991), with little counter-balancing positive imagery, members of stepfamilies – especially the adults – often want to present themselves as just 'ordinary' families, and not as ones that are stereotyped as problematic. As a result, alternative terms have been developed to represent this family form, including for example 'reconstituted families', 'remarried families', 'blended families' and 'second-time families'. However none of these terms has developed into normatively dominant labels, leaving the problem of nomenclature unresolved (Ganong and Coleman, 2004).

The second broad problematic element around terminology in step-families concerns the labels given to specific relationships and the naming procedures involved. While descriptive labels such as 'step-mother' and 'stepfather' appear quite clear-cut, there are uncertainties about the appropriateness of these descriptors. When, for example, does a mother's new partner become a stepfather? Is it when co-residence starts? Is it only on marriage? Is it the same if the child is not normally resident in the mother's household? More importantly, what conventions or norms govern the names used in interaction? What should a resident stepfather be called? By their first name? As 'Dad' or some equivalent term representing fatherhood? What should a non-resident stepfather or stepmother be called? How should the parents of a step-parent be addressed? Families resolve these issues in their own ways, but that is Cherlin's point. There are no strong social guidelines governing these matters (though also see Jacobson, 1995); in this regard, stepfamilies remain incompletely institutionalised.

Apart from language, Cherlin (1978) also highlighted the absence of legal and policy interest in stepfamilies as a prime indicator of their incomplete institutionalisation. Cherlin was discussing the situation in the US, but the situation was – and is – similar in Britain and elsewhere. In effect, the state is largely unconcerned with stepfamilies. In some respects it treats stepfamilies as though they were equivalent to natural families, in effect ignoring 'the special problems of families of remarriages after divorce' (Cherlin, 1978, p. 644). At the same time though, the state usually treats step-parents as though they were not part of the family at all (Bainham, 1999; Atkin, 2008). There are for example no clear guidelines about incest within stepfamilies. No legal prescription forbids marriage between a step-parent and his or her step-child, a matter which aroused much public interest when film director Woody Allen married Soon-Yi Previn, the adopted daughter of his former partner, Mia Farrow. Similarly, there is no legislation forbidding sexual relations between stepsiblings, whether or not they have been brought up in the same household.

Equally in cases other than adoption, step-parents have no privileged rights or responsibilities for involvement in decisions about their children's lives. These remain parental responsibilities, not step-parental ones (Edwards, Gillies and McCarthy, 1999; Mason et al., 2002). Indeed, as we shall discuss in more detail below, the current emphasis on continuing parental responsibility irrespective of marital status, as well as increased discouragement for stepfamily adoption, have in some regards rendered the public or 'official' recognition of step-parents even more peripheral; as Malia (2005, p. 298) argues, step-parents and the step-parent/stepchild relationship remains 'largely invisible in the law'. For instance, step-parents have no specific rights to be consulted by school or medical staff about decisions that affect their stepchildren. Equally, while in Britain and elsewhere, the state is very much concerned with regulating natural fathers' financial support for their children, it has no policies or guidelines (aside from those involved in household welfare payments) that indicate a step-parent's financial obligations to their stepchildren.

Elements of the incomplete institutionalisation of stepfamilies are also evident in other spheres of stepfamily life, including lack of consensus over how second weddings should be celebrated and, more significantly, over appropriate ways of ordering relationships between ex-spouses and their new partners. Cherlin's arguments about the 'incomplete institutionalisation' of remarriage helped establish the importance of viewing remarriage as different from first-time marriage and stepfamilies as more complex than natural families. At the same time as Cherlin was writing, family therapists were also beginning to explore the dynamics arising in stepfamilies. In particular, they focussed on the systemic properties of stepfamilies and the different 'boundaries' that were constructed within them. Walker and Messinger's paper 'Remarriage after divorce: Dissolution and reconstruction of family boundaries' published in 1979 developed many of the key themes emerging from this perspective.

Walker and Messinger use the term 'boundary' to represent the factors that encourage a shared sense of identity within families. They argue that within the nuclear family model dominant in Western societies, there are strong boundaries separating the nuclear family household from the outside world. These include the physical boundaries of the home, but also more implicit boundaries of intimacy, dependence, authority and ritual which symbolise and represent the solidarity of the family and serve to distinguish it from other families and households. Separation and divorce alter the nature of these constructed boundaries; in Walker and Messinger's (1979, p. 187) terms, 'the space-time boundedness of family life is disrupted', with the non-resident parent no longer included within the constructed 'boundaries' of family in the previously taken-for-granted fashion. He (or she) nonetheless retains rights for involvement with children which necessarily involve a greater degree of permeability in post-divorce family boundaries than was the case prior to the separation (Burgoyne and Clark, 1984; Smart and Neale, 1999).

But in turn, remarriage or repartnership increases the permeability of family boundaries further. Within the new marriage, boundaries cannot be established in the usual ways they are in first-time marriages. The activities, feelings and loyalties of the child(ren), the non-resident parent and, arguably, the immediate kin of the step-parent ensure that the boundaries which separate the 'family' from those outside it are far less clearly demarcated than in natural families. Issues of 'home' as a 'family' space become more complex, as do the generational relationships sustained within the family. Classically these are represented in terms of disciplinary actions by the step-parent, though actually they reflect boundary difficulties at all levels of identity and belonging within the family. As Walker and Messinger (1979) emphasise, much as Cherlin (1978) did, each stepfamily has to develop its own means of managing these boundary issues, in part because of the diversity of factors which impinge on any resolution. Establishing a family system with more permeable boundaries in this way is inherently a difficult, complex and emergent process that requires patience, accommodation and, perhaps most crucially, time for adjustment.

The arguments of these two papers by Cherlin (1978) and Walker and Messinger (1979) are clearly compatible. They are both premised on functionalist ideas about the nature of the family in contemporary society. Both are concerned with the systemic properties of families and with the ways in which different families are able to construct and sustain family order. A key element for both papers, and one which has remained central in stepfamily research since they were writing, is the issue of *unity* within different types of family. There is, in other words, a concern about the sense of solidarity and commitment that different members feel towards one another and about the extent to which these feelings signify a shared or fragmented family identity. These two papers, along with others from the era (e.g., Fast and Cain, 1966; Visher and Visher, 1978; Furstenberg, 1980; Giles-Sims, 1984), also reflect the *ambiguity* there is about the ways in which step-parent roles in particular should be performed. The issue was captured well by Fast and Cain (1966) who first posed the question of just how much of a parent a step-parent should be. It is also pertinent to ask how much of a parent they are allowed to be. We will return to the issue of family boundaries in Chapter 4.

Burgoyne and Clark

In line with Cherlin's analysis, this uncertainty about step-parental roles is indicative of their being at best only partially institutionalised. However it also raises questions about the social, policy and legal contexts in which step-parenting is undertaken. This is a matter highlighted very clearly in Jackie Burgoyne and David Clark's (1984) groundbreaking British study *Making a Go of It: A Study of Stepfamilies in Sheffield*. As well as capturing the key elements in stepfamily research of the time, it was the first major study of stepfamilies in Britain and has thus served as a prime point of reference for consequent British research on the topic. It remains a classic account of how stepfamilies constitute themselves, as well as of the various issues, dilemmas and contradictions they face.

The fieldwork for Burgoyne and Clark's study was undertaken in the late 1970s. It was based on an interview survey of 40 couples in which at least one of the couple had previously been married and had custody of one or more children from that marriage. In all but three of the couples, each partner was interviewed individually on three separate occasions. Initially drawing on a life history perspective, the study generated a large amount of qualitative data about the respondents' previous experiences of marriage and family life and of the varied processes involved in recreating a 'new' family through remarriage or, in one case, continued cohabitation. Obtaining a sample for the study proved to be extremely difficult, requiring a range of different sampling strategies including the use of personal contacts. As the authors note, these sampling problems reflected a common dislike of the 'stepfamily' label and a desire not to be seen or treated as somehow 'odd' or 'exceptional'. While for this and other reasons the final sample could not be regarded as representative of stepfamilies more widely, it did contain a diverse range of couples in terms of marital histories, family constitution and material circumstances. It thus enabled Burgoyne and Clark to develop a broad-ranging understanding of the different experiences members of stepfamilies have.

The difficulties of obtaining a stepfamily sample reflect one of the strongest themes to emerge from Burgoyne and Clark's study: the desire of the couples in stepfamilies to construct an 'ordinary family life'. This entailed a number of different elements, all drawing on normative understandings of how family life should be. In particular, it signified a nuclear family model of an adult couple with dependent children, largely left alone to make decisions and organise their family routines as they considered appropriate without undue interference from others. This applied across all spheres of family life, including the mutual creation and development of the couple as a couple, responsibility for the proper development and socialisation of children and the creation of an emotionally and materially secure home environment. The place of children, however, was especially pertinent within these constructions of normal family life, as within conventional models of the 'ordinary' nuclear family children were commonly recognised as symbolising the shared achievement of the couple and consequently the successful performance of 'family life'.

However the ability of the couples in the study to construct an 'ordinary' family life was routinely compromised – for most if not all – by the need to accommodate the actions of others, be these individuals or agencies. For most of the couples, there was, in other words, a sense of 'interference' in the family routines and practices they were trying to establish. Those things over which it was perceived natural families had autonomy could not be as freely developed or managed as the couple would have liked. Importantly here, the degree of 'interference' that occurred need not have been particularly high for the differences between natural families and stepfamilies to become apparent, for in many respects the contrast being made was with an idealised image of 'ordinary' family life. Equally though, the notion of 'interference' and the sense of difference from 'ordinary' family life stem from exactly those issues of 'family boundaries' and 'family unity' discussed above.

Burgoyne and Clark (1984, Chapter 4) provide a lucid analysis of the different ways in which their respondents found the maintenance of the boundaries they wished to create around their family life problematic. Essentially, there were three root components to this: non-resident parents, social agencies and children. The study is extremely good at portraying the ways in which ex-spouses continued to have an impact on the respondents' family experiences. To begin with, when there was continuing contact between a child and the non-resident parent, the need for co-ordination of these activities of itself served to highlight difference from the freedoms associated with organising 'ordinary' family life. While in some instances access time allowed the couple precious space to be alone, it could equally result in minor irritations or more serious conflicts, especially when the non-resident parent was thought to be contravening established agreements. Disputes about maintenance payments also served to create tension and spotlight the continuing relevance of the previous relationship.

In addition, various social agencies were often more involved in familial matters than was usual in 'ordinary' families. Solicitors, courts and other aspects of the legal system were prime instances of this, certainly in those cases where less formal resolutions had proved difficult to agree. Thus the need to settle custody, maintenance and access arrangements required that normally 'private' family information had to be divulged and debated, sometimes over a considerable period of time. Similarly, at different times education and welfare agencies could be experienced as intruding into family life because of their need to be informed of the 'unusual' circumstances of the stepfamily. Overall, while a flexible approach to childcare arrangements might be beneficial for the children involved, the consequence of such flexibility was usually a higher level of 'interference' in the 'ordinary' life of the stepfamily.

From an adult/parental perspective, an evident 'solution' to these effective intrusions into the construction of an 'ordinary' family life would be somehow to 'close the book' on the past and start afresh, away from the encumbrance of previous relationships. For children, though, this was less the case. Indeed at the time of the study, policy initiatives and common-sense understandings were moving in the opposite direction with increased emphasis placed on the value of continuing parental relationships and a rejection of 'clean break' solutions. As Smart and Neale (1999) were later to argue, in effect this cultural shift in notions of children's best interests following separation and divorce made it more difficult to disentangle parental interdependence, thereby rendering the construction of a new, distinctly independent family life harder. (Also see the discussion of Simpson's (1994, 1998) research later in this chapter.) But for children, the desires they have of their stepfamily are likely to be different. For them, their idea of 'family' does embrace their continuing relationships with the non-resident parent (and usually his or her kin). In other words, the 'boundaries' constructed around their family are generally not synonymous with those constructed by the resident parent or the step-parent. Thus, as Burgoyne and Clark indicate, matters of family unity often cannot be resolved in the same taken-for-granted ways they are in 'ordinary' families. Not only is there an evident lack of unity, but importantly not all stepfamily members share the same desire to achieve it. These issues become more complex when the remarried couple both have children from previous relationships.

Burgoyne and Clark's (1984) approach to collecting data was framed around a life history perspective. A major advantage of this approach was that it allowed them to highlight the importance of time – or process – within the construction of stepfamily life, an obvious point but one which is sometimes underplayed in analyses of stepfamilies. There are two related issues warranting consideration here. First, as with all families, time alters the nature of stepfamily relationships simply as a consequence of ageing. In particular, as children age and progress into independence and adulthood, so the dominant concerns, joys, dilemmas and satisfactions of family life alter. Some issues remain salient for long periods; others that once loomed large fade or get resolved. Second, and following directly from this, relationships between step-parents and stepchildren are themselves dynamic. As stepfamilies evolve, so too do the individual relationships involved, whether negatively or positively. Burgoyne and Clark recognise that these processes are central components within the diversity of stepfamily experiences, as indeed are the biographical histories and life-course locations of the different individuals involved at the time of the stepfamily's formation.

In concluding their research, Burgoyne and Clark (1984, pp. 191–4) construct a five-fold typology of stepfamilies which attempts to integrate some of the key themes they have analysed, including aspects of biographical time. More specifically, their typology distinguishes stepfamilies in terms of children's ages – their categories 'Not really a stepfamily' and 'Looking forward to the departure of the children'– and the degree to which the couple desire and are able to achieve a form of 'ordinary' family living – their categories 'The largely successful conscious pursuit of an ordinary family life together'; 'The "progressive" stepfamily'; and 'The conscious pursuit of an ordinary family life frustrated'. One of the advantages of this typology is that it inherently highlights the diversity there is in stepfamily experiences and the dangers there are of treating stepfamilies as though they were a single form of family. At the same time, the ability to construct the typology also indicates that common issues and concerns are confronted by members of different stepfamilies, albeit not in all cases, not to the same extent and not at all times.

Negotiation and practice: British family sociology in the 1990s

In their study, Burgoyne and Clark (1984) highlighted the efforts made within their stepfamilies to develop a consensus about the appropriate ordering of family life. In other words, their analysis recognised the construction of family order as the active accomplishment of its various members, usually but not exclusively inside the household. This approach was developed by other writers in the 1990s, a decade which saw something of a renaissance in British family sociology. We want to focus here on two highly influential books which shaped the approach we are taking to the study of stepfamilies. These books are *Negotiating Family Responsibilities* by Janet Finch and Jennifer Mason (1993) and David Morgan's *Family Connections* published in 1996. Both of these books emphasised the extent to which family relationships, and consequently family life, were constructed by the actions of those involved rather than being simply the result of socialisation into particular family norms. They reflected the greater flexibility there was in family organisation, together with a strong emphasis on the interplay of structure and agency in generating social order. In many ways Finch and Mason's (1993) discussion of family 'negotiations' and Morgan's (1996; see also

Morgan, 2011) focus on family 'practices' served to voice a fresh under-standing within British sociology about the ways families operated.

Finch and Mason's (1993) study of family responsibilities was concerned with analysing the nature of the solidarities that existed between family members. Based on extensive fieldwork involving structured and unstructured interviews with a wide range of inform-ants, Finch and Mason's key thesis was that people do not follow 'a set of pre-ordained social rules' (1993, p. 60) premised on their genealogi-cal position within a kinship network (see also Finch, 1989). Instead family behaviour needs to be understood more contextually, recog-nising the choice – or agency – which people have over their family responsibilities. However such agency is not unbounded. People's understandings of morality and social obligation will inform the decisions they reach about appropriate behaviour in the context in question. So too, the way they respond will be influenced by the actions of others, especially others involved in the same family networks. As Finch and Mason explain,

> the concept of negotiation emphasises that individuals do have some room for manoeuvre, though it is never entirely open-ended and sometimes it can be quite tightly constrained. In this perspective, each individual is seen as actively working out his or her own course of action, and doing so with reference to other people. It is through human interaction that people develop a common understanding of what a particular course of action will mean.
>
> (1993, p. 60)

In addition to agency, Finch and Mason's concept of 'negotiation' also highlights process. Rather than interpreting family behaviour as a series of discrete responses to specific contingencies, as a normative model would suggest, their model of negotiation recognises that how people behave is linked to the emergent history of their relationships. And as is evident from the quotation above, the relationships in question are not just those most directly involved in the particular event, but rather the network of relationships in which these individual ties are embedded. Thus in emphasising process, Finch and Mason recognise that patterns of family commitment are generated over time and result from the out-comes of serial and repeated negotiations conducted with others who, through their membership of the kinship network, also have knowledge of previous responses. In other words, at any time people enter particular episodes of family negotiation with existing 'reputations' and 'moral identities' which help to frame – for themselves as well as for others – the stance they are likely to take in consequent family interactions (see Finch and Mason, 1993, Chapter 5).

Finch and Mason recognise that negotiations can be managed in different ways, both within and across family relationships and networks. Some negotiations are explicit, others implicit; many contain elements of both, lying somewhere in the 'spectrum' between these categories (1993, p. 64). They highlight three categories of negotiation, but are at pains to emphasise that these do not represent a formal or 'pure' typology but instead provide a framework for understanding processes of negotiation. The three categories are *open discussions*, *clear intentions* and *non-decisions*. As the name suggests, *open discussions* are the most explicit form of negotiation Finch and Mason specify, and also the form which most reflects everyday understandings of 'negotiation'. Typically it involves two or more family members coming together to discuss openly a particular family issue or problem. As Finch and Mason recognise, while open discussions are commonly reported, they are frequently combined with other modes of negotiation which may be more crucial in actually determining outcomes.

Clear intentions refers to processes where individuals themselves determine how they are going to act, but then convey this to other members of the network without any open discussion. Thus, an individual may decide they are (or are not) going to provide support for a relative, and act accordingly, without discussing this with anyone else involved. The final category, *non-decisions*, is, like 'clear intentions', implicit rather than explicit. However it is distinctive in that decisions emerge without anyone apparently having formulated a clear intention or discussed it openly with others. Instead, it would seem the constellation of different people's circumstances and family or kinship 'biographies' are such that it becomes 'obvious' to all that a particular course of action is the one to follow.

While neither 'clear intentions' nor 'non-decisions' really signify 'negotiation' as it is commonly understood, both involve processes in which kin are actively positioning themselves *vis-à-vis* one another over time. It is this aspect of negotiation, distinct from normative injunction, within the development of family practices that has attracted the attention of researchers concerned with different aspects of family life. While the 'negotiation' may not be explicit, the decisions made emerge as a result of understandings people within the family network have of each other's family-relevant biographies, locations and proclivities. It is in this sense of longer-term processes of action and inaction, including discursive constructions of family responsibility, identity and reputation, that both 'clear intentions' and 'non-decisions' can be recognised as 'negotiated', despite their implicit character. As will become evident in later chapters, Finch and Mason's (1993) emphasis on processes of active relational construction across time is one that informs the analysis of stepfamily relationships we develop in this book.

David Morgan's book *Family Connections* (1996) is quite different to Finch and Mason's (1993) study. It is subtitled *An Introduction to Family Studies*, though it is far more than just an introductory text. Rather it is a theoretical treatise which captures very clearly many of the competing issues which have been central to family sociology in recent decades. For our purposes, there were three key elements within Morgan's approach. First Morgan highlights the continuing importance of family relationships and family activities within people's routine lives, notwithstanding the very significant changes that had been occurring within the family realm. He does this by demonstrating the inherent connections there are between family matters and a wide range of other components of social and economic life, including gender, work and employment; the body; and different aspects of consumption. He is thus not making a claim for the importance of 'the family' *per se*, but rather arguing that family matters are important precisely because of their connection and interweaving with other equally key facets of social organisation. Second, and closely related to this first point, Morgan also emphasises the inappropriateness of treating family relationships as given or fixed. In this regard, while there is regularity in family behaviour, 'family' is not best understood in terms of 'family structure' as this implies too 'concrete' or reified a view of what happens in families. Instead there is a need for greater emphasis on agency, on family relationships as socially constructed and 'achieved' and on movement, fluidity and process in family life.

This leads to the third – and most novel – element in Morgan's account of family life that we want to highlight here: his conceptualisation of the term 'family practices' for analysing family relationships. Morgan draws on this term to convey a number of different themes. The most important, as noted, is to move beyond the idea of 'family' as fixed. Indeed in understanding the realm of family, it is necessary to pay heed to what it is those directly involved define as being about 'family' rather than to impose external criteria. In other words, while the researcher's (or observer's) ideas of what constitutes *family* behaviour are of consequence, so too are the actor's own ideas, and the two perspectives – researcher's and participant's – may not be wholly synonymous. Equally the notion of 'family practices' conveys a sense of *routine* in the constitution of family life, first in terms of the significance of unexceptional, everyday activities, and second as a consequence of these activities being regular and repetitive rather than one-off or episodic.

Thus the term reflects the idea of family life being constructed by its members through their relational behaviour and activities – that is, their practices – rather than simply being normatively governed or socially imposed. Yet, equally, it implies that patterns of behaviour develop which have a continuity and a constraining reality for different family members. These are the largely unquestioned ways in which those involved 'do' their family. In other words, the use of the term 'family practices' represents a means of engaging with the structure/ agency dichotomy. It represents an understanding of family matters which embraces the idea that different family networks achieve their goals in different ways, that family patterns are consequent on the actions of those involved and that there is fluidity and change possible within these patterns. At the same time, it recognises that this fluidity is not unbounded. Ways of being within different family contexts, ways of doing different family activities, ways of organising different family relationships become established as a response to both historical and biographical factors. Families are not constituted by members in a structural void, but rather in response to the social and economic opportunities, constraints and contradictions which confront them individually and collectively (Widmer and Jallinoja, 2008). In this way, patterns become established, both within what might be termed the 'culture' of particular families and within their broader sociocultural milieu. Overall, the concept of 'family practices' represents a bridge between fluidity and stability, structure and agency, change and continuity in understanding the character of family relationships. These are issues which Morgan has developed fully in his later work – see Morgan, 1999, 2002, but especially Morgan, 2011.

It is evident that there are commonalities in the ways Finch and Mason (1993) and Morgan (1996) sought to understand family matters through their concepts of 'negotiation' and 'family practices'. It is no coincidence that these two concepts have received a good deal of attention from family sociologists and have been drawn on in a variety of studies (e.g. Silva and Smart, 1999b; Seymour, 2007; Becher, 2008; Chambers et al., 2009). They reflect very well concerns about the dangers of reifying family organisation and ignoring issues of family diversity, family change and the relationship between agency and structure in constituting family life. Moreover, in terms of understanding stepfamily relationships, the perspectives they embrace are well-suited to an analysis of family members' different commitments and solidarities. Indeed it is evident that the concerns Morgan (1996) and Finch and Mason (1993) are addressing were also ones which exercised Burgoyne and Clark (1984) in their study of stepfamilies. While they did not talk about 'family practices' as such in their book, Burgoyne and Clark were very much concerned with the idea that these families were engaged in processes of negotiation, without actually framing this or developing the concept as explicitly as Finch and Mason do. We will be drawing on these ideas in later chapters, not least when we explore the relevance for stepfamilies of 'family order' in Chapter 5.

Constructing unclear families

Stepfamilies have not been widely studied in Britain. Indeed it is only in the US that this family form has been a significant sociological focus of interest (see Ganong and Coleman, 2004, and Pryor, 2008, for reviews of much of this work). Since Burgoyne and Clark's (1984) research, there have only been a small number of major studies in Britain focussing on stepfamilies. One of the most important of these is Simpson's (1994, 1998) anthropological examination of post-divorce family and kinship, though his study focusses on the kinship consequences of divorce rather than on stepfamily issues *per se*. However, much of his analysis is of direct consequence for understanding important aspects of stepfamily organisation and relationships. And although its focus is very clearly anthropological, it shares with the research discussed in the previous section a concern for the ways in which family and kinship ties are actively constructed through the routine activities they involve, as well as a concern for the ways in which relationships alter over time as new contingencies and practices emerge.

Simpson's study has the advantage of being longitudinal. Respondents initially contacted as part of a project on divorce conciliation were interviewed over a seven-year period about their post-divorce family experiences and relationships (Simpson, 1998, pp. 13–22). A key theme underlying his analysis is that divorce, and the issues and dilemmas it produces, help to make explicit the principles around which marriage, family and parenting are normally constructed, principles that are not always so evident while the marriage is extant. More specifically from a kinship perspective he argues that marriage represents a reordering of relationships, property and rights. Divorce consequently also represents a (further) reallocation of goods, rights and people, relocating 'people and relationships in space and time' (1998, p. 25). In turn, of course, any consequent remarriage also relocates people and relationships in this way.

One of the benefits of this perspective is that it focusses on continuities as much as on discontinuities. Normally when we think of marital separation and divorce, the focus is on endings, on establishing new family orders and on the breaking up of previous relationships. At one level, as Simpson notes, this discontinuity is apparent in the language of separateness which characterises aspects of divorce, for example, in terms such as 'fresh start', 'single' or 'lone' parent, 'absent father (or mother)' and 'clean break', as well as 'separation' itself. However for those involved divorce is very rarely just about endings, even though at times many may wish it were. Instead the relationships entailed within the marriage, especially but not only when there have been children born to the union, continue in different guises long after the marriage is legally ended. Such matters as parenting arrangements, property and income rights and the reordering of kin relationships represent and embody continuities as well as discontinuities. So too, any identity (re)construction following divorce is patterned both by the presence of these post-divorce family continuities and by the ongoing biographical significance of the material and emotional legacies of the marriage.

Consequently it is mistaken to see divorce as just an 'ending', the closure of a now unsatisfactory relationship. Because of the different continuities there are, establishing family practices post-divorce necessitates negotiation and management of existing relationships to place these on a new footing, the more so when there are children involved. This is rarely a straightforward matter. Most people experience it as a highly problematic, emotionally fraught and complex process requiring substantial time before any real sense of resolution is achieved. The resonances here with Finch and Mason's (1993) and Morgan's (1996) work are clear. In particular, rather than following established ways of responding, those involved are engaged in actively reconstructing a kinship narrative, as well as a narrative of the self, involving the repositioning of people and relationships. Importantly, this is not an individual achievement; it is highly social. Simpson draws on Finch's (1989) term 'working out' of relationships in his analysis, though he equally could have referred to the idea of 'negotiation' (or 'renegotiation') of family relationships and practices. And as he makes clear, such 'renegotiation' needs to be seen as active and multifaceted. At times it involves explicit negotiation, perhaps with the involvement of external agents – solicitors, counsellors, judges; at other times it is a far more implicit process of action and reaction to the demands and behaviour of the ex-spouse or other family members.

Simpson (1994; 1998, Chapter 2) captures this brilliantly with the inversion of the standard '*nu*clear family' into the idea of the '*un*clear family'. The 'unclear family' represents the form of family becoming increasingly evident in late modernity (Giddens, 1992). It reflects especially well ideas of movement and flexibility encapsulated in arguments about the shifting nature of relational commitment and the decreasing influence of a strong normative ordering governing family constitution. Moreover, the idea of the 'unclear family' signifies confusion over the distribution of family responsibilities, rights and obligations, a position many post-divorce families find themselves having to manage. As Simpson (1998) highlights, the negotiation and balancing of material and emotional commitments, responsibilities, interests, claims and rights to ex-spouses, children, new partners, and in some cases their wider kin, is inherently complex and frequently fraught, an issue also developed by Smart and Neale (1999) in their study of the aftermath of divorce. Without socially accepted guidelines about how ex-spouses should treat one another or even about how post-divorce parenting should be managed, each unclear family emergently constructs their own family practices and resolutions, often in a conflictual context overlain with unresolved feelings of guilt, blame, recrimination and failure. To express this in the language used earlier in the chapter, the 'unclear family' encapsulates issues of family boundaries and family unity which are emergent, complex and consequently difficult to negotiate or resolve.

In focussing explicitly on stepfamilies, Jane Ribbens McCarthy, Ros Edwards and Val Gillies's (2003) book, *Making Families: Moral Tales of Parenting and Step-Parenting*, integrates some of the key themes raised by Burgoyne and Clark (1984) with the theoretical advances made by Finch and Mason (1993) and Morgan (1996). As their title indicates, Ribbens McCarthy, Edwards and Gillies were concerned with investigating the 'lived realities' (Chamberlayne, Bornat and Wengraf, 2000) of people's experiences of parenting within a stepfamily context, and the different ways in which 'family' was actively constructed and maintained by those involved. As in Burgoyne and Clark's study, there was significant variation in these matters, reflecting in part the strength of the 'boundaries' that were constructed around the family/household complex and in part the nature of the commitment that had developed between step-parents and stepchildren. (See also Bornat et al., 1999.) These variations also reflected class differences in what respondents considered desirable, with working-class respondents tending to draw more on a discourse of 'social (or replacement) parenting', while those from the middle class were more likely to emphasise the continuing significance of 'biological parenting'.

Whichever of these views of parenting was embraced, the respondents in the study sought to construct a 'shared family life', a domestic unit in which children were properly parented and given appropriate attention, care and security. Parents and step-parents collectively engaged in negotiating how children's welfare was to be managed, with elements of tension, disagreement and conflict frequently evident in these continuing and emergent negotiations. In turn though, resident parents and step-parents were accepting from an early stage of their relationship that their evolving commitment to one another also entailed a degree of commitment to the children in the household. In Ribbens McCarthy, Edwards and Gillies's (2003, p. 72) words: 'As the commitment to the new partner developed, this was understood as implying an equally developing commitment to her or his child/ren.' The ways in which that commitment came to be expressed varied, by both gender and class, as well as over time. The traditional stepfamily concerns of who holds rights and responsibilities for discipline and authority were evident in this study, with the working out of these matters influenced by the class-linked issue of whether a 'social' or 'biological' notion of parenting dominated.

Ribbens McCarthy, Edwards and Gillies (2003) also debate how issues of fairness are handled in stepfamilies. While the general moral imperative that everyone in stepfamilies, especially children, should be treated 'fairly' was a powerful one among their respondents, how this was achieved in practice was frequently problematic. Here 'boundary' issues of inclusion and exclusion loomed particularly large, sometimes concerning the different ways parent and step-parent within a household treated their own and each other's children, and sometimes about how children were treated outside the household by their non-resident parent. Cross-cutting this were also attempts to balance the needs of particular children at particular times versus the idea of treating all children equitably. How such issues of fairness are negotiated and resolved – and indeed the extent to which they are resolved – serve to encapsulate divisions within stepfamilies, reflecting some of the boundaries which limit their internal cohesion.

Like Burgoyne and Clark (1984), an important issue that Ribbens McCarthy, Edwards and Gillies (2003) address concerns changes within stepfamilies over time. This is a topic that has not received as much attention as it warrants in stepfamily studies (Baxter, Braithwaite and Nicholson, 1999; Braithwaite et al., 2001; Van Eeden-Moorefield and Pasley, 2008). Ribbens McCarthy, Edwards and Gillies (2003, pp. 87–90) highlight the importance of time in their respondents' views about the construction of commitment and trust within stepfamily relationships, particularly those between step-parents and stepchild(ren). In giving time to children, a 'proper' family could eventually be created; here concepts such as 'investing time' and 'building relationships' were drawn on by respondents to express their views about how an emergent sense of 'family' – as distinct from the couple tie – could be established.

The imagery here is highly positive. The outcome of giving time to such family matters – both in the sense of devoting time to them and of allowing time to do its work – was envisaged broadly by respondents as the successful creation of 'family solidarity' within the stepfamily. Of course, in practice, time may not have this effect; its impact may be more destructive. Analytically the key issue is that to understand stepfamily experiences, those experiences must be seen as 'process'. Stepfamilies are no more static than other families. Within them, as within other families, family practices may become somewhat settled, but it is important to recognise that stepfamilies have their own dynamic. In examining the patterning of stepfamilies, attention needs to be paid to the varied 'pathways' and 'careers' that stepfamilies can take. This is an issue to which we will return in the later chapters, particularly Chapter 8.

Conclusion

This chapter has been quite disparate in the range of issues it has addressed. Its aim has been to inform the analysis of stepfamily patterns considered in the chapters that follow through highlighting some of the key developments in recent family sociology in Britain and core themes from previous stepfamily research. In doing this it has emphasised process and fluidity. The structuring of family experiences of course remains important, but there is also a need to see such structuring as the consequence of the actions and decisions of the individuals involved. While such actions and decisions are evidently constrained by broader social and economic circumstances, family members have the capacity to influence the relationships and practices which constitute their family. They bring to their families their own interpretations and understandings, desires and principles, which collectively help to inform and pattern how their families are organised.

This is the value of concepts like 'negotiation' and 'family practices'. They highlight the degree to which family relationships are emergent rather than fixed. They indicate the role of agency in shaping family patterns without thereby neglecting the structural characteristics within which that agency operates. In looking at stepfamilies in the chapters that follow, we will be following a similar path. In drawing on material from our own empirical study, as well as on published research into stepfamily experiences, we will be seeking to illustrate how members of stepfamilies construct a family life, the divisions and tensions that there are in this and the diversity there is in the family solidarities generated.

However before turning to this, we are first going to provide some case examples of stepfamily relationships from our own study of stepfamily kinship. In later chapters of the book, we will use these case examples to illustrate and develop some of the arguments we are making. The examples we provide here are not selected for their typicality or representativeness. Rather we have chosen them to illustrate key processes within different stepfamilies and to convey some of the diversity there is in the construction of stepfamily relationships. But while not selected as representative *per se*, we would argue that the different concerns raised in them do reflect experiences common within stepfamily kinship.

3
Case Illustrations

In this chapter we present four case illustrations from our interviews. As noted at the end of the last chapter, these examples cannot be regarded as necessarily typical of some wider population of stepfamily networks. However we have selected them to represent key aspects of the issues which our respondents discussed in their interviews, and to reflect key debates which can be found in the research literature. They consequently provide a sense of the different relational dynamics which occur in stepfamilies. We will draw on these examples to illustrate arguments made in the chapters that follow. In this chapter we will not comment on what is being reported, instead we are simply summarising the issues as they were expressed in the interviews. The names and certain other identifying details of the individuals in these case illustrations have been changed to protect the anonymity of the respondents.

It must be remembered, of course, that the accounts we have are just that: accounts. They represent the views of the people we interviewed. They are our summaries of their narrative constructions. As such they are also 'moral tales' (Ribbens McCarthy, Edwards and Gillies, 2003). In presenting their understanding of their family relationships, the interviewees are also positioning themselves as moral beings and judging other people's motives and behaviour from this perspective. If the others being discussed had been interviewed, their accounts may well have been in substantial agreement about what can be thought of as the collective family experiences, but equally there would in many instances be differences in the motives they ascribed. Because we interviewed a number of individuals who were 'linked' to one another, we were at times able to see this. In general, differences in these accounts were relatively subtle and largely understandable in terms of the different positions the respondents occupied in the family networks (see, for example, the cases of Steve and Christine Richards below). However the case illustrations we are presenting need to be seen as in this sense partial, as narrative constructions which reflect the perspectives and views of the person being interviewed.

Steve and Christine Richards

Both Steve Richards and his stepdaughter Christine Richards were interviewed as part of our study. Their accounts of their family life shared many elements in common but also differed in a number of important and sometimes subtle respects. We are going to provide a summary of the main issues raised in Steve's interview first. We will then turn to Christine's account of her family relationships, highlighting the different ways in which she expressed the character of their family relationships.

Steve

Steve was 53 at the time of the interview. He had been married in his twenties but had divorced five years later. He had married Sally in his early forties. She too had been married previously and had three children from this marriage, David, 21; Christine, 18; and Ben 17 at the time of the interview. Christine was also interviewed as part of our study (see below). Nick, now 8, was born two years after Steve and Sally married. The only other family Steve now had were his sister, Lesley, now divorced, and her two children Chris, 24, and Sandra, 21. Although Steve had been close to Chris and Sandra before his marriage to Sally, he now saw relatively little of them unless they happened to be there when he visited his sister

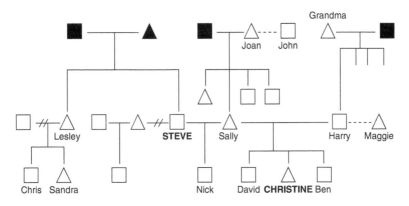

Diagram 3.1   Steve and Christine Richards

who lived near Coventry. Like Steve's parents, Sally's father had died before she met Steve. She had a difficult relationship with her mother, Joan, who lived in Portugal with her new partner, John. At the time of the interview, Sally and her mother had hardly spoken to each other for more than a year. Sally's relationships with two of her three siblings were also problematic and entailed little contact of any significance.

Sally and Steve had met in Ireland when he was working there. Sally's first husband, Harry, still lived there with his current partner Maggie. Sally had returned to Britain immediately after marrying Steve, bringing her children with her. David, Christine and Ben had visited Harry two or three times a year over most of the next ten years, though recently this had become less frequent. When they were in Ireland, they often stayed with Harry's mother. Although she lived some distance from Harry, her lifestyle was more child-centred than his and she also lived near her other children and grandchildren – David's, Christine's and Ben's cousins. Aside from answering the phone on occasion, Steve had no contact with Harry or his mother. It was clear from the interview that Steve felt that Harry was irresponsible and unwilling to provide financially or otherwise for his children. Sally's relationship with Harry was also fraught, in part because he did not pay the regular maintenance that had been agreed at the time of their divorce.

When Steve had first married Sally, he had hopes that they would all become much like his vision of a 'normal' family. Not only had they all moved to England as a family, but he also regarded himself as 'taking on' the three children. Moreover the surname of all the children had been changed to Richards by deed poll soon after he and Sally married. He reflected how he had

> tried very hard to treat them all the same and as my children, as Sally's children and I … I mean I consciously married Sally knowing she had three children, knowing that I was taking those on, and happy to take them on, I thought they were great children … I knew I had them for the duration! … We [changed their surname] because Sally and I agreed … it wasn't really done to be selfish to me at all. I felt that the family looked as a united family as far as the UK was concerned. We as a family had just moved from Ireland, and there was no need for anyone to know that they were not my children and that we were called 'Richards' and always had been.

However rather than becoming closer over time, new divisions had emerged within the family. In particular, Steve recognised that there were significant differences in his relationship with Nick, his natural child, and with his three stepchildren. Equally though, his relationships with Christine, and to a lesser extent Ben, were also more positive than his relationship with David. He found David particularly difficult: 'He's my problem. He's the biggest blot on my landscape if you like!' While this was a reference to David's size, it was also a reflection of the – apparently mutual – suspicion, if not outright dislike, there was between them. In part he put this down to David being older at the time of his marriage to Sally, but in part he also saw it as a result of David's personality. He felt David should take more responsibility for himself, make more effort to get a job and spend less time 'dossing around'. 'He doesn't seem to be wishing to take control of his future. He isn't putting in the effort, to try and control his destiny. And that worries me. A lot.' It was evident that Steve and David now found it difficult to be civil to each other; currently Steve felt it unlikely that he and David would continue having any involvement with each other were Steve and Sally's marriage ever to end.

While he felt much closer to Christine and Ben, Steve recognised that he had never played a 'full' father role to them in the way he had with Nick. There were five themes in his interview that illustrated this quite clearly. First, and most importantly, his emotional commitment to Nick was of a different order to the other three children. Throughout the interview, it was apparent that Nick was 'his' child. He said that while trying to treat them the same, he 'favoured Nick'. In contrast, while recognising he was very fond of Christine in particular, he hesitated about using the word 'love', saying: 'I, I'm, yeah, I'm um, yeah I would have to, really. … It's a difficult word to choose to use'. Moreover he recognised that he had rarely shown Christine or his stepsons physical affection. In particular he remarked that Christine had never given him a hug until recently when she came back home during her first term at University.

> [She] came home for a week in November, and on her arrival she gave me a hug – which is probably the first time she's given me a hug, and she gave me a hug again when she came home at Christmas … she hasn't hugged me – as far as I know – in the past, ever.

Second, he was aware that he had always taken – or been given – a back seat as far as discipline was concerned. This was Sally's responsibility:

> They wouldn't accept me disciplining them. So we quite quickly, I stopped. Sally would do the telling off, with my back-up. In fact we did it differently at different times. But I tried to discipline them

initially, and as I say it didn't, they wouldn't accept the discipline from me. They, I don't think – I suppose their age is inversely proportional to their respect for me – David the oldest has the least respect for me. As to my authority in the household and I said this in the early years, and Sally always said 'Oh, well you have to earn their respect' ... Sally did the telling off, the day to day um [disciplining].

Somewhat similarly in terms of his 'outsider' status, Steve recognised Sally's importance for managing what he termed 'family cohesion':

[It] is very noticeable, that if Sally's not in, the family cohesion falls apart very quickly ... when there's only Ben, Nick, and Sally and I, um, then the family cohesion is quite good, even when Sally's not there. But if the other two are there, like David and Christine, David particularly, Sally's not there for a meal or anything like that you can feel ... a whole different atmosphere and things are deteriorating and if she goes away for, you know, for a day or two days you can see the, the significant change and deterioration in the whole sort of [situation]

Fourth, it was clear from the interview that Steve and his three step-children had quite different kinship solidarities. To begin with, they called him Steve rather than 'Dad', though he did say he referred to them as his children rather than stepchildren. More importantly, according to Steve they had little to do with his sister Lesley – the only other close family Steve had. They did not regard her as an aunt or appear to feel any real connection to her. In turn, Steve knew few details about his stepchildren's kin on their natural father's side. Thus, in pointing to how much his stepchildren loved their paternal grandmother, his comparative lack of knowledge about this important arm of his stepchildren's family highlighted the divergences there were between his and their sense of family:

They like their, they love their Grandma, yeah. They do, they like their Grandma and they like a few of the brothers and their cousins – there's cousins and things. A big family there and they like, I don't know the exact numbers but there's, but names that crop up would suggest there's like three cousins that are quite close or maybe four cousins that are quite close.

Finally, Steve recognised he faced dilemmas over inheritance. He had not made a will, partly because he was unsure how to reconcile the competing claims. However in discussing the issues, it was clear he prioritised Nick over the others and felt it was up to him to protect Nick's interests. In this, he drew on the notion of 'blood' fatherhood:

> No I haven't made a will but it wouldn't be equal. It is awfully complicated. I would even in my own mind I have trouble reconciling what I want to do. On the one hand, you sort of say well Nick's my son I should leave it all to my son, then blow the rest [of them]. But I don't feel that strongly enough to actually say it. I, I feel I owe it to Nick that he should get the lion's share or he should certainly get a bigger proportion, even if you just base it on the technicality that the others will inherit from their blood father.

In these and other ways, it was evident that Steve had a different type of relationship with Nick than he had with his stepchildren. In a real sense, Nick was his family in a way the other three were not so fully. The following lengthy quote, taken from the end of the interview, captured Steve's view of his and others' experiences of being in a stepfamily:

> I still believe I'm the sixth member of my family. I am the bottom of the pile in Sally's eyes. Because my children are more important to her than me. I mean you can understand that to some extent, but if you were the blood father then you do have um, you were necessary for those children to exist, therefore there would have to be, you have to be there ... whereas when you're a stepdad you're not necessary, the only thing that you're important for is the money. Really. If that's what you're providing, you may not be, but if you are, then that's what's important. ... It takes time. Don't assume that they're going to love you, they won't, they don't, I don't think. I mean I'm putting a lot of information in here, not just my own experience, but there is no reason for them to like you, at all. In fact I would say there's every reason for them to not like you. Because they, I won't say – there's, there's a ... in their eyes there's a good reason to blame you for breaking up their previous relationship. Even though you have had nothing to do with it. At all. You're there. You are the replacement. Therefore if you weren't there, mum would still be with dad. Probably. I mean probably not, but they see it as that. I don't think they do in later life, but in the early time. There's a critical age. I would say I think possibly why I had problems with David, is the age at which I came on the scene.

Christine

Christine was 18 at the time of the interview and attending University. She had lived in Ireland with her mother, father and two brothers. Her parents separated when she was 6, and she and her brothers then lived with her mother, Sally. Sally married Steve when Christine was 8 and shortly after that the family moved to England. As noted above, all the family's surnames were changed at that time to Richards, Steve's surname. Some two years later, Nick, her half-brother, was born.

Christine's account of her experiences in her stepfamily echoed many of the themes that Steve discussed in his interview. In particular, she recognised the escalating conflict that had developed in recent years between Steve and her brothers, especially David. She also recognised very clearly the central role her mother, Sally, occupied within the family/household complex. Despite the similarities in their accounts, we want to address four issues from Christine's interview which warrant fuller consideration.

First, her use of the term 'stepdad' highlighted quite subtly Steve's more marginal position within her sense of family:

Interviewer:	One of the things that keeps cropping up is that people don't like to use the word 'step' – they don't like to think of themselves as 'steps', what do you think?
Christine:	I don't mind using it because I don't regard Steve as my dad, I don't like the idea of calling him my dad, I'd rather call him my stepdad.
Interviewer:	But you do describe him as your stepdad?
Christine:	Oh yes, if someone asked me who Steve was I'd say he was my stepdad, I wouldn't just say he's someone my mum's with or married to.

Similarly, in line with Steve's account, she also acknowledged that Steve's sister, Lesley, was not related to her. She was in her words 'just Steve's sister'.

Second, and building on this, Christine also pointed to the different ways she felt Steve responded to Nick, implicitly emphasising in her account the fact that Nick was Steve's 'own' child which marked him off as quite different to a stepchild.

Interviewer:	And how did you feel about [Nick's birth] at the time, can you remember?

Christine: Mmm – I was quite happy, I think. I wasn't bothered really. I didn't feel any – I wasn't surprised, I think I knew Steve wanted his – one of his own. It didn't bother me at the time so much as it does now sometimes. Steve makes it quite obvious that Nick can do no wrong but we can sometimes – more than he [Nick] does.

Interviewer: Why is that do you think? Because he's the youngest? Or because he's Steve's?

Christine: Well it might be that but I just think it's because Nick is Steve's. He doesn't like to think of him doing anything much wrong.

Later in the interview she returned to this theme, recounting how Steve's protection of Nick could serve to highlight Steve's different relationship with her:

> But I can be quite off with Nick. There was, quite recently, a stage I went through when I didn't like him at all. Mainly because – I think it was Steve's fault – because Steve had told me off, in front of Nicholas, a couple of times, for telling Nicholas off for something he'd done when Steve wasn't there. And then Steve hears me tell him off, came in and criticises me. And then after that Nicholas would say 'You can't tell me what to do, you're not the boss.' and he didn't listen to me at all. ... I was someone who was good enough to baby-sit though but not good enough to control Nicholas in any way.

Third, as this last quotation indicates, Christine did not feel that Steve was 'on her side' in the way her mother, Sally, was or, indeed, in the way Steve was on Nick's. She pointed out how she would always go to her mother, rather than Steve, with any problems: 'I'd wait for mum to come home'. Later in the interview, she was asked if she felt that Steve would 'champion' her if something went wrong at University. She responded: 'Mmm, I suppose if it was really serious he might, but he would probably find some way in which it could be my fault – the problem.' The conditionality of their relationship for her was also captured in the following response:

Interviewer: So how would you describe your relationship with Steve?

Christine: Mmm, it's OK most of the time. Sometimes I can get very frustrated with him – like he doesn't like me ever going out and if I want something or I want to go out then I don't ask him because I know the answer will be 'no'. So I always go to mum. I don't have a strong relationship with Steve – I do love him because he does a lot for me but he's just not – you know.

Fourth, Christine, like Steve in his interview, acknowledged that Steve played no direct part in disciplining her or her brothers as they grew up. However her account of the part he played here was subtly different from his, though equally revealing of the divisions and boundaries operating within the family. Whereas Steve had emphasised his background support for Sally, Christine highlighted the way in which Steve's disapproval of various activities and behaviour resulted in a degree of collusion between Sally and the three older children. She recognised in particular the 'buffer role' Sally played and how her protection of them often led to rows between her mother and Steve:

Christine:	I hate that...well, I think the major effect on me from Steve's discipline point of view – that it causes arguments between mum and Steve. And it can cause major rows.
Interviewer:	Do you know when these are going on?
Christine:	Usually yes, because mum tells me. ... Sometimes we hear about them but usually she'll be upset and then she'll tell me.

The following quotation from Christine's interview captures well the sense of 'belonging' and 'division' evident in her account of Steve's position in the family.

Mum always says that we're quite lucky in that Steve's not our real dad because she's always going to be on our side but Nick will have to put up with the fact that mum can't be on his side, she can't turn around and say 'Yes' if Steve says 'No' because with him it will have to be joint.

Mark Burton

Mark was 26 at the time of the interview and living alone. His natural parents, Michael and Ann, separated when he was less than a year old. He lived with his mother and her parents, Pop and Nana, briefly until

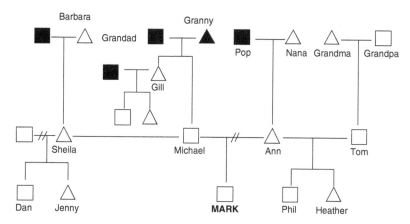

Diagram 3.2 Mark Burton

Ann married Tom Wellington. Ann and Tom had two children, Phil and Heather, aged 20 and 18 at the time of the interview. Michael had lived in different parts of the country as a result of his work in the armed forces, but had maintained regular fortnightly contact with Mark throughout his childhood. Michael had married Sheila when Mark was 14. Sheila had two children from a previous marriage, Dan and Jenny, now aged 25 and 20, who until recently lived with their mother and Michael.

From the very beginning of the interview, Mark made it clear that he regarded his core family to be Ann, Tom, Phil and Heather, the members of the household in which he had grown up. These were the people who were his family and who he felt most at home with. He said 'Yup, what happened was parents divorced when [I was] very young, and my mother remarried very quickly, to Tom who's always been "Dad" to me.' While he had not changed his surname from Burton, that is, Michael's surname, at various stages in the interview he emphasised how he had always thought of Phil and Heather as full siblings, and as Tom's parents, Grandpa and Grandma, as full grandparents. He had always been treated by them as a grandson and was still very close to them. Indeed in the course of the interview Grandpa rang him up to make arrangements to go out together.

Interviewer: Now Tom's parents, you were very young when your mum and
Mark: That's Grandma and Grandpa.

Interviewer:	Right. And they were in effect your stepgrandparents. But did they feel like stepgrandparents?
Mark:	No, no, we spent a lot of time with them. Still do see them though, saw them on Sunday, you know we see them a lot really.
Interviewer:	So they're your grandparents?
Mark:	Yes. There's no real distinction on that side of the family, if you like everything that side [referring to the Wellington part of the genogram] is family.

This sense of who his family was was pervasive throughout the interview. He clearly perceived a strong boundary around the Wellington family group and included himself as a full member. In contrast, his relationship with his natural father, Michael, was quite different. As noted, Michael's work had taken him to different parts of the country but he had still visited Mark very regularly every two weeks when he was younger.

Mark:	Yes, every two weeks. Visited every two weeks, every second Sunday.
Interviewer:	Right and always you went
Mark:	Well, he always came to visit me usually
Interviewer:	In your home?
Mark:	Yes … We'd go out for a day or something.

Later in the interview Mark added that 'With the exception of once or twice, I don't think I've ever been driven over there, he was always coming over this way'. This pattern began to change when Mark was in his mid-teens as a result, according to Mark, of three factors: his father's marriage to Sheila; Mark's increasingly independent social life as a teenager; and a very serious crash that Michael had had that had left him partially disabled. Indeed once Mark had learnt to drive, the pattern changed further with Mark now visiting Michael and Sheila – albeit somewhat less frequently – at their home some 60 miles away, rather than his father driving to see him.

Thus Mark's portrayal was one in which Michael came into his world, rather than him (Mark) going into Michael's. Interestingly this pattern seemed to continue even after Mark started driving to Michael's and Sheila's home. For example, he said that he had never actually stayed at Michael's and Sheila's, despite getting on well with Sheila's son, Dan.

Interviewer:	Of course you and Dan are almost the same age.
Mark:	Yes.
Interviewer:	So did you start then to go and stay with them?
Mark:	No, never stayed with them.
Interviewer:	Never have?
Mark:	I have always been a bit hesitant if you know what I mean.
Interviewer:	You didn't want to do that?
Mark:	No, not really. That is very definitely McDonald [Sheila's surname] family, this is really – friends, if you know what I mean. It's a different
Interviewer:	So for you it's a different – role?
Mark:	Yes.

At other times in the interview, Mark also indicated a hesitancy about his involvement with or incorporation into his (natural) father's new family. This was not a consequence of 'traditional' stepfamily problems; he described Sheila as 'very nice' and appeared to have an entirely cordial, though not strong, relationship with her. As in the passage above though, he implied that with his marriage to Sheila and sharing a home with her two children, Michael's genealogical location had shifted. It was as if Michael had been removed that much further from the orbit of Mark's family Wellington into Sheila's family McDonald. As we shall discuss below, Mark did not see this as problematic; instead he rather welcomed it as a solution to the complexity of his *'unclear'* (Simpson, 1998) family circumstances.

As in the passage above, one of the ways in which Mark expressed his commitment to his natural father while still asserting his full membership of the Wellington family was through using the language of 'friendship' rather than 'family' to describe his relationship with Michael.

Interviewer:	And your relationship with [Michael], is it a good, close relationship?
Mark:	Yes, more like we're friends really. ... It's more like a – friends really.

Similarly in discussing his relationship with Dan, Sheila's son, he also drew on the language of friendship as a contrast with 'family'.

Interviewer:	So do you feel that Dan – when you talk about this side [McDonalds] as friends – does Dan feel more like a brother?

Mark: Er – Dan feels like a good close family member, yeah.
Interviewer: ... like a brother, of course, it's different for everybody anyway.
Mark: Yeah. I wouldn't, I mean it may be wrong of me but I wouldn't put Dan in the [pause]. How would you say it – friend of special consideration – I don't know.
Interviewer: Special friend?
Mark: Special friend, something like that ... Except we don't, as I said because of time and everything, we don't see each other a lot, I've got other friends I see a lot more.

In contrast, Mark, felt no ambiguity about his relationships with his three sets of grandparents, all of whom he had had strong relationships with, though three of the six were now dead. Like Tom's parents, Ann's parents had lived close and been important to him throughout his life. Michael's parents lived over 100 miles away, but Mark had had regular contact with them throughout his childhood. Indeed not only had Michael taken him to visit them on some of his contact visits, but Ann had been active in sustaining this relationship as well as Mark's relationship with his paternal aunt, Gill. Grandad and Granny sometimes came to stay with Ann and Tom, and, according to Mark, Ann and Gill had remained good friends despite her separation from Michael. In addition, Mark had frequently stopped off at Grandad and Granny's on his way to and from University in the north of England. He said of his three sets of grandparents:

Mark: And in some respects it's much easier with grandparents.
Interviewer: In what way?
Mark: Well it's easy to have a more normal relationship with grandparents, 'cos grandparents usually see, you know, a couple of dozen times a year perhaps, maybe not even that, a dozen times a year for a day or something and therefore you can have quite a normal grandparent-type relationship with stepgrandparents or whatever.

In contrast to these ties, Mark had no real relationship with Sheila's mother, Barbara, having only met her on a small number of occasions.

What Mark is alluding to here was the difficulty he experienced of having two 'fathers'. As noted, he regarded his stepfather, Tom, as his 'dad', and used a friendship analogy to characterise his relationship with Michael. In part, this reflected his everyday experience in growing up, but it was also a reflection of his sense of who had taken on most 'parental responsibility'. He was very aware of Tom's commitment to him and the way he had never differentiated between Mark and his two natural children, Phil and Heather. He was also aware that Michael, despite being in a well-paid job, had contributed relatively little maintenance. Tom, by contrast, had been very generous, among other things paying for expensive private education. At the end of the interview, Mark was quite forthcoming about the tensions he felt around these relationships. He reported how when Michael married Sheila he wanted to stop his regular access visits. For him, this seemed to offer something of a watershed, an opportunity for Michael to become more 'embedded' in his new family and for Mark's family relationships to become more normative and 'ordered'. When he was asked if his relationship with Michael had ever caused any trouble with Ann and Tom, Mark replied,

> Caused more aggro with me actually, the number of occasions I thought 'This is it, I've had enough'... Once or twice I said, 'That's it, don't want any more to do with it'... [Mum] was responsible for keeping the links open. Had it been up to me I'd probably... [have kicked] it into touch, just lose it really.

He ended the interview with a reflection that captured well his views of how family should be:

> I think you've got to pick one side of the family for being family, you can't have two families I don't think. You've got one group of a family, and the other group are going to be friends. ... You've got to put your flag in the – on this level you've got to put your flag in the ground one side.

Louise Buchanan

At the time of the interview Louise Buchanan, a social worker, had been married to Alan for almost four years, having previously cohabited with him for a little under five years. She and her first husband, Dave, had divorced some 14 years before the interview. She and Dave had had two children, Ellen, now 18, and Mark, 15, who lived with her and Alan. Her parents, Jim and Betty, lived locally and were important figures within her support network. Alan had previously been married to Yvonne. They had had three children, Dan, now 26, Adam, 23 and Layla who

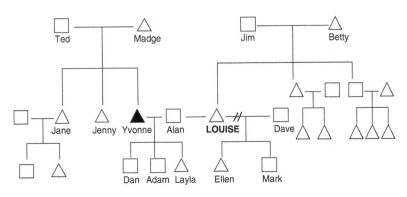

Diagram 3.3   Louise Buchanan

was 15, the same age as Mark. Yvonne had died quite unexpectedly of kidney failure 13 years before the interview. After Yvonne's death Alan lived with his children in Devon, close to Yvonne's mother and father, Madge and Ted Abbott, and her two sisters, Jane and Jenny. They provided a good deal of support for him at this time and were very committed to the children. When Alan and Louise started cohabiting, Adam and Layla moved with him, though Dan, then 16, chose to live with his maternal grandparents.

Louise said that when she and Alan first started living together, she thought the process of forming a new family would be relatively easy. As well as having her own children, she had through her work gained a good deal of experience of children coping with transitions and thought that this would mean she could avoid some of the pitfalls others experienced. She now recognised that she had been very naive; the process had been far more difficult than she had ever imagined.

Louise:	And I was very naive. Because I work with loads of children – and I thought it would be like it was at work – but it's not because they are there with you twenty-four hours a day. I thought it was going to be easy but it wasn't.
Interviewer:	No, I'm sure but because you had experience of children …
Louise:	Yes, and I get on really well with children usually and I don't really have much problems with them, any children, all ages and that, and I thought it would be the same – giving a home to a child and the child coming to live with you. But it's easy to forget that they have different rules

that they've had in their house – and different ways of being brought up. It's not the same.

In reality, Louise and Alan faced many problems. At the beginning, it was clear that the children were not happy with the new arrangements. Mark, who was described as very easy-going, appeared to have fewest problems and quite quickly formed a good relationship with Alan. Ellen, on the other hand, showed her resentment with the new family in various ways, according to her mother 'doing some terrible things' including cutting some of Alan's clothes and poisoning Layla's pet goldfish. In turn, Louise found Layla to be very dependent and demanding of her time. Adam also felt some unhappiness with the new arrangements:

Adam never could settle. And when he came to live here he didn't like the house we had. And, like, his father had done everything whereas I had been out at college and my children were used to, sort of, doing their thing – and then when his college course finished he decided to go and live back in Devon. But now he gets on really well with me [laughs].

Over time, some of these issues abated with relationships between Alan and Louise and their children generally improving. However there remained significant issues within the family, principally related to tensions consequent upon the strong relationships that Yvonne's parents and sisters maintained with Dan, Adam and Layla. As noted, the two boys had both decided to live in Devon rather than with their father and Louise in Middleston. Layla continued to live with Alan and Louise, but had a close relationship with Madge and Ted. She spoke on the phone to them frequently and usually went to stay with them (and her brothers) for a week in school holidays. While Louise recognised the importance of these relationships for Layla, she also resented the continuing impact they were having on her attempts to construct a joint family life.

According to Louise, a number of factors were at play in this. To begin with, she recognised the very strong sense of family solidarity which the Abbott family in Devon, especially Madge, had. 'Yes, they are a very, very close-knit family. ... Madge, she thinks it's very important that all the family stays close and all together.' They saw Layla as very much part of their family and were consequently very supportive and protective of her. From Louise's perspective, this served to undermine Layla's sense of commitment to the 'Family Buchanan' which she (Louise) had been trying to establish within her household. Louise felt that this had become particularly pronounced since she and Alan had married. 'Well, in the beginning they did [treat the children equally] but once we got married it faded out. They stopped and they said it should be separate families'. Thus she felt that while she had (implicitly) been trying to establish common boundaries within her household, Madge and the rest of the Abbott family sought to ensure that Layla continued to recognise that she was part of the Abbott family. Moreover Louise felt that Layla's visits to Devon were often emotionally upsetting, as well as being disruptive of the routines that she (Louise) was working to achieve.

> When she goes to this lot – like if she's had a whole week with that Nan and they're trying to keep this image of her mother alive and visiting the grave and that. It makes Layla really upset. And then she comes back and she is really awful, out of routine and everything.

Linked to these concerns about family boundaries, commitment and solidarity lay significant disagreements over how Layla should be treated, disagreements which were rooted in different ideas about childhood socialisation generally and Layla's immediate needs more specifically. Louise emphasised how with Ellen and Mark she had prioritised education as well as expecting them to contribute domestically from an early age. She felt Layla had been over-indulged by Madge and her family – and by Alan – and been given too little self-responsibility.

> It's just that, to me, it was too much molly-coddling and I suppose I didn't have time. Where I was going to college and that – my children had to help and fend for themselves a lot more.

Differences in their respective expectations about how children should be treated, along with concerns over who in her family should exercise control over Layla's development, emerged throughout the interview. They signified different family cultures and in the process both expressed and reinforced the divisions existing between the two families.

Interviewer: Right, so Madge, and Jenny and Jane – when Alan was on his own, he must have been on his own for about six years, were they his main means of support and help?

Louise: Yes, they supported him all the time and that's what they got mad about when we got married. They felt that I was taking over Layla in the way of – well, like her clothes because I felt that a lot of her clothes were really babyish, and I didn't want other children to laugh at her; she needed to be the same as other children down here – and her hair and everything. Alan ... relied on them to decide everything, and then when I came along I decided stuff and they didn't like it.

Interviewer: So over here, when Layla says these are all hers – the people in Devon – do they include Ellen and Mark at all?

Louise: They used to – up to about two years ago – they send Christmas cards now and one of the aunties sends presents to Ellen and Mark because she's got children. ... They just stopped because when Layla was going up for half term and that she had quite a bit of homework – and I sent up quite a bit of homework and they said that they feel that she doesn't get enough love and attention and I am more into education, so they didn't like it.

Interviewer: So they are critical of you?

Louise: Yes, they don't like, they wanted Alan to stay on his own with those children and they didn't want me to – when I had Layla she could hardly read or write or anything and I spent hours and hours with her reading and writing – and she still has a bit of special needs at school but she's getting on pretty good.

As implied in these quotations, Alan played little part in Layla's routine emotional or practical care. He appeared to have adopted a 'traditional' father role, seeing childcare as essentially a female responsibility. After Yvonne's death, his mother-in-law and sisters-in-law stepped in to care for his children, with Louise taking over this role – at least for Layla – once she and Alan started to live together.

Louise: I think when his wife was alive he seemed very close to [the children]. But when she died I don't think he really knew what to do. With Layla, like, he doesn't seem to know what to do with her or how to talk to her.

Interviewer: So do you feel that he leaves a lot of the day-to-day stuff to you?

Louise: Oh, he does. I do it all.

Interviewer: So earlier on Jane and Jenny and Madge stepped in. And then you came in – which they weren't very happy about – but there were no problems there with Alan.

> They could do it or you could do it – because he was a bit at sea, you think?

Louise: Yes, he did it all like a robot, what he had to, what he should be doing. But as for talking to her, finding out what she liked and what she didn't like and everything, well, that was sort of immaterial. And when she's talking to him but he doesn't listen, he just switches off, blanks out. ... he'd buy her stuff – ice creams or chocolates or anything just to keep her quiet.

Alan's relative lack of involvement seems likely to have exacerbated the tensions Louise experienced with the Abbott family. With Alan acting passively and consequently not mediating as parent, the diverse claims to authority over Layla and the judgements of her best interests that Louise as stepmother and Madge as grandparent made could not easily be resolved. Moreover, as well as their different perceptions of Layla's needs and how she should be treated, at play here too were the competing pulls of 'family as household' and 'family as kinship'.

From Louise's perspective, she was trying to treat the children fairly and equally within the 'family as household', but found this difficult when the Abbott family were emphasising divisions. She felt her parents and sisters, on the other hand, were supporting her efforts by not differentiating between Ellen, Mark and Layla.

Louise: Well, she says eight [grandchildren], my mum always says eight because she includes Layla as well.

Interviewer: But not Dan and Adam?

Louise: No, probably because they're older and have moved away. But she always tells people she has eight.

Interviewer: And again you said they were fair with presents giving the same to each – and tell me, was that a conscious decision, did you ever ask for that or talk about it at all?

Louise: No, but my mum would always treat everyone the same – and my brothers and sisters. And Madge and Ted and Jane and Jenny they started off like that in the beginning but then once we got married they felt it should be separate – and they also feel resentful that Alan doesn't spend enough time with his sons. But that's very difficult when they're older to try and arrange weekends when you can all – you know, they've got things to do and college and ...

Yet while Louise strongly emphasised the need to treat the three children in the household equally, she also indicated that this was difficult because of the different backgrounds of the children, their different personalities and, importantly, her different feelings towards them.

> *Interviewer*: And would you say that there's a difference – between how you are with your children and, perhaps, how you are with Layla?
>
> *Louise*: I think in the beginning, yes, because she used to be so obnoxious but I think now, you know, I just class them as all three the same. ... Well, Layla used to irritate me because she wasn't how I wanted her to be. She had no confidence, and she never had many friends and she was always falling out – and she was always lying, she used to steal money ... and any sweets or anything, when she's upset about anything she steals sweets and keeps eating sweets all the time.

Perhaps most revealingly, when Louise was asked what she thought would happen if she and Alan separated, her response was as follows:

> *Interviewer*: If this marriage ended Louise – and I do hope it doesn't – but if it did, do you think that you would still carry on having contact with your stepchildren?
>
> *Louise*: No.
>
> *Interviewer*: You don't, and not see Layla either?
>
> *Louise*: No, [pause] because it's forced.
>
> *Interviewer*: And Alan and your two?
>
> *Louise*: No, I don't think so. He's like me, once something's finished then it's finished.

Although Louise did not say it, it would seem probable that in these circumstances, Layla would, like her brothers, (re)turn to the secure base of the Abbott family.

Sandie Noonan

Sandie Noonan, a stepdaughter and a stepmother, was 39 at the time of the interview. She had been married twice. Her first marriage was to Paddy. They had had two daughters, Reb, 20, and Alex, 18, though Paddy had left Sandie for another relationship before Alex was born.

Shortly afterwards Sandie left the town they were then living in and moved back to Middleston where she had been brought up and where her family still were. Since then neither she nor her daughters had had any contact at all with Paddy, though Sandie had heard he had remarried. Sandie had also repartnered, marrying Simon some 12 years before the interview. She and Simon had had two children, Gina, 5, and Tim, 2. Simon had also been married previously, having a son Liam, now 18. Liam lived with his mother, Kate, her second husband and their two children, some 30 miles from Middleston. Sandie's daughter Reb now also had a child, Jamie, who was 18 months old at the time of the interview. Reb was not partnered, though Jamie's father had access visits every two weeks. Sandie's parents had divorced when she was 12. Neither she nor her older sister, Susan, had had any contact with her father, Martin, after the divorce, and Sandie now knew nothing about him except that he lived in Spain. Her mother, Angela, had married Andy shortly after this. When Sandie was 18, Angela and Andy had a son, Colin, Sandie's half-brother, who was now 21.

In some regards, Sandie's family was one of the more complex that we came across in the study. In other ways, however, it was curiously straight-forward, though not traditionally so, in part because of the complete absence of both Sandie's father, Martin, and Sandie's ex-husband, Paddy, as significant others in her and her children's lives. After her mother's marriage to Andy, Sandie had lived with Angela and Andy until she married Paddy. From her account of her adolescence, there had been no difficulties in her relationship with Andy. He was effectively seen as a 'replacement' father and fully a member of her family. She had called him 'Dad' since he and

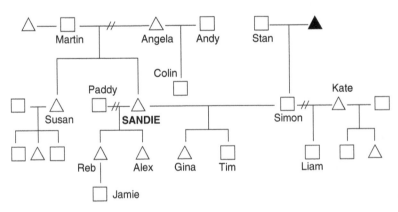

Diagram 3.4   Sandie Noonan

Angela married. Likewise, for all her children he and Angela were 'Nan and Grandad'. They now lived some 20 miles from Sandie, but maintained an active relationship with her:

Interviewer: And how often would you see them?
Sandie: Um, well sometimes it'll be perhaps a fortnight before – I'll speak to them on the phone but I won't actually see them, and then perhaps we'll see them two or three times in the week and then I won't see them again for a little while. Because they live – it's not that close – you know it's not as if it's just popping down the road.
Interviewer: It's a trip, isn't it?
Sandie: Yes, but it varies, sometimes I'll see them, like I said I'll see them a couple of times, two or three times in the same week, and then I won't see them perhaps for a fortnight.

Her relationship with Colin, her younger brother, was also important here. Sandie emphasised how Colin was a full brother:

Interviewer: And do you have a lot of contact with Colin?
Sandie: Yes.
Interviewer: You do ... would you describe him as your brother?
Sandie: Yes.
Interviewer: Or your ...
Sandie: No, he's my brother, yeah.

She also added that she had never felt that Andy treated Colin differently from the way he treated her, though of course there was a large age difference. She had left home by the time he was born, and shortly afterwards had her own child, Reb.

Thus Sandie's 'family-as-child' took a relatively 'standard' form, even though from her teens onwards she had no contact with her 'natural' father. This pattern was similar to the relationships constructed in her 'family-as-parent', though this was somewhat more complicated by Simon's previous marriage. According to Sandie, and also Reb, who with her son Jamie was present for some of the interview, Simon was fully accepted by all as her and Alex's *de facto* father. The use of kinship labels in the family also reflected the degree of solidarity experienced in it. While Reb called Simon 'Simon' rather than 'Dad', Alex had always referred to him as 'Dad'. Equally he was recognised without hesitancy or qualification as 'Grandad' for Jamie. Reb's and Alex's relationships with Simon's father, Stan, and his son, Liam, also reflected the degree of integration there was in this family. Simon's mother had died before Simon met Sandie, but his father lived near them. From the accounts given in the interview, it was clear that Stan was a grandfather figure not just for Liam, Gina and Tim, but also for Reb and Alex.

Sandie:	Yeah. They see him. Yeah, [he lives] next door to Gina's school. ... Yeah because Reb and Alex look upon him as their grandad.
Interviewer:	Right. Because of course I suppose he's your stepgrandad, isn't he really?
Reb:	Yes
Interviewer:	But you don't think of him as that? You think of him as your grandad, not your stepgrandad?
Reb:	Yes
Interviewer:	And you'd go and see him often?
Reb:	As often as I can.
Interviewer:	And you see him, you quite often see him when he's out, don't you?
Reb:	Yeah.
Interviewer:	And is he a grandad to Jamie as well?
Reb:	I refer to him as grandad. Grandad Stan.

Liam lived with Simon when he and Kate first separated, though from the age of five had lived with Kate. Initially this had caused friction between Kate and Simon, though now their relationship was unproblematic if not particularly warm. As a child, Liam had regularly spent weekends and some holiday periods with Sandie and Simon, though now he visited more when it suited him. Sandie felt that Liam had always fitted in well when he came to stay, with the fact he was a stepbrother causing no difficulty. Reb's comments at the end of the following passage provided a clear insight into Liam's position in the family.

Sandie:	Yeah, people are all different aren't they, so you're bound not to agree all of the time – or not agree all of the time. But you know most of the time I think we were quite lucky really, because we all got on really.
Interviewer:	And you didn't have any trouble getting on with Liam?

Sandie:	No.
Interviewer:	He just fitted in?
Sandie:	Yeah.
Interviewer:	And how about Reb and Alex and Liam?
Sandie:	Yeah, they were all right. There used to be either Liam and Reb, or Liam and Alex, if the three of them got together they used to ...
Interviewer:	That's threes though, isn't it?
Sandie:	Yes, but that was just the ordinary, just the normal sort of children thing. But there wasn't any problems because of um, because they were step – yeah they were stepbrothers and sisters. No there wasn't any problems there.
Interviewer:	So if you were going to say, Reb, how many brothers and sisters you have, what would you say?
Reb:	Two brothers, two sisters. Uncle Liam as well. ... Well, we call him Liam, but he's uncle Liam.

Thus across the two generations of divorce and remarriage, Sandie's families had been reconstituted in ways which from her account appeared to have presented few significant difficulties. The introduction of stepfathers into these families had been accomplished without the friction or tension that others can experience. Of course these events had happened many years before the interview. Any difficulties that had arisen at the time may have come to be regarded as now of little consequence. Yet as we saw in the other case illustrations presented above, other respondents often recounted in some detail the emotional and practical issues they had confronted in creating new stepfamilies. In contrast, it appeared that Sandie's experiences of stepfamily formation had been far less problematic.

In both her own and her parents' marriages, separation and divorce had followed the more 'traditional' clean break model. Neither Paddy nor Martin had made significant efforts to see their children after the divorce and neither had contributed any maintenance. Both had effectively disappeared from their children's lives. While both families experienced a degree of poverty until the respective mothers, Angela and Sandie, repartnered, neither had the complexities of access or role conflict to negotiate. Only between Simon and Kate had such post-divorce conflicts emerged and they had been settled some years previously. But equally it seemed that Simon's continuing, strong relationship with Liam had been facilitated by Liam's ready integration into Sandie's, Reb's and Alex's family network.

Towards the end of the interview, Sandie was asked what advice she would give to others in her position:

> I wouldn't offer any advice to anybody about things like that. No, because, I don't know, well I'm not qualified to offer advice really I don't think. ... I think ... the only thing I could say, you've got to be flexible. Because if you, if you're not flexible, and you're not willing to compromise and you're not willing to – you know you want it all your own way all of the time, you're not going to get anywhere, really.

The level of acceptance and tolerance this expresses was reflected in Sandie's responses throughout the interview. It seemed that this outlook permeated her family's relationships and was central in the successful construction and management of this 'unclear' family across three generations.

Conclusion

We are not going to comment further on the cases illustrations presented in this chapter. In presenting them we have tried to represent accurately the tone and content of the different interviews and of the ways those we interviewed understood their family relationships. Of course, these are doubly constructed accounts. They are our summaries of the versions of the family 'reality' the respondents presented to us. But the interviews are themselves constructed versions of family relationships and practices. Each respondent portrayed their understanding of their family relationships from their own perspective with their own implicit 'moral glosses'. Such portrayals may not have been shared or accepted completely by others in the family network. For example, Steve and Christine Richards' accounts contained their different viewpoints. Nonetheless as with Steve and Christine, in the other 'linked' interviews we conducted, what might be termed the 'deep structure' of the different accounts were essentially supportive of each other. The respondents had their different views of the relationships in their family networks, but overall the issues they raised and the ties they described were similar. In the chapters that follow we will draw on the examples given in this chapter to illustrate different elements of our analysis, as well as introducing material from other interviews.

4
Family Boundaries

As we saw in Chapter 2, the idea of family boundaries has been influential in theorising about stepfamily relationships since the 1970s (Walker and Messinger, 1979). Indeed much of the early research into stepfamilies, in the US especially, was based upon therapeutic models, which were typically informed by family systems approaches. The premise of such systemic perspectives on family life was broadly in line with the type of theorising that had been dominant in family sociology, especially with the rise of Parsons's influential analysis of family interaction (Parsons and Bales, 1955). Put simply, the model was one in which families could be understood as highly complex yet integrated systems in which the constituent components – people and relationships – complemented each other in achieving their individual and common goals. In turn, from a therapeutic perspective, when families were not functioning well, attention needed to be directed at the (mis-)integration of these component elements rather than (just) at the pathological behaviour of individuals. (For a classic statement of this approach, see Minuchin, 1977.)

In this form of analysis, issues about the nature of the boundaries constructed around the family and, as importantly, around the sub-systems of relationships within the family – between parents; between parents and children; between siblings – played a major part. Where inappropriate boundaries were constructed and maintained within a family, the consequences for that family's overall functioning and organisation could be quite damaging. That is, if the boundaries maintained within a particular family were unclear or overly rigid or too permeable or inconsistent, then that family was liable to experience problems and difficulties. Specific individuals might be scapegoated for causing the family these difficulties, but their root causes lay in the systemic interactional properties the members of that family sustained collectively.

Without going into any further detail here of the benefits of family systems theory or the critiques that have been aimed at it (Morgan, 1985; Whitchurch and Constantine, 1993), the idea of analysing stepfamilies in terms of the differences in the character of the boundaries constructed in them as against other family forms has become an established perspective. It appeals particularly because it allows an insight into both 'internal' and 'external' relationships sustained by members of a stepfamily household. That is, the approach encourages a focus on the relationships existing between members of the stepfamily household and those outside it, as well as on the different sub-groupings and alliances developed within the household. This chapter will utilise the concept of family boundaries to analyse some of the dynamics of stepfamily living, in the process drawing on the case illustrations provided in Chapter 3.

The idea of family boundaries

Traditionally, different societies have their different family systems, structures and cultures. Some are more patriarchal than others; some are matrilocal; in some, marriage is the key relationship; in others, maternal or paternal kinship ties dominate (Parkin and Stone, 2004). At a simple level, each different type of family system can be thought of as involving different boundaries being constructed around who normatively is considered as family and who is not, or perhaps more accurately around who, within any family system, is considered 'more' family and who 'less' family'. In other words, family systems comprise the classification of others into those who are identified as being part of 'family' and those who are not, with the classification and consequences of membership being interpreted with greater or lesser rigidity within different systems (Carling, Duncan and Edwards, 2002; Cheal, 2002). Thus the idea of family boundaries reflects inclusion and exclusion, with some being 'insiders' and some 'outsiders', but also allows for differing degrees of 'flexibility' and 'permeability' in the manner in which such boundaries are constructed.

For example, the normatively dominant model of family system within industrialised Western societies has been the nuclear family one. This comprises a form of family organisation with comparatively limited membership yet quite strongly marked boundaries, at least at an ideological level. Within this nuclear family model, the primary family unit consists of parents and their not-yet-adult children living together as a domestically and economically independent unit in a separate family home with comparatively low levels of involvement – 'interference' – from other kin. In Parsons's (1943) famous phrase, this family unit is 'structurally isolated', in that its primary responsibilities are to its members rather than to any wider kin. In this sense, the nuclear family is characterised by strong boundaries. Its membership is clearly demarcated and the rights of others to intervene, even where they have a kinship connection, are limited.

As discussed in Chapter 1, the nuclear family model is no longer as dominant in countries like Britain as it was for much of the twentieth century. Since the mid-1970s, family constitution, especially in terms of family-as-household, has altered significantly, principally as a result of changing patterns of partnership formation and dissolution. For many people, the boundaries around family can be understood as becoming less rigid and more permeable. In other words, with increases in separation and divorce, lone-parenthood and stepfamilies, there is now greater flexibility in who is regarded as constituting family. In turn, over different phases of life course there is greater flux in family membership and, additionally, reduced overlap in shared family membership. For example, a child's parents may no longer be family to one another, though they once were; similarly following divorce, parents-in-law are likely to be regarded as less 'family' than they were previously, even if relationships remain cordial (Duran-Aydintug, 1993; Fischer, De Graaf and Kalmijn, 2005). In all these ways, the boundaries constructed around 'family' are now often more flexible, less rigidly ordained and more permeable than they were under the classic nuclear model specified by Parsons.

Though the boundaries constructed around 'family' within nuclear and other family systems are clearly metaphorical rather than real, they are nonetheless real in their consequences (McKie and Cunningham-Burley, 2005). As with the boundaries constructed around different communities (Cohen, 1985), they serve to inform people's identities as family members and to exclude 'outsiders' from such shared membership. In this regard, the sense of boundaries that are maintained both reflect and re-enforce, encapsulate and project, people's ideas of identity and belonging. Most importantly for our purposes, the active construction and maintenance of these family boundaries serves to generate feelings of family connection and unity. Clearly, the sense of family unity that people have is influenced by various factors and experienced more fully by some individuals and in some families more than others. Nonetheless the idea of unity itself plays a significant part in our understandings of what family means. In this regard, the construction of boundaries is inherent in our differentiation of family membership, and consequently in informing and representing our sense of who, in family terms, we are and where we 'fit' or belong (Stewart, 2005a).

While family boundaries are symbolic, one sphere in which they come to have a material, physical representation is in the home, particularly – though not only – in contemporary Western societies. While as we have argued 'family as household' is distinct from 'family as kinship', the home nonetheless embodies some key aspects of family boundaries. At an obvious level, the walls of the home serve to keep 'outsiders' outside, with only 'insiders' routinely having rights of uninvited entry. Similarly hedges, fences and garden walls serve as barriers to mark the boundaries of private family space from public space (Davidoff and Hall, 1987). So too, the internal organisation of physical space within the home can be read as representing boundaries of inclusion and exclusion. Who is invited into the home, on which occasions, under what terms and into which parts, reflect ideas of family membership, belonging and inclusion and thus also serve to signify exclusion and non-membership. In such ways the social construction of the physical space that is the home comes to represent and reflect our common-sense understandings of family unity and belonging (Allan and Crow, 1989; Allan, 1998).

Yet while there is a clear resonance between the notion of 'family boundary' and conceptions of the home as a physically bounded and organised space, it is the symbolic constructions of family boundaries that are of greater relevance. Such boundaries are, of course, more ephemeral and thus more difficult to specify; there are no walls or hedges demarcating the different areas. Indeed it is the nature of family boundaries that the divisions represented by the boundaries are rarely rigid or clear-cut. Even in family groupings that are strongly bounded, such as those that approach the Parsonian model of the nuclear family, grandparents and others are usually incorporated into various aspects of the family's life. The more that 'incursions' like this happen, the less 'solid' the symbolic boundaries constructed around the initial group – in this illustration, the nuclear family – are. Indeed as the involvement of, say, a grandmother in the routine of (nuclear) family life increases, there comes a point when the main family boundary of inclusion and exclusion would need to be reformulated to include rather than exclude her. Moreover, of course, within the initially specified family grouping, there can also be sub-divisions or boundaries of inclusion and exclusion, as well as competing alliances between some of its members and others outside the specified group.

While these issues will become of significance later in the chapter, we do not need to focus on them now. It is important though to reflect further on the meaning and status of family boundaries, at least in the ways we are drawing on them here. As we have argued, the concept of family boundaries refers to symbolic understandings that individuals embrace, which reflect the extent of their identification with others as shared family members. It is not necessary that such boundaries are recognised explicitly by those involved, though they will be evident in their behaviour. Equally from an analytical perspective, these boundaries can be understood as heuristic devices drawn on by the analyst to represent the degrees of identification and solidarity existing between family members. And unsurprisingly given that it is heuristic, the analogy of 'boundaries' needs to be treated with some care. Two issues are particularly important.

First, as with all boundaries, there is of course a concern with where the boundaries are drawn, with who is included and who is excluded, who is considered an insider and who an outsider. Yet while issues of boundary placement are of evident importance, other aspects of the boundary are also of consequence. In particular, some boundaries are more strongly demarcated than others. Some are 'policed' more thoroughly. Some are 'fuzzier', though of course how 'fuzzy' any boundary is depends on the degree to which the criteria of inclusion and exclusion can be clearly specified. Similarly, some boundaries are more permeable or more penetrable than others, so that those who are recognised as outsiders still have a capacity to 'enter' to differing degrees.

Second, it is important to recognise that the boundaries being discussed here are emergent properties of the families being considered. That is, family boundaries do not exist independently of the family relationships they are being used to characterise, in the way spatial boundaries do. Rather these symbolic family boundaries are evident and identifiable only through the actions of those involved. They have no independent existence. In this regard, they are social constructions generated and made apparent through the relationships developed between those involved, their interactions and communications (Afifi, 2003; Ribbens McCarthy, Edwards and Gillies, 2003). Sometimes people are conscious of the ways in which their actions constitute these boundaries; at other times they are not. Thus family boundaries are at one level ephemeral. They are constituted only through the words and actions of the people involved. But at the same time they achieve a different 'reality' through informing those words and actions, which in turn reconstitute the boundaries in question (McKie, Cunningham-Burley and McKendrick, 2005).

Here Morgan's (1996, 2011) ideas about 'family practices' are extremely helpful. It is through the family practices which families develop that each family generates the boundaries that characterise their family life. That is, it is through the everyday, routine organisation of domestic and family relationships that the boundaries of insider and outsider, of belonging and not belonging, are formed. In this regard, to portray any family in terms of the boundaries that are maintained is a genuinely heuristic exercise. It involves making decisions about the strength and inclusiveness of different relationships by assessing the assumptions that are built into their different family practices. It is through their different family practices that the solidarities and commitments of different family members, and hence of the family collectively, are expressed and in this sense become evident. It is through these family practices that family boundaries are policed and maintained to the differing degrees they are.

This can be seen quite readily with regard to 'families as households'. The routines of everyday family life, including mealtimes, access to family space, domestic leisure pursuits, family money management and the like, all serve to indicate who belongs to this family and who is outside it. Through such taken-for-granted activities, including the management of conflict about any of them – for example, over the timing and constitution of meals, the tidying of rooms or the temporal priority given to different activities – family/household order is generated in ways which reflect and symbolise the boundaries that exist between family 'insiders' and family 'outsiders'. The constructed nature of this family order is revealed most clearly when, for whatever reason, it is questioned or challenged, for example by children of different ages seeking to alter existing family rules governing their freedoms. The processes of negotiation around such issues – which themselves are aspects of the 'family practices' in play – involving persuasion and discipline as well as love, intimacy and trust signify and help constitute family belonging and membership (Jamieson, 2005).

Equally though, the existence of internal boundaries within families is also made evident through the family practices generated by the family's members. As above, the boundaries represent the different feelings of identification, belonging and commitment which exist within the family, with these being made manifest through the actions and relationships of those involved (Jacobson, 1995). The exercise of authority and discipline in the creation of family order provides a classic example of boundary formation and 'boundary work' within families. Thus, how different forms of control and disciplinary action are organised and patterned within the family, who exercises authority under what circumstances, what forms of resistance are mounted and the like can all be understood as constitutive of the internal boundaries existing within a family, a theme developed insightfully by Nelson (2006) in her analysis of 'doing' family in lone-parent families in America. But so too, the patterning of comfort and support, love, warmth and affection, respect and dependence which are made manifest in the various family practices established over time within different families can be seen as reflecting the boundaries there are within that family.

It must be emphasised again here that the concept of family boundary is heuristic; these boundaries do not share the same properties of rigidity and precision that physical boundaries possess even in the absence of explicit material markers. Moreover they are emergent and liable to shift across activities as well as over time. Nonetheless the idea of family boundaries does provide a useful means for interpreting aspects of family identification and differentiation. It is particularly helpful for analysing the structural dynamics of stepfamilies where patterns of belonging and commitment are more complex than they typically are in more standard nuclear families. To illustrate this, and to highlight the range of relational patterns that occur in different stepfamilies, we will now turn to consider some of the boundary issues evident in three of the case illustrations outlined in Chapter 3. We will start by focussing on Steve's (and Christine's) family relationships, and then consider Mark's and Louise's.

Steve

As reported in Chapter 3, when Steve first married Sally, he had a very clear notion that they would form a conventional family. He saw himself as fitting quite easily into a relatively standard husband/father role. While he recognised this may have taken some time to establish, Steve appeared to have seen it as comparatively unproblematic. The move to England and the change of the children's surname to his was part of the process of establishing the new family as a 'united family'. In other words, what Steve was envisaging here was a successful integration of Sally, him and the three children into a strongly bounded grouping in which their different family backgrounds would quickly become irrelevant. Others outside this grouping would have no reason for thinking differently about this family. From his perspective, no one would need to know that the children were not biologically his children, especially given the common surname they all adopted.

The reality was somewhat different, particularly with regard the degree of unity that could be established within the new family. Whatever the perceptions of others outside the household, it was evident that the unity which Steve initially foresaw was not achieved within the family. Indeed instead of decreasing over time, in many regards the divisions between Steve and the children became more apparent. In other words, rather than breaking down, boundaries of belonging, identity and difference became more strongly marked as the family established its patterns of domestic and familial routines. Indeed as the children became more autonomous with adolescence, the extent to which Steve felt marginalised, and sometimes excluded, from the centre of this family network grew. Steve's location here as adjunct rather than core member was not coincidental. It was a clear consequence of the boundary-maintenance behaviours that were actively perpetuated by the family members in the construction of their shared family practices.

The issue of discipline was an important aspect of this. Christine's, Ben's and especially David's refusal to accept Steve's authority over them appeared not only to have resulted in continuing tensions but also in Steve recognising the limitations of the 'fathering' he could play to his stepchildren. It is clear from both Steve's and Christine's accounts that Sally was the main parent in the family; it was she who the children turned to, it was her authority and discipline that they accepted. Moreover it would seem that it was to her that they appealed when Steve tried to exert his own discipline over them. At one level, this can be recognised as Sally and her children forming an element of alliance against Steve, consequent upon their different sense of who constituted 'family'. Steve's attempts to assert his mode of parental order within the family appeared to have been successfully subverted, in part because the 'rules' he wished to impose were at variance with the family practices Sally had established with her children.

Thus with regard to issues of discipline, it is evident that the family created boundaries which led to Steve being relatively marginalised. This was not solely a result of Steve's attempts to discipline the children *per se*, but also a response to the different content of the disciplinary code he attempted to impose. According to Christine's account at least, this led to Sally intervening to protect the three children from some of Steve's disciplinary measures and colluding with them to circumvent their impact. Such collusion can of course arise in families of different forms, not just stepfamilies. However the alliance between Sally and her children in these matters served to mark the greater legitimacy attached to Sally's parenting practices. In other words, at the heart of these tensions lay Steve's *right* to exercise authority over the children and, in particular, his right to apply his own forms of disciplinary code within the family. Thus as Steve indicates, he felt David especially, but Christine and Ben to a lesser degree, lacked respect for him. He in turn focussed on what he saw as their personality traits and their age as being problematic for establishing unity in the family.

While these issues certainly appear to have been of consequence in undermining Steve's original desire to form a united family, there is a deeper issue behind them. As Christine's comments in Chapter 3 make evident, she – and by implication, her brothers David and Ben – did not feel that Steve was as committed to them as individuals in the way their mother, Sally, was. In effect, her love for them was unquestioned; she was unequivocally on their side. Such emotional commitment was not so evident in the relationships Steve had with Christine, Ben and David. Indeed while Christine said she did love Steve because of all he did for her, she recognised that her relationship with him was not a strong one. Moreover it is significant that Steve hesitated to use the term 'love' in characterising his relationships with David, Christine and Ben. These marked differences in Sally's and Steve's perceived emotional commitment to the children were crucial in generating and sustaining the family boundaries which encapsulated Steve's marginalisation. Without this sense of love – Schneider's 'diffuse, enduring solidarity' – Steve's inclusion as 'family' was always likely to be partial. In his terms, he would inevitably remain something of an outsider – 'the sixth member of my family'.

In contrast, of course, Steve felt highly committed to his natural son, Nick. In their interviews, both he and Christine clearly acknowledged that his relationship with Nick was qualitatively different from his relationships with Christine, Ben and David. There was no question that Steve was fundamentally 'on Nick's side' and felt protective of him. His kinship was, in no doubt, with the blood connection being seen as intrinsic to this. He was 'family' in a full sense. But Steve's differential attachment to Nick and his differential treatment of him expressed and confirmed the divisions there were within the family overall. With Nick, Sally's protection was unnecessary; Steve's love and commitment was clear. Moreover the differences were understood. They appeared to be seen by all involved as legitimate precisely because Steve was Nick's natural father. It was legitimate for him to act as such in a way that was distinct to his fathering of the other three, even though this caused some irritations at times. Conversely Nick could not sideline Steve in the way the other children had, but, as importantly, he had no need to.

Furthermore, as discussed in Chapter 3, the issue of inheritance, and in particular Steve's dilemmas over his desire to favour Nick, provided a material reflection of the boundaries that existed within this family. While as wife and mother Sally was strongly bound to all, Steve's ties with Christine, David and Ben were in numerous ways more limited and more contingent than his connection to Nick.

Mark

Family boundary issues for Mark were relatively straightforward and quite different from those arising in Steve's case. The issue for Mark was not the degree of involvement of his stepfather in his family life, but rather the involvement of his natural father. Mark was unusual in this regard within the sample, certainly with respect to the strength of the feelings he expressed. He found the arrangements that had been made over his childhood and youth created problems for him, principally involving differential loyalties. The matter of where his family's boundaries were drawn was central to this. As he made clear in his interview, at various times in his adolescence he felt his family experiences would have been less disruptive and easier to manage if his natural father had played no further role in his life. Symbolised by his fortnightly visits, his natural father's involvement in his parenting undermined the clarity of Mark's preferred family boundaries.

In some regards the strength of Mark's feelings seems surprising. On the basis of what he said in the interview, it appeared that the involvement of his natural father, Michael, in his life caused other family members few difficulties. They appeared not to be concerned with family boundary issues in the way he was. As he said, his mother encouraged his contact with his father, Michael, even when Mark wanted to limit it. Moreover his mother maintained positive relationships with her ex-parents-in-law, Michael's parents, until their deaths, with Mark fully expecting his halfsiblings, Phil and Heather, to be recognised in his paternal grandfather's will once probate was settled. Importantly too, both his stepfather and his stepfather's parents seemed to treat Mark as much a part of their family as they did Phil and Heather. Thus Mark's account of relationships in this family was quite different to the accounts given by Steve and Christine of their family experiences. In Mark's case, there appeared to be no differentiation made between natural and stepchildren in terms of behaviour or emotional commitment; here 'family as household' also entailed 'family as kinship'.

Mark's identification of the Wellington family – his mother, stepfather and half-siblings – as his prime family, and his suggestions that his natural father belonged more to the realm of friendship than family, is particularly interesting given his easy acceptance of his relationships with his paternal grandparents. It would appear from his comments that these relationships did not pose any threat to his identification with the Wellington family group. Not only as grandparental ties were they readily manageable, but from Mark's perspective at least they also seemed to present him with no conflicts of loyalty. Despite his mother's and stepfather's apparent openness to his natural father's participation in his life, Mark would have preferred to have had less 'interference' and clearer lines drawn. He felt he did not need the 'aggro' that his regular contact with his natural father generated.

Mark's reference to 'aggro' here mainly related to the disruption that fortnightly visits with Michael caused to his weekend social and sport-ing schedules, in particular in the context of the demands that his school made of him on Saturdays. Yet it ran deeper than this. In com-menting in this way, Mark was also referring to the personal tension he felt that arose from his having two 'fathers'. He was very conscious that at a day-to-day level his stepfather, Tom, had not only been the 'father figure' in his household, but more importantly had always treated Mark as he had his other children, apparently never differentiating between them or causing Mark to feel he occupied a 'stepson' status. One further issue that influenced Mark's feelings concerned the financial contribu-tion that Tom had made to Mark's upbringing. While Michael was in a well-paid job, he had contributed comparatively little maintenance for Mark, having something of a reputation for being 'careful', if not mean, with money. In contrast, Tom had, from Mark's perspective, been extremely generous, not only treating Mark as he did Phil and Heather at a day-to-day level, but also paying for his education in a private school and for his university course.

Thus despite his natural father's continued presence in his life, Mark presented Tom as fully being his 'social' father. He was wholly integrated into Tom's family and kinship, the family practices generated over time in this family were entirely inclusive of Mark, and Tom had willingly contributed significant amounts of money to provide Mark with an advantaged upbringing. Moreover although this was not discussed at length in the interview, it appeared that Mark felt more at ease with Tom than with his natural father. Tom and Mark enjoyed each other's company, as well as having more business and leisure interests in common. As a result of these factors, Mark had a high degree of respect, trust and affection for Tom. From Mark's viewpoint, Tom was fully 'family' and had been a father to him throughout his life in a way that Michael had not. Because of this, Mark had felt uncomfortable with Michael's regular intrusion into his 'family life'. What it did for him was act as possibly the only reminder or signifier of his different position within the Wellington family. As he stated so clearly, Mark would have preferred clarity and to have maintained the family boundary by placing his 'flag in the ground one side'.

Louise

Louise's family involves the most complex boundary issues of the four case illustrations provided in Chapter 3, but also in some regards the most obvious. They operate at a number of different levels and were apparent from the time Louise and Alan first started living together. The issues Louise and her family faced were ones which lay at the core of family identity and the differential loyalties that people inside and outside her household held. One aspect of them, particularly in the early days of her partnership with Alan, concerned Alan's integration into Louise's family/household. The negative response of Ellen to both Alan and Layla can be readily seen in Ellen's destruction of Alan's clothes and Layla's pet fish – almost 'classic' acting out of her opposition to their membership of her family. While little was said in the interview about Alan's perspective on family issues, from Louise's account it would seem that he had accepted a relatively marginal role within the family, leaving day-to-day issues of domestic management and family relationships mainly to Louise.

However it was in Layla's relationships with her natural mother's family that issues of family boundaries, identity and belonging were most evident and most problematic. While we only have Louise's account of the dynamics involved here, she portrayed very clearly the tensions and difficulties which arose as a result of the competing claims they made of Layla's loyalties. Although to begin with, conflict over Layla's well-being appeared to have been limited, after Alan and Louise's marriage the divisions had become more marked. In this regard, it would appear that the formalisation of their union through marriage, with the symbolic consequences this potentially had for the construction of a different modality of 'family', resulted in a mutual re-enforcement by the two family groupings of their divergent views of who knew best how to care properly for Layla, given the disruptions she had experienced in her life as a result of her mother's death.

From her interview it was evident that Louise had wanted to create a united family when she formed a committed partnership with Alan. With her experience of childcare, she had imagined that with time she could mould the members of her stepfamily into an integrated family group, one which, in other words, had shared and established boundaries of belonging and commitment. This had not happened largely because of the competing sway on Layla's family membership that Yvonne's family exercised. The older boys, Dan and Adam, were able to resolve these dilemmas by staying with the Abbott family rather than living permanently at Louise's and Alan's – in the language Mark used above, by clearly placing their flag in Abbott ground. At the time of the interview, Layla was too young to exercise such agency even if she had wanted to. This though then led to a degree of interference in the child-rearing practices Louise wanted to establish which cut across the family boundaries normatively associated with parenting.

At one level, the tensions that arose resulted from the different views Louise and Madge, in particular, held about the value of education. However they were also concerned with the expectations that could reasonably be placed on children in general, and Layla in particular. As Louise makes clear, she expected her natural children, Mark and Ellen, to be more independent and to make a fuller domestic contribution than Layla's grandparents expected of Layla. Such differences in family practices were imbued with moral connotations, reflecting views about appropriate and inappropriate ways of preparing children/adolescents for adulthood. In other circumstances, such grandparental indulgence may have been acceptable. In this instance though, it represented a significant interference and undermining of the family order Louise was trying to achieve. Moreover it also represented differences in the way the three children were being treated, differences which themselves were seen by Louise as unfair as well as inappropriate.

While Louise experienced Madge and her family's 'spoiling' of Layla as subversive of her attempts to create family unity, it would seem from their viewpoint they were providing Layla with some of the love and support she needed given her mother's death. Inherent within this was also the question of who, in family terms, Layla was and where she belonged. Following Yvonne's death, Alan appears to have relied heavily on Madge particularly, but also Jenny and to a lesser extent Jane, for support with his three children, Dan, Adam and Layla. The three children thus remained firmly rooted in their mother's kinship. Her memory was protected; the children's place in the close-knit Abbott family secured. Alan's remarriage to Louise with her very different ideas of children's needs threatened all this, the more so as it became apparent over time how much Louise sought to change Layla. Not only did Louise challenge how Layla had been brought up, and thus the Abbott 'family culture' more generally, she also wanted to make Layla part of the new family she and Alan were creating, thereby reducing the influence of the Abbott family and thus Layla's membership of it.

Issues of family boundaries and family identity were consequently highly significant in this case, as were disagreements over appropriate family practices. Over time these issues became more marked, arguably more so as a result of Alan's seeming lack of participation in Layla's care. As Alan's wife and Layla's resident stepmother, Louise considered herself to be Layla's legitimate guardian, the person who was in the best position to determine and meet her needs. As close family who had known Layla all her life, cared for her through traumatic experiences and whose love for her was unconditional, Madge, her husband, Ted, and her daughters also had a legitimate claim to know best what Layla needed.

Given the differences there were in family practices and culture, there could be no easy resolution to these competing claims. The result was both that family boundaries became more firmly marked over time and that perceived boundary interference generated more resentment. As an example, Layla's visits to her grandparents were now no longer seen as just routine expressions of kinship solidarity; from Louise's perspective at least, they had become imbued with a far greater significance. In undermining the routines of Louise's family order, such practices as the 'spoiling' of Layla, the lack of co-operation over her schoolwork and the reminders of her natural mother all served to symbolise Layla's continued belonging to the Abbott family, alongside her two natural brothers.

Family membership in stepfamilies

As these examples have illustrated, there is wide variation in the boundary issues which emerge in different stepfamilies. Indeed in some stepfamilies boundary issues seem to be of little consequence, as appeared to be the case with Sandie Noonan's family, the fourth example given in Chapter 3. Yet despite the differences in the ways that boundary problems were experienced in the other three families – or, more accurately, by the individuals we spoke to in those families – there was also an underlying commonality to them. What all these respondents were reporting as problematic concerned the degree to which the practices within their families diverged from the practices they took to be normative in more 'standard' forms of family life. In particular, they all indicated some unease or frustration with the divisions inherent in the network of familial relationships in which, as part of a stepfamily, they were enmeshed. In line with this, Coleman et al. (2001, p. 71) indicate how disagreements in stepfamilies often appear to be 'the manifestation of the underlying issue of negotiating the boundaries around and within the stepfamily'.

From our respondents' perspectives, the tensions they experienced were often linked to their ideas of family membership, connectivity and belonging – in essence issues of family unity (Church, 1999). These are not minor matters. As discussed above, in many regards unity is one of the core elements of what 'family' represents symbolically and normatively. Much of the time in many families, family unity is simply assumed, taken-for-granted as a result of the structuring of family practices. In the cases discussed here, family unity was more problematic. It could not be assumed; indeed some of the family practices within these families clearly undermined any easy acceptance of family unity and shared family identity. However much some of those involved might want to have been seen as a united family, structurally the complexities of their family networks at times served to generate an awareness of difference rather than commonality. In turn, awareness of difference subverted any simple construction of 'family'.

But the ways in which aspects of family proved problematic varied across the three cases. For Steve, it was a case of not having the same sense of belonging to his family that the other members had. As step-father he felt he played a minor role within the family, effectively being excluded from full participation in a range of family issues. Interestingly this awareness of difference was exacerbated by his commitment and love for his natural son, Nick, feelings which were far less strong for the other three children. Mark's boundary issue was quite different. As he made apparent through drawing on the concept of friendship, he wanted a greater closure, and thereby clarity, in his family relationships. For him, his tie with his father and his father's new family represented a somewhat unwelcome intrusion into the family where he felt most 'at home'. He experienced a tension in having two 'fathers', especially as he so admired his stepfather and felt such an affinity with him. The boundary issues experienced by Louise were different again and in many ways the most clear-cut. In this case the tension arose from the degree of 'interference' in family life experienced as a result of the competing claims that were legitimately being made for Layla's family membership. Although only Louise's perspective is known, it seems likely that all involved experienced similar dissatisfactions through having to cope with 'outside' intrusions into their desired family order.

Although there are other variations of family boundary issues arising in stepfamilies, these examples do represent three of the most common forms of boundary dilemmas which occur. In this regard, the example of Mark can be seen as one of *passive intrusion*; that of Louise can be seen as one of *active intrusion*; and the example of Steve as one of *exclusion*. In general, the issue of *passive intrusion* frequently results from separation and divorce rather than the creation of stepfamilies *per se*, though the issues may be exacerbated in stepfamilies. As with the example of Mark, its most common form stems from the continued involvement of the non-resident parents in the lives of their children. As is now widely recognised, the maintenance of this relationship has consequences for the scheduling of activities in the resident household and makes apparent the different loyalties and obligations of its members (Simpson, 1998; Smart and Neale, 1999). Usually though it is the resident parent and their new partner who find the intrusion most problematic, especially if they are seeking to create a stepfamily in the mode of Burgoyne and Clark's (1984, p. 193) 'pursuit of an ordinary family life'. But adolescents can also experience the scheduling of contacts with a non-resident parent as problematic, especially if it involves a clash with their other activities and pastimes. However it seems Mark was unusual in so clearly experiencing this as disruptive of a desired family unity, both in his adolescence and now in adulthood.

For Louise the intrusion into her family life was far more of an *active intrusion*. As we have seen this was not just a case of visits to other family members causing disruption to schedules. It was a clash of family practices, family values and family ideologies. It was, of course, an unusual stepfamily in that it resulted from parental death rather than separation through divorce. This undoubtedly coloured the responsibility that Yvonne's mother and sisters felt for her children as well as their desire to honour her memory. However such active intrusion is not limited to cases where a parent has died, nor to intrusion by a stepchild's wider kin group. Indeed as we shall discuss in the chapters that follow, usually a non-resident parent's wider kin have little opportunity to influence – or interfere – in how a child is brought up within a stepfamily.

Instead *active intrusion* is more commonly associated with the involvement of the non-resident parent in the child's life and the disruption to the stepfamily's family practices that this can generate. This stems less from the type of scheduling issue linked to *passive intrusion* discussed above and typified by Mark's relationship with his natural father Michael, but more to a non-resident parent's own practices undermining or contradicting those established in the stepfamily. For example, children may be allowed to do things that they are not allowed to do in their main home; the 'rules' established governing their behaviour may be flouted; they may be 'spoilt' in a range of ways that are inconsistent with the preferred practices of the stepfamily. Again while not restricted to stepfamilies, such conflicts between the treatment and permitted behaviour of children across the different households can be experienced as highly intrusive and disruptive, especially when it seems to reflect and express continuing conflict and tension between the now separated parents.

As with the example of Steve, *exclusion* refers to instances where the family practices emergent over time in a family lead to one or more of those involved being – or feeling – 'distanced' from other family members and less incorporated into the network of family relationships than those others are. Of course in all families individuals are excluded from different activities – parents exclude children from adult matters; siblings may exclude one another or parents from some of their activities. But the exclusion referred to here is more systemic and divisive than this. Typically it concerns the way in which a step-parent, and most commonly a stepfather, is excluded from aspects of parenting with the consequence that their family 'membership' is seen as somewhat peripheral. The issues that appear to arise most frequently involve the authority to exercise control and discipline over stepchildren and consequently to influence 'family order'. Children's agency, especially in adolescence, is important within these dynamics, as is the natural parent's desire to 'protect' their children. But so too, the step-parent's actions in attempting to change the practices established by the natural parent and the children can lead to greater collusion between the latter. This may serve to reinforce, and sometimes further exacerbate, the divisions experienced within the family, as Christine reported was the case with Steve.

When family therapists draw on the concept of family boundary they are typically concerned with some form of individual or family pathology. An important point about the stepfamily boundary issues we have been discussing in this chapter is that they have a quite different status. They are structural to the circumstances of the families rather than an indicator of family pathology *per se*. They may cause friction and be difficult to manage as we have seen, but they do not stem from any dysfunctional or inappropriate behaviour on the part of the individuals involved. In other words, the issues which have emerged in these families are the result of the distinct family positions the individuals involved occupy. Others occupying similar positions in different families may have played these roles differently. The dynamics of their families may have led to different family practices; different sets of relationships may have been negotiated. Some of these may have resulted in less tension being experienced; some may have generated more. The point here is simply that the dynamics of the relationships in these families were not the consequence of normatively inappropriate behaviour. Rather they are better understood as resulting from the interplay of legitimate but conflicting family actions.

In other words, they represent inherent dilemmas in the management of relationships within these families. Perhaps this can be seen as a lack of institutionalisation of roles within stepfamilies. But such institutionalisation requires a level of socially sanctioned agreement over the 'right and proper' responsibilities of the different actors involved. And the key point about the examples we have been discussing is that there can be no such agreement because of the competing claims there are around family membership, loyalty and identity. For example, Mark appeared to want less involvement with his natural father, Michael. Yet for this to happen would mean Michael acting against his own perception of what being a father entails, as well, seemingly, of those of Mark's mother. It would also be counter to current social beliefs about the importance of the continuation of such paternal contact. Similarly, Layla's maternal grandparents could be, from Louise's perspective, less interfering of her attempts to integrate Layla into her (Louise's) family, but for them to do so could also be interpreted as their sacrificing Layla's family heritage and failing to be caring grandparents.

Importantly, while many of the dilemmas and frustrations that arise within stepfamilies are deep-rooted, they are also likely to alter over time, in particular as children grow into adulthood. It is not simply that time allows for new 'solutions' or '*modus operandi*' to emerge, but also that the demands made of family membership alter across the life course. Using the two examples just cited, while Mark is still concerned with having dual paternal claims, in reality these issues appear to have become less problematic as he has become more independent. He sees his natural father at times it suits him rather than regularly every two weeks, and in many ways appears to have successfully negotiated the transformation of his father's new family into the realm of 'friendship'. Similarly Layla's brothers, Dan and Adam, have avoided some of the conflicts there were by deciding to live with their grandparents rather than in Louise's household. As Louise reported, now Dan and Adam 'get on really well with me'. Layla may not choose to move back to Devon when she becomes older, but whatever decision she reaches, it seems unlikely that the tensions that currently exist between Louise and Yvonne's mother and sisters about Layla's welfare will figure as large as they now do. However Layla then feels about 'family', the competing claims there on her family identity are unlikely to be experienced with the same force.

Conclusion

This chapter has been concerned with the boundary issues that arise in stepfamilies. The notion of boundary is a complex one built around understandings of family identity and connection. It allows us to focus on who counts as family members to whom under what circumstances and in what respects. Our argument has been that family boundaries are linked both to shared social understandings of what 'family' means in different contexts and to the emergent family practices which arise within a particular stepfamily. Within stepfamilies, establishing the degree of unity that is largely taken for granted in natural families – despite the conflicts and antagonisms which arise in different periods – is often problematic. The different family memberships of those involved, their different constellations of commitment and solidarity, their different kinship histories cannot be so readily moulded into a shared, collective sense of belonging and connection. Yet it is this shared sense of belonging, connection and commitment that constitute people's notion of family. It is what 'family' means.

In arguing this way, we are certainly not trying to suggest that such feelings of 'family' do not emerge in stepfamilies. We are very clear in not wanting to pathologise stepfamilies. Many individuals in them do experience what we have identified as boundary difficulties of exclusion, and passive or active intrusion, at least for some periods. Yet others do not, or do so only to a degree that causes them comparatively few difficulties (Bornat et al., 1999). To conclude this chapter, consider the fourth case illustration discussed in Chapter 3, Sandie, whom we have so far not discussed in this chapter.

According to Sandie's account at least, her family seemed to face few, if any, issues of family boundaries or family unity, despite two generations of marital separation and stepfamily formation. In part, this may be a consequence of their greater experience of managing stepfamilies, combined with a degree of tolerance and acceptance of more varied family patterns. Equally though, the absence of boundary issues was almost certainly influenced by the complete absence of both Sandie's natural father from her life after he separated from her mother and her first husband's absence from her daughters' lives. There still had to be an acceptance of both Andy and Simon as new father figures within their families, but this did seem to have been accomplished without the concerns that arose in the other three examples discussed in Chapter 3. However it is noticeable that even though Simon's relationship with his first wife Kate had been difficult when their son Liam was young, there now seemed to be few difficulties consequent on Liam's involvement in both households. From both Sandie's and her daughter Reb's accounts, Liam was recognised unproblematically as being family. Indeed within Sandie's kinship, there appeared to be a full and unambiguous recognition of Andy, Steve and Liam as 'family'.

In the chapters that follow we will develop further some of the issues raised in this chapter. In the next chapter, Chapter 5, we focus on stepmothers and stepmothering. As in this chapter, we will draw on examples from our study to highlight key themes in the family practices that arise in stepmother families. In Chapter 6, we will turn our attention to stepfather families. In each of these chapters, we will be concerned with exploring step-parenting in both 'resident' and 'non-resident' contexts and consequently with the construction of relationships and practices in both family-as-kinship and family-as-household realms.

5
Stepmothering Stepchildren

Traditionally the position of stepmothers is seen as more problematic than that of stepfathers, largely because standard gender divisions within households typically result in stepmothers having greater responsibility for, and involvement in, childcare and domestic matters. Yet as indicated in the case illustrations in Chapter 3, in practice there is a good deal of variation in the relationships that develop between stepmothers and their stepchildren. Many factors are reported as influencing the patterning of these ties – some concerned primarily with internal household dynamics, some more with aspects of individual personality and biography and some with family relationships external to the household. Moreover the character of any stepmother–stepchild relationship will alter over time, both through the relationship becoming more established and as a result of childhood transitions. Often research has focussed quite appropriately on stepmother–stepchild relationships in dependent phases of childhood, but how the relationship develops in the younger generation's adulthood is, in kinship terms, also of interest. Before discussing these issues more generally, consider again here the case illustrations we introduced earlier.

In many ways Louise provided an almost stereotypically 'classic' example of the difficulties of resident stepmothering. As we discussed in the Chapter 4, the key problems she was facing comprised competing ideas of family and domestic order, boundary difficulties around the construction of family and conflicts over who had authority to determine how her stepchild, Layla, was to be socialised. And interacting with these issues was a largely unspoken recognition of the differential emotions of love, commitment and identity she felt for her natural children, Ellen and Mark, and for Layla, together with an element of resentment regarding the negative impact that Layla's presence was having on their family life together.

On the basis of his account, Mark's relationship with his stepmother, Sheila, was quite different to this, though, as we shall see later in the chapter, in its way not unusual. The key to this relationship lay in its limited involvement. While Mark had good relationships with Sheila and with his stepsiblings, Dan and Jenny, his relationship with Sheila had not formed until he was in his teens. Moreover while Mark visited regularly, he had never actually stayed with his father and Sheila. Consequently there had never been any reason why issues of domestic order, socialisation or responsibility for maintaining household rules should have become matters of concern in this relationship as they had between Louise and Layla. Sheila was in no sense a maternal figure in Mark's childhood. What she was was simply his father's new partner; his involvement with her was mediated by this relationship, but also limited and readily contained. Consequently its management presented few difficulties, particularly now that Mark was adult, as it was framed in quite large measure by the degree of their personal compatibility and liking.

The third illustration of stepmothering provided in Chapter 3 was different from either of the above cases. Sandie's stepson, Liam, was young when she and Simon married. Simon's relationship with Kate had also been turbulent at this time. However 12 years on, Sandie recalled no significant difficulties with integrating Liam into her family during his regular weekend and school holiday visits. She, of course, had experience of being a stepchild herself, so perhaps this enabled her to anticipate potential difficulties. Equally though, at least from her viewpoint, there appeared to be few conflicts with regard to discipline, domestic order or personal antagonism, other than those which she saw as standardly occurring within any sibling group. Even in discussing her relationship with Kate, she downplayed any difficulties that had arisen. Her views about Liam's position within the family were clearly endorsed in the comments her daughter, Reb, made about the strength of her own relationship with Liam, as well as that between her sister, Alex, and Liam. From the interview, it certainly seemed that Sandie had experienced little difficulty in developing a positive stepmother relationship with Liam and incorporating him into her family and kinship networks.

These three case illustrations provide some indication of the wide variation there is in the relationships that develop between stepmothers and their stepchildren. One aspect of this is the quality of the relationships that evolve – the commitment there is, the satisfactions they provide, the extent to which they are defined as 'family', as well as any tensions that develop (Church, 1999). We will explore these issues more fully below, though one point worth emphasising at this stage is that these relationships are not static. Like all family relationships they change over time, especially as children mature through adolescence and into adulthood. In particular, as we shall discuss, tensions and difficulties experienced between a stepmother and one or more of her stepchildren may in some cases still colour their relationship in the child's adulthood, but often these issues are rendered of less consequence once the stepchild is no longer dependent.

A second aspect of the variation there is in stepmother–stepchild relationships concerns their degree of familial and domestic involvement. Some stepmothers and stepchildren, like Mark and Sheila, have relatively little involvement; others, like Louise and Layla, have a great deal. Obviously a key factor here, aside from the age of the stepchild, is the child's living arrangements – whether or not they are part of the stepmother's household. But this is not the only issue generating diversity. There is significant variation within each of these categories as well as between them. At one extreme, there are those stepmother 'relationships' which exist at a 'genealogical' level but have no social or personal content. Thus in the study sample there were a number of respondents, like Sandie, who had had no contact with their father since their parents' marriage ended, but who knew that their father had repartnered. Others had limited contact with their fathers, but only a basic 'social' relationship with their stepmother and did not regard them as family.

Most non-resident stepmothers in the sample had fuller relationships than this with their stepchildren, with most stepchildren visiting their father for shorter or longer periods depending on the circumstances and history of their relationship. Clearly when a stepchild lives in the same household as a step-parent, their relationship is likely to be more complex as well as more fully rooted in family and kinship networks. Yet here too there is a good deal of variety in the arrangements made, ranging from those who are, like Louise, full-time stepmothers to those where the stepchild stays for shorter periods, residing most of the time with their natural mother. A small, though increasing, number of stepmothers are involved in joint care arrangements, with their stepchildren dividing their time proportionately between their mother's and father's homes. Again, though, it is important to recognise that the patterns of parenting and residence established at any given time are liable to alter, with consequences for stepmothers' relationships with their stepchildren. During different periods of their childhood and adolescence, stepchildren may become more or less involved in their stepmother's household in line with their changing circumstances and other commitments. Similarly in adulthood, their relationship with their father and stepmother will be influenced by each side's changing domestic, social and geographic circumstances. The history of their relationship is likely still to have some bearing on the present, but it does not determine it.

Mothering and family order

In Britain, as in many other Western countries, there have been significant changes over the last two generations in women's participation in employment. In particular, the idea of married women's work being confined to the domestic sphere now holds little popular credence. Nonetheless paid and unpaid work continue to be highly gendered. Men not only occupy more advantaged positions within professional, bureaucratic and other occupational organisations, they also systematically earn more at every level of the occupational structure (Grint, 2005; Crompton, 2006). As a consequence, wives and mothers continue to have prime responsibility for household organisation and management. While husbands/fathers now participate more than in previous generations, most domestic activities necessary for the day-to-day reproduction of home life – cleaning, washing, food preparation, shopping, meal planning and the like – continue to be allocated primarily to women. Mothers are also more fully involved in childcare tasks, especially when children are younger. Most importantly, responsibility for the co-ordination, management and planning of domestic and childcare activities, as distinct from undertaking specific activities at any given time, is routinely assigned to wives and mothers (Walzer, 2004).

A significant element within women's greater 'managerial' responsibility for the smooth operation of family and domestic life concerns the 'emotional' or 'relational' work they do (Duncombe and Marsden, 1993; Wood, 1993). The issue here is that households do not just need to be organised at a practical and material level; the interactions and relationships they involve also need successful 'managing' if harmony is to be sustained. Such management of relationships involves a wide range of skills and activities – monitoring, smoothing, cajoling, persuading, calming, negotiating, organising, etc. While all family members may undertake these tasks at different times and to differing degrees, such 'relationship work' is usually integral to women's role as wife and mother. In line with their earlier and later socialisation experiences, women become 'relationship experts', knowledgeable and skilled at 'reading' and managing their families. Indeed, such expertise represents a key component within their expression of family love and care and becomes part of their gendered familial identity. Although rarely recognised culturally as significant, this 'relationship work' is crucial for the mundane, largely unproblematic, maintenance of family life.

Thus these standard gender divisions within families usually lead to wives and mothers having prime responsibility for domestic organisation and family relationships. To put this slightly differently, it is they who are most involved in the successful creation of family order. As we are using it here, the term 'family order' is both complex and somewhat imprecise. But, in line with the above, what it seeks to highlight are the ways in which any family establishes a routine mode of living and relating. This involves the ordinary activities and procedures which emerge within the family governing how family matters are normally handled; the forms of control and authority which are exercised within the family; and the family 'rules' and values which are typically applied and followed. In this, it reflects a concern with the family practices (Morgan, 1996, 2011) which are established in a family and which encompass its members' shared understandings of how their family operates, understandings which can on occasion be challenged but which most of the time are simply accepted uncritically as being the way things are (Dempsey, 1997).

The notion of family order as we are conceiving it is useful for examining the experiences of stepmothers, especially resident stepmothers, for three reasons. First, it allows for the emergent, 'active' construction of family life, while still serving to emphasise the sense of 'orderliness' or 'structure' which typifies much of it. In other words, it helps highlight the degree to which that 'orderliness' is a family accomplishment, enacted through the generally routine and gendered management of the panoply of family matters. Second, it implicitly recognises that the 'order' being created within families is not unchanging. Because it is the result of the different practices established in any family, it alters over time in line with the changing interests and commitments of the individuals within that family. And third, use of the term family order connotes the possibility of 'disorder'. That is, elements of the 'order' established in families are always open to being challenged, undermined and disrupted by different members of the family. How such challenges are handled may itself be seen as reflective of aspects of family order.

Consider briefly here the construction of 'first-time' families. When two individuals come together to form a new partnership, whether through committed cohabitation or marriage, they develop their ways of doing 'household' and doing 'family', albeit ways informed by gender ideologies and experiences (Mansfield and Collard, 1988). These gradually established family practices will alter when children are born to the union. And as these children become older, so the family order will alter further, reflecting the different circumstances of the particular family and the different ways they organise their collective domestic/ familial life. It is helpful to think here of Finch and Mason's (1993) ideas of 'negotiation' in the gradual transformation of these family practices and the achievement of family order. While parents have more control than children over the management of family activities, implicit as well as explicit processes of negotiation involving different family members contribute to the construction – and reconstruction – of family order. In line with Finch and Mason's position, this sometimes involves open conflict, sometimes more standard discussion and debate and sometimes more intuitive or tacit action. As suggested above, it is generally wives/ mothers who play the dominant part in the exercise and management of these negotiations.

The key point is that usually in these 'first-time' family contexts, the negotiation and establishment of family order is a matter for those included in the family – typically those directly involved in the 'family as household'. Of course, others may also influence the ways in which different family practices develop within the household, but the family order generated is principally a 'family' matter. Indeed in many ways, the family comes to be recognised as 'family' by its mutual construction of the practices that constitute the family order – the taken-for-granted world which is the family. However in families other than 'first-time' families, it is not always possible to construct a family order independently of non-household members. Others outside the household can have an impact on the 'orderliness' that is being established. In part this is simply a further reflection of the idea that stepfamily boundaries, like the boundaries in lone-parent families, are more permeable than the boundaries in 'first-time' families (Nelson, 2006). However the point here is not only about the permeability of boundaries, it is also about the conflicts which can arise as a result of different family groupings upholding divergent family orders (Jacobson, 1995; Henry and McCue, 2009).

As we saw in discussing family boundaries in the Chapter 4, such conflicts can be the result of adults in different households asserting their distinct views about how particular children should be treated or expected to behave. Equally though, the children involved are also active in these processes. That is, with the exception of those who are still very young, children who become part of resident stepfamilies already have understandings of how family and domestic life is ordered, based on their own previous experiences. In stepfather families, this is likely to be congruent with the mother's views and perspectives on family order and to this extent not represent a particularly radical shift in family order for the children. Of course different stepfathers can play a more or less active part in generating a new family order and placing different expectations on children. However, generally, because of a mother's greater responsibility for family order within the domestic division of labour, the transition to a stepfather family may, from the children's perspective, be less disruptive of existing family practices.

Resident stepmothering

As research on stepmothering recognises, family order issues are liable to loom larger in stepmother families than in stepfather ones. A resident stepmother usually assumes greater responsibility for family order, and this typically means a far greater involvement in the day-to-day routines which pattern their stepchildren's lives. Influenced by the age of the stepchildren, this operates at a number of different levels. One of the most important concerns domestic servicing and household management. Given the dominant division of domestic labour, such matters as room cleaning, tidying and vacuuming; washing, ironing and other laundry work; and shopping for food, preparing meals and ensuring balanced diets are usually understood to fall within the woman's realm. As above, this does not mean that all these tasks and activities are necessarily undertaken only by wives and mothers, but it does mean that they are usually seen as the ones with greater responsibility for their accomplishment.

These domestic activities make stepmothers' relationships with their stepchildren more complex because they inevitably entail routine, day-to-day involvement. Simply in order to complete the tasks, a stepmother requires a degree of co-operation with her stepchildren which shapes her relationships with them. Indeed, in managing these activities, she will need to establish 'rules' governing the routines and standards to be applied, the behaviours seen as acceptable or inappropriate and the contribution the children are normally expected to make. Thus more than stepfathers, stepmothers become involved in getting children to put clothes away, keep rooms tidy, eat appropriate meals and the like. Importantly these aspects of domesticity are ones which frequently generate irritations and arguments as children passively or actively resist the demands being made of them. As a consequence, resident stepmothers inevitably become involved in ongoing 'negotiations' with their stepchildren around the scheduling and satisfactory completion of these mundane domestic activities.

In a similar way, resident stepmothers are likely to be involved in a wide range of childcare tasks. Indeed many of these flow over from aspects of household management and domestic servicing. For example, dress, appearance, clothing, personal hygiene and other such matters are typically seen as facets of domestic responsibility. Equally resident stepmothers are likely to play a significant part in the routine management of children's time, though clearly the specifics of the tasks involved in this will depend on the children's ages and commitments. Meeting the demands of schooling is one element here. As with Louise, for example, stepmothers may be the ones who ensure that children are ready on time, that they have whatever is needed for the day and maybe even that homework is completed appropriately. Similarly they are likely to be involved in getting children ready for their different out-of-school activities and in co-ordinating these within the broader household schedule.

Generally then, resident stepmothers are likely to be active in their stepchildren's lives in various ways. In particular, they are likely to be incorporated into a degree of nurturing and socialising appropriate to the child's age. In this regard, their involvement with their stepchildren is usually of a different order to stepfathers with their resident stepchildren. Indeed resident stepmothers' centrality for ensuring family order, as we have conceived of it here, means that they are likely to be routinely involved in the day-to-day monitoring and supervision of their stepchildren. In other words, in doing these 'mothering' tasks, they come to occupy a clear position within the disciplinary framework that is exercised over the children. This does not mean they are necessarily the ones to respond when serious breaches of accepted familial standards of behaviour occur. Their disciplinary role is generally more mundane but also more pervasive. They are the ones who ensure order at a more immediate level – through cajoling, nagging, reminding, persuading, threatening and negotiating, in other words the unexceptional complex of techniques which mothers especially draw on to exert control over children and maintain family order.

All the features of the stepmother role that have been raised here are entirely routine and normal aspects of mothering. They are what mothers do in generating and maintaining family order as a result of the standard division of labour within most families. There is of course a good deal of variation in the ways different mothers perform the role, but, however performed, the activities and practices involved are part of what routinely constitutes mothering. For stepmothers though, these activities and practices can prove more problematic than they do for natural mothers. In particular, the forms and standards of family order they seek to establish are more open to challenge than is normally the case with natural motherhood, as are their rights to impose a specific order. There are two broad aspects of the stepmothering experience that we wish to highlight in exploring this. To be clear, we are not claiming that these two aspects of stepmothering are always of consequence, merely that they are issues which can in various ways impact on stepmother–stepchild relationships.

The first one concerns the difficulties which arise as a consequence of the stepchild(ren)'s history and in particular their existing experiences of a previously established family order. There are a number of elements to this. To begin with, there is the issue of the child's agency in constructing a family order in a stepmother family. Rather than a developmental taken-for-granted awareness emerging of the way 'family' is done, as typically happens in natural families, any attempts by a resident stepmother to establish different family practices and different ways of behaving are capable of generating a reaction from the children. Rather than endorsing the new mode of family life, children may instead seek to protect the practices that are familiar to them. They may also challenge the right of the stepmother to impose change, as is so graphically captured in versions of the somewhat clichéd but apparently still common assertion: 'You can't make me do that. You are not my mother.'

Conflicts over a resident stepmother's attempts to establish a different family order can also be compounded through the stepchild's continuing involvement with his or her natural mother, whether through access visits or shared care. As quite frequently reported by natural mothers of their dealings with non-resident fathers following divorce, facilitating any such contact is potentially disruptive of the resident family's routines (Smart and Neale, 1999). However where there are competing practices within the different families, efforts by a stepmother to establish a distinct family order may be further undermined or resisted. How this happens and what responses are made will vary, in part depending on the child's age, but negotiating and resolving such competing practices across households is liable to prove particularly difficult. While disputes between parents and children – and especially adolescents – about family behaviour are common in all families, those that are rooted in competing claims about the legitimacy of different family orders can be particularly disruptive.

The second aspect of stepmothering we want to highlight concerns the nature of the commitment that exists between a stepmother and her stepchildren. In kinship terms, a natural mother's tie to her children is routinely constructed as premised on an unquestioned and inalienable love. This unconditional bond of love, generally seen as arising 'naturally' through birth and early nurturing, is taken as the defining characteristic of mother-child relationships. In contrast, the stepmother–stepchild relationship is not seen as naturally imbued with the same level of commitment and solidarity. Indeed dominant cultural representations often portray the bond between a stepmother and her stepchildren with a degree of suspicion (Hughes, 1991), as one in which there can be no easy assumption that a stepmother will automatically – 'naturally' – act in the best interests of a stepchild.

There is of course no reason why a stepmother should love her stepchildren. As is frequently pointed out, the stepfamily results from the commitment between the father and the step-parent; the stepchildren are merely 'part of the package'. In most cases there will have been a shorter or longer period of courtship during which the stepchildren and stepmother will also form a relationship. A range of both positive and negative emotions may be experienced during this process, but love as it is usually understood is unlikely to be one of them. Similarly once the stepfamily is formed, both the stepmother and her stepchildren will normally be involved in processes of gradual adjustment and accommodation to one another. While this may entail a growing commitment between them, there is no inherent reason why it should. In some cases these relationships may be coloured more by tensions and disagreements that result in dislike rather than solidarity (Robinson and Smith, 1993).

Indeed in general, it is common for both stepmothers and stepchildren to have ambivalent feelings about one another, at least for periods in their relationship. While natural mothers may also at times have contradictory feelings about their children – for example, resenting the ways in which motherhood alters their lives while nonetheless having strong feelings of love and attachment to their child – the ambivalence that stepmothers experience is likely to run deeper. Their stepchildren are not 'theirs' in the way natural children are; they may find them intrusive and their behaviour irritating. Yet they are expected to care for them and nurture them, and generally provide them with the requisite degree of security and warmth. Similarly, at times, the children may be loving and rewarding, and at other times equally rejecting and irksome (Giles-Sims, 1984; Hughes, 1991). Structurally the central feature of these relationships is that they are created through commitment to a third party – the father. They are in this sense conditional, and not of themselves based on strong feelings of attachment. Though at least in some cases this may develop, it cannot be assumed (Doodson and Morley, 2006).

The example from Chapter 3 of Louise and Layla that we have already referred to above is a good illustration of these types of issue. In her account, Louise presented herself as trying to provide Layla with the experiences and upbringing that would equip her best for adult life. For Louise, this involved developing levels of independence and educational accomplishment that she felt Layla had been ill-prepared for and was failing to achieve. As we have seen, she saw the influence of her natural mother's family as undermining her efforts here. However it is also reasonable to argue that what lay behind the difficulties Louise experienced in this relationship was the failure – whatever the reason – of Layla to embrace the family order that Louise was trying to generate within her (i.e. Louise's) family. This of itself symbolised the difference there was between, on the one hand, Ellen and Mark, her natural children, and Layla, her stepchild.

There can be no doubting that Louise demonstrated a high degree of commitment to Layla. This was not a relationship that was of little significance or involved a lack of care. Even allowing for the fact that Louise was giving her own 'moral tale' in her interview account (Ribbens McCarthy, Edwards and Gillies, 2003), it would be difficult to argue that Louise was not committed to Layla's welfare. Yet at the same time, there was clearly a difference in the way she understood her relationships with Ellen and Mark and her relationship with Layla. At times Mark's and Ellen's adolescent behaviour may have proved to be problematic, but this did not colour her love for them. They were not judged in this way. Put bluntly, her commitment to them was unconditional. She understood them and shared a sense of communion with them. With Layla, her commitment was evident but it did not have the same all-encompassing quality. Layla was not 'hers' in the same way. Louise's 'love' for her did not reflect that same unconditionality. While she was doing her best for Layla practically and emotionally, acceptance of her and her ways proved more of a struggle. The feelings she had were simply different.

Resident stepmothers in the study

In order to explore in greater depth the complexities that resident stepmothers experience, we will examine the material that was generated on this in our own research project. In the study sample, seven respondents were or had been resident stepmothers. A further two had had resident stepmothers when they were children. Of these nine cases, three (including Louise's) had followed maternal death, and six parental separation/divorce. Two involved shared care, with the stepchildren typically spending alternate weeks with their mother and their father respectively. While the age range at the time of the interview was wide, the majority of the children involved had been of broadly primary school age when they first lived with their stepmothers. In addition, in seven of these nine cases, the stepmother had children of her own living in the household, while in one of the remaining two cases there were children from the new partnership, that is, half-siblings to the stepchildren involved.

'They're such bloody hard work'

As might be expected, the resident stepmothers interviewed reflected on how 'difficult' or 'hard' they had sometimes found stepmothering to be, though in doing so they emphasised different aspects of their experiences. Some of the difficulties the resident stepmothers recounted were recognised as being more a consequence of having comparatively large numbers of children in the household than the result of any stepfamily tensions *per se*. These included increased levels of bickering and argument between the different children; shortages of time, space and money; and problems in adequately meeting the different needs and demands of the children. In addition though there were problems associated with 'melding' the two families together and caring for children who had been used to a different family order. A number of these stepmothers recounted their difficulties in coping with aspects of their stepchildren's behaviour, at least for some of the period their stepchildren had been living with them. Some found that one or more of their stepchildren were particularly demanding; others that their stepchildren had taken a long while to adjust and become accommodated to their new circumstances. The following quotes capture some of this:

> I mean the kids are hard work, full stop. Whether you have two or ten, but it just sort of – I'm doing my best to bring up two other children.
>
> (Emma, mother of three and co-parenting stepmother of two)

> It is a lot to take on and I'm not blowing my own trumpet but I think it's harder to be a stepmother than it is to be a stepfather. Because

the mother does most of the disciplinary role – nine times out of ten, and this is no disrespect to Tony, but the father's out at work and the mother's doing everything in the house.

> (Deb, mother of four and stepmother of four)

I would say just think very, very hard and if there's a lack of cash just think extra hard, find out whether you've got the wherewithal to keep going at it all. There were days, I don't mind telling you now, when I wept at [Woodlands]. ... I look back on it sometimes with absolute horror. We were struggling because we had almost no money.

> (Madge, mother of three and stepmother of one).

It took him [stepson] a long time to accept me, a long time.

> (Linda, mother of one and stepmother of one)

She's not a difficult child but she's overpowering. She wants a lot of attention all the time.

> (Louise about Layla)

Quite often the overall difficulties these stepmothers were reflecting on could not be specified that easily. They were not so much the result of a particular issue or problem, but more the consequence of cumulative pressures. As the quote from Deb above suggests, these pressures were integral to the varied and multiple tasks of 'mothering'. Thus, particularly early on, it was the combined burden of sustaining domestic order, overseeing household schedules and monitoring children that stepmothers found practically and emotionally draining: providing different children with appropriate care; monitoring their activities and relationships; ensuring their developmental and other needs were being met; providing meals they liked; stopping arguments and keeping the peace; cajoling and persuading them to do whatever was required, all the while trying to maintain some balance and treat them equally. Emma, who cared for her own three children full-time and her two stepchildren on alternate weeks, captured the weight of this when she was asked at the end of her interview what advice she would give to someone in her position. She responded in a subdued voice:

Don't do it. No! I don't know. I don't know. Um, when it works fine, it's fine. It's just you have your ups and downs and sometimes they're such bloody hard work. You know?

Discipline and personalities

As we have discussed above, resident stepmothers are likely to be responsible for family order as well as childcare. Inevitably this involves them in the routine, everyday disciplining of stepchildren in ways which are less common for resident stepfathers. Interestingly though, discipline *per se* was not often cited as a major *stepfamily* issue by the resident stepmothers in the sample.

> I mean natural families will do that whether they're step or not. But it is harder for Tony's [her partner's] children than it is for mine, mine are a lot younger. James is the stubborn one, he will say, 'Hers can't tell me what to do, hers isn't my mother' (laughs). And I'll say, 'Hers can tell you what to do and hers is telling you', but disciplining them, yes, they take it, they take it.
>
> (Deb, mother of four and stepmother of four)

> Yes, well, I discipline them the same as I discipline my own. And if I need to deal with one of them then I do. It doesn't matter which one it is [laughs]! But then I'd have a word with anybody's kids if I saw them misbehaving!
>
> (Rachel, mother of three and resident stepmother of two)

> I don't think it's probably any more testing than any biological parent. I have never had one turn round and say to me: 'But you're not my mum, I don't have to do that'. And I probably am lucky. But I have been tough right from the word go.
>
> (Carla, mother of two and co-parenting stepmother of three)

Certainly these stepmothers reported having problems at times getting their stepchildren to behave appropriately and to do as they (the stepmothers) wanted. However while these issues were sometimes attributed to their stepchildren's wilfulness or their ability to play different parents off against the other, in the main they were understood to be either normal aspects of childhood behaviour or else seen as the result of their previous experiences, much as Louise had understood Layla's behaviour in these terms.

> I mean, I don't take any nonsense from him, never have done, I don't believe in that with kids. They've got to have something to kick against, they've got to know where they stand with you. ... We get on alright now. It's been a struggle, and he can be shitty but then so

can mine. It goes with the flow, it goes with the age. It's their job, it's what teenagers do [laughs].

(Linda, mother of one and stepmother of one)

Thus the emphasis in these stepmothers' accounts was on discipline as an integral part of mothering. Like their natural children, stepchildren could induce feelings of irritation, anger and frustration; as Madge said, they could reduce you to tears. But in a sense these problems, difficult though they were to handle at times, were seen as normal. As Linda said, they were what children do. But equally what mothers do is manage domestic life. That is their job. To put this differently, the resident stepmothers in the sample accepted that as the 'woman in the household' they had the responsibility to impose order and ensure that all the children in the household behaved appropriately. Importantly it seemed from the stepmothers' accounts that their stepchildren also recognised this. At times they may resist their stepmother's wishes and look to undermine their authority; some may require comparatively high levels of monitoring and vigilance. Nonetheless it appeared that there was a general acceptance of their stepmother's right to supervise, instruct and control.

However it was also apparent that at times stepchildren, or more accurately specific stepchildren, had a particular capacity to irritate their stepmothers. The following quotes are illustrative of this.

But Alex is, he'll wind them up and, and just be nasty sometimes. I'm not – I know my kids aren't perfect, but he does wind kids up. He's known for it. Winding everybody up.

(Emma, mother of three and co-parenting stepmother of two)

Oh, I have been so upset with him [stepson], that I've said to Geoff [partner] I don't want him round our house. I mean I know he's only 11 years old, I know it's completely irrational. But I have been so upset by his manipulation and his wheeler-dealing.

(Carla, mother of two and co-parenting stepmother of three)

I've really hated him [her stepson] sometimes [laughs]. ... Even now I don't like him very much – as a person. He's not got the compassion for others that Alan [her son] has. He's very 'me, me, me'. And I know it's because he was with John for so many years and John's mum did so much of the bringing up. And I think there was too much spoiling. Whereas I said to Alan: 'Listen mate, it's you and me now kid. Don't hang on to my apron strings. You've got to stand on your own two feet. I'm not always going to be there', so there was no, I realise that spoiling them, you know, it really does spoil them. It's a good word. You can spoil a character.

(Linda, mother of one and stepmother of one)

The resident stepmothers in the sample could also be critical of their natural children. However when they discussed the problems they had with their own children, they tended to be somewhat more understanding and somewhat more forgiving. For example, in the case of Linda above, it appeared from her account that Alan, her natural son had caused far more problems at school and at home than her stepson. Yet it was her stepson whom she saw as having the more deep-rooted personality problems. Alan might get up to more 'mischief' and be harder to control, but from Linda's perspective, this was seen as positive; it was indicative of the strength of his personality, his independence and his willingness to express himself – all positive character traits that she saw as somewhat lacking in her stepson. Although often quite subtle, the different ways that stepchildren's and natural children's behaviour was accounted for was indicative of the different commitment and solidarity these mothers felt – in essence, the different love they had. However as we shall see, this did not mean that the resident stepmothers were not committed to their stepchildren. There was a difference between natural and step-children, but usually there was still a strong sense of caring about (as well as for) their stepchildren (MacDonald and DeMaris, 1996).

Proper mothering and inadequate mothers

While stepchildren were at times criticised by the resident stepmothers in the sample, as with the quote from Linda above and the example of Louise and Layla in Chapter 3, many of the issues that arose were seen as a consequence of the stepchildren's earlier socialisation experiences. In particular, the children's natural mothers were generally the ones who were held accountable by the stepmothers for whatever difficulties their stepchildren were experiencing, at least in those cases where the marriage had been ended by divorce rather than the mother's death. Although not universal, they tended to be presented as 'inadequate' or even 'bad' mothers who demonstrated a lack of 'proper' mothering skills. The stepmothers interviewed were particularly judgemental and scornful about natural mothers who had 'walked out' on their children to form another relationship. In these cases, what ended up being questioned were both the mothers' capacities for mothering and more generally their moral standing as women. In bringing forth these judgements, the stepmothers were not only highlighting their own 'good' mothering capabilities in comparison, as well as their ideas about femininity and family order, they were also expressing their frustration at having to cope with the continuing impact of the natural mother on their attempts to instil appropriate discipline, responsibility and family order in their stepchildren.

> [L]ike when they're with their mum they always look dirty and it's not important, I know, but you just can't help seeing it. And they go to school with their hair all stuck up and she won't sort of take time to make sure they look all right. ... Well it's just like, I don't know they've got no, they seem like wild children sometimes, you know. They, you try and instil good values all the time, and, I don't know, she just makes it so easy to slag her off!
>
> (Emma, mother of three and co-parenting stepmother of two)

> When she left, Sarah [the stepchildren's natural mother] wrote a letter saying, 'I grew up in this house and leaving it is the hardest thing I've ever done'. Not 'I hope the kids don't take this too hard', or 'If there are any problems this is where you can contact me and I'll come round and see them every day'. No, nothing like that. It's just 'me, me, me', 'my house' and 'poor Sarah' really. When I read that letter I said, well I thought she was the Tin Man, she just hasn't got a heart, she just hasn't. ... I mean I have put my children through a lot, especially Sonia. I mean, she's had two stepdads and I've been married and divorced and, you know, and she's been through a lot. ... Basically she's been through hell and out again. But like I said to Sarah, his ex-wife, 'I've put my kids through S-H-I-T and out again, just to keep them with me, just to keep them with me'. But she [Sarah] says, 'I couldn't do that to my children, I love them too much'. So she left them here instead! But the grass was greener. Well, it's not, but she thought it was. It's been mowed down now (laughs).
>
> (Deb, mother of four and stepmother of four)

> She's never treated them as a mother. I mean, they don't know their times tables, they can't read very well. I mean that, to me, is something that you do from the age of when they can talk. Spend time with them. All they do, or all she's ever done with them is to sit on the settee and watch every soap that's going. ... So you can see how their life has changed. When they first came over here, they said

to me once 'What are you doing?', and I said 'I'm peeling potatoes. What do you mean what am I doing?'. They'd never seen that before. I said to them 'What would you like for a pudding? You can have lemon meringue pie or an apple cake.' Well, they said 'We've never had apple cake before, we'll have apple cake.' And of course, I just made an apple cake. And their eyes nearly fell out of their heads. To think that I'd just made something, put it in the oven and then they ate it. You know, they'd never seen that before. She'd never made a cake in twenty years.

(Rachel, mother of three and resident stepmother of two)

Very clearly the stepmothers here are involved in constructing their own 'moral tales' about their mothering. In presenting their accounts the way they did, they are evidencing their own moral worth and higher standards of childcare. Interestingly too, in depicting the comparative inadequacy of the natural mothers' mothering (or in those two cases where the natural mother had died, the child's other previous carers), they were distancing themselves from blaming the stepchild. He or she may at times be irritating or difficult, but the cause of this lies not with the child *per se* but more with the natural mother's inappropriate standards of childcare. The anger and frustration experienced was directed at her. Similarly, any continuing problems in mothering the stepchildren and getting them to behave were also often attributed to her continuing 'interference' and the conflicts that arose over how the child(ren) should be treated (Hughes, 1991; Simpson, 1998).

This was an issue for all five resident stepmothers where the natural mother was still alive, as it also was for Louise with regard Layla's maternal grandparents. Each recognised – albeit sometimes grudgingly – the right of the natural mother to be involved in their children's lives, but equally they experienced their involvement as taxing and, from a personal view, unwelcome. Even when everything ran smoothly, the need to co-ordinate with the natural mother over access visits not only placed constraints over the freedom and control the stepmother and her partner could exercise, but also tended to make their lives 'busy', and sometimes fraught. The stepmothers – and frequently they were the ones who were directly involved in these negotiations – resented the amount of effort that went into managing these arrangements, especially when change was necessary to their agreed routines or when they perceived these routines had been unnecessarily sabotaged by the natural mother. Particular episodes where arrangements had gone awry were recounted with a degree of antipathy in the interviews in ways which highlighted the perceived practical and moral unreasonableness of the natural mothers.

Sharing care and family order: an example

There were only two resident stepmothers in the sample who co-parented with the children's natural mothers, both having their stepchildren on alternate weeks. One was Emma whose interview was drawn on in the previous section. The other was Carla. The following excerpts taken from the interview with Carla illustrate some of the tensions and difficulties that she and her husband, Geoff, experienced. Many of these were similar to those other resident stepmothers reported, but, as will be seen, they were exacerbated by the need to co-ordinate activities and co-operate with her stepchildren's natural mother, Laura. Carla had two children, aged 2 and 5 with Geoff, and three stepsons, aged 8, 11 and 14, from Geoff's previous marriage to Laura.

> Yeah, I'll pick them up. Sometimes I go to school twice. ... But what I do is when I drive – where we are is sort of here, where she [Laura] is, is six minutes there and school – for me to go to call in at her house on the way to school is about a three minute detour. So I just say leave everything you don't need at mum's and I pick it up on the way through to school. ... And it just has panned out and she has a little bit at the back of her house which she doesn't lock, and I don't think she locks it whether I'm coming or not. ... I just can go in ... and pick up the stuff ... And the same thing on the Wednesday morning. So they don't have the stigma of carting thousands of things round. We drop it on the way to school. Just leave it at the back of the house. ...
>
> He [Geoff] doesn't talk to her any more. I talk. Because he can't talk to her, he's so angry with her. He's so angry at her about the original thing and then he's so angry at her about the way she is now that she doesn't – she gets ... quite a good deal financially. And she doesn't look after them the way he thinks. She would leave them at home by themselves. Even the eleven-year old and eight-year old. ... So there are some bad bits about it, and it does really rile him. So I tend to be the organizer in saying 'Do you want them for the first week of school holidays or second week of school holidays?' And when I say she is in control it's like if she wants something, she'll have it. If she wants to make a fuss about it, it's very hard for me. I'll try and, you know, manoeuvre it, but the bottom line, she's their mum. ...
>
> It wasn't our weekend, but you can't really say that to someone on the phone 'Oh it's not my weekend, but their mother wants to go

to something so it's now our weekend, so could ... '. You know, you do have to walk a bit of a tightrope. So we did it. But because we did that, I then said to Geoff, 'Well look, when we want to swap something, we'll just swap it. And we'll just say'. And as long as we give her enough advance. I think the problem is that she's not organised and she has recently said 'Oh I don't run my house like a military camp like you do'. And my answer would be 'Well, unfortunately, we have to. Because even when we don't have the three big boys, we have the two little ones, we're going in different directions.

It would be much easier for me if she disappeared off the face of the earth. But it probably wouldn't be easier for them. ... Ten times easier. Ten times easier if she went to London, got a job in London and just had them every six weeks or every school holiday. Just from a discipline point of view, from different standards and different values and, you know, getting homework done. Our idea is that you get in, get it done, do it to the best of your ability, whereas her idea is you just get it done. And that must be hard on a kid. ... To try and think well, why should I work really hard when she says I can just do it? ... And they see the differences. I mean we live in a much nicer house. But there's me and dad and both work very hard in hard jobs.

There is no need to comment extensively on this illustration. Carla's words speak powerfully for themselves of the issues she faced. Clearly organising and managing children's care in this way demanded a great deal of tolerance. It necessitated a high level of organisation, flexibility and co-ordination. As stepmother, Carla did seem to be in the middle, trying hard to juggle different demands and ensure that complex familial arrangements worked. Although not mentioned explicitly in the interview, it is perhaps worth noting that Laura also demonstrated a tolerance and flexibility in accommodating Carla's quite different domestic regime, even if from Carla's viewpoint Laura held the upper hand.

Commitment

Carla's commitment to her stepchildren was evident in the amount of time she spent doing practical childcare activities, as well as in the way she spoke about them. As she said, her preference would have been to care for the three of them full-time, even though at times she found the middle one quite difficult and demanding. This same sense of commitment was evident in the accounts most of the other resident stepmothers gave of their relationships with their stepchildren (Ribbens McCarthy, Edwards and Gillies, 2003). As we have seen above, this did not mean that they always found parenting them easy or without its problems. Nonetheless there was a commitment to them and a desire to see them do well. In this, the stepmothers defined themselves as genuinely 'mothering', and not simply acting as housekeeper or temporary guardian. They were concerned with their stepchildren's needs and with providing them with a secure environment in which to grow up. They may not have loved them with quite the same emotion or understanding that they felt for their natural children, but they none-theless demonstrated a strong attachment to them. In this, they clearly included them within the umbrella of their 'family' (Ribbens McCarthy, Edwards and Gillies, 2003).

It would, however, be wrong to see this as simply a consequence of the individual attachment that existed between the stepmothers and their stepchildren. The sense of commitment and of family membership was also consequent on the other relationships that developed within the family. As would be expected, the bond between the stepmother and her partner, the stepchildren's natural father, was important in this. However the relationship that developed between the stepmother's own natural children and her stepchildren was also important, whether they were half-siblings or stepsiblings.

> They [her son and stepson] get on like a house on fire, just absolutely brilliantly. ... They call each other brother, they say they're brothers. The problem was, you see, they would gang up against us. That's what they'd do. They knew exactly how to wind us up! And by golly, we did have to have a very united front. You know, you daren't let them crack you open!
>
> (Linda, mother of one and stepmother of one)

> But we get on like a house on fire, don't we? And they [her children and stepchildren] do. They argue like natural brothers and sisters but when we first got together there was a lot of 'that's mine and that's mine', but that's all stopped.
>
> (Deb, mother of four and stepmother of four)

> I think we're actually very lucky because this boy (her oldest stepson) is such a good boy. He has always adored her (Carla's natural daughter) and he totally adores him (Carla's natural son).
>
> (Carla, mother of two and co-parenting stepmother of three)

Interestingly too, in the small number of cases we had in the sample, the bonds that developed between resident stepmothers and their step-children endured strongly in adulthood. Admittedly there were only three cases in the sample where children who were now adult had lived with resident stepmothers, one stepmother (Madge) and two step-children. However in all three cases, a strong and significant commitment continued to exist between stepmother and stepchild long after the latter left home. For example, Ruth, 43 at the time of the interview, had had a very troubled relationship with her natural mother and at the age of seven had chosen to live with her father and stepmother, Pam. While their relationship had been difficult in the beginning, Ruth had become very close to Pam as a teenager. Even though Pam was no longer married to Ruth's natural father, she now not only regarded Pam as her mother figure but also as a best friend who she could turn to whenever she needed help. 'Because you see I had a relationship not only as Pam, I regard Pam as my mother, but we're best friends as well.' Beryl, who was in her sixties at the time of the interview, also recounted the strength of her attachment to her stepmother, Freda, who had become Beryl's stepmother at the age of eight following her natural mother's premature death. It was evident that Freda was in every sense a 'full' mother to Beryl right up until the time of her death, some 15 years before the interview. In Beryl's words: '[Freda] was extremely good to us. ... She loved us ... She was wonderful, absolutely wonderful. ... Well I couldn't have had a better, she was, my mother couldn't have treated me any better. Probably some mothers wouldn't have.' In turn, Beryl nursed her through her final illness. Although there were only three respondents in the sample who had direct experience of resident stepmother – adult stepchild relationships, it seems unlikely to be just coincidence that all three were clearly sustained as 'family' ties.

Non-resident stepmothers

In the sections above, we have focussed on stepmothers and stepchildren living in the same household. We now want to consider relationships between non-resident stepmothers and their stepchildren. We will do this in two parts. First we will examine stepmother/stepchild relationships in which the child is (or was) still dependent at the time of their father's repartnering but lives (or lived) principally with their natural mother. We will then conclude the chapter by considering briefly the relation-ships that develop between stepmothers and stepchildren when a father repartners after his child(ren) have become adult. As in the previous section, we will draw on some of the empirical material we collected in our stepkinship study to develop the arguments we are making.

Dependent children

The most obvious point to make about non-resident stepmother/stepchild relationships concerns the diversity there is in them. Like other stepfamily relationships, their patterning depends on their individual histories and the complex of relationships in which they are embedded. As noted earlier, some of these relationships are effectively non-existent. There may be knowledge about the step relationship, but there is little or no interaction between the stepmother and her partner's children from his earlier marriage. Almost invariably this is a consequence of a father playing little part in his children's lives after the parental separation, whatever the reason might be for this. Interestingly, eight of the 16 respondents in our study whose fathers had repartnered while the respondents were still children reported having no relationship of consequence with their stepmothers. While some of the eight had met their stepmother on occasion in the past, knowing their names and some other personal details about them, none of them had any involvement with them. As they now had no deliberate or intentional contact with their natural father, there was no reason to develop a tie with his new partner. Similarly they might know of the existence of half-siblings, but they did not have any sibling-type relationships with them. As we have noted, it is likely that this pattern will become less common over time given the normative encouragement there now is for non-resident fathers to maintain active relationships with their children.

Leaving aside such non-existent or moribund ties, there is still a good deal of variation in the character of the relationships sustained by non-resident stepmothers and their stepchildren (Doodson and Morley, 2006). Clearly though, these relationships are structurally quite different to the relationships that resident stepmothers and stepchildren have. In particular, they usually entail a far lower level of involvement, less responsibility and consequently less concern with socialisation, family order and family identity. Indeed, generally notions of family and kinship are seen as less relevant to them. Consequently while irritations and conflicts can still arise, the intensity of the relationships means that these can be accommodated much more readily. A good example of the limited involvement of non-resident stepmothers and their stepchildren was provided in the case study of Mark presented in Chapter 3. His relationship with Sheila was not particularly strong but little was demanded of it, so it remained cordial.

In other cases there may be more tension or, conversely, a greater compatibility and liking. However in the main, these relationships are recognised as being mediated relationships, both by the stepmothers and stepchildren involved. They are consequent on the relationship each party maintains with the stepchild's father rather than ties which exist for their own sake. One of our respondents, Sammy, who was 30 at the time of the interview, captured this well when she said of her stepmother who was now separated from her father: 'She was never particularly close. ... She was my father's partner. ... There was no independent relationship there.' Sammy's notion of there being no 'independent relationship' between her and her stepmother mirrored the comments that other respondents made about their relationship with their stepmothers. They were rarely integral within their ideas of 'family', more often, they were just their 'father's partners'. To express this slightly differently, there tended to be acceptance rather than any degree of either fondness or kinship expressed about these relationships by the non-resident stepchildren in our sample.

On not being a mother

Non-resident stepmothers and non-resident stepchildren are of course likely to perceive their relationship differently. The issues and pressures they face overlap but are not the same. Moreover often stepmothers have a fuller and more sophisticated perspective of how their relationships with their stepchildren have developed than their stepchildren have. They are also likely to be more reflective of the impact of the different family experiences the stepchild has had. Certainly this was so within our study. While the numbers were small – there were seven non-resident stepmothers in our sample – the accounts they gave us were fuller than those provided by stepchildren and entailed more complex histories. Moreover these stepmothers recognised the extent to which their relationships with their stepchildren were patterned by the wider network of relationships in which they were mutually involved, not least of which was the current relationship between the stepchildren's natural parents.

This is one of the issues we want to develop in this section. First though, we want to discuss ways in which non-resident stepmothers with dependent stepchildren negotiate the idea of 'mothering'. One of the issues long identified in the research literature on step-parenting concerns the complexities of managing a pseudo-parental role when you are not fully recognised as a parent. There can be a tension around how much of a parent to be, to draw on Giles-Sims' (1984) terminology (see also Weaver and Coleman, 2005; Doodson and Morley, 2006). This was a concern for the non-resident stepmothers in our sample, though one which they claimed to have resolved by stepping back from a mothering role.

In particular, most of these respondents emphasised the importance of not 'interfering' too heavily and of being 'flexible' in their responses to their stepchildren's ways, difficult though this might be at times (Henry and McCue, 2009). In the main, they made it clear that they were not directly involved in 'mothering' in any strong sense. Unlike resident stepmothers, most felt they were not responsible for enforcing rules or promoting discipline. The children's natural parents were responsible for these matters. Indeed a number of the respondents emphasised how important it was for them to be seen as something other than a mother figure (Orchard and Solberg, 1999). For example Jane, who at the time of the interview had been a non-resident stepmother to her husband David's children, Lizzie and Charlotte, aged 12 and 10, for some three years as well as now being the natural mother of a 15-month-old daughter, expressed her views as follows:

Interviewer: Do you think of yourself as a stepmother?

Jane: Not really, I try not to I think, because I don't like the wording and I know that Charlotte and Lizzie probably don't like the wording either. We've talked about it and they call Jeremy [their mother's second husband] 'Jeremy' and they don't see him as a stepfather so I don't think they think of me as a stepmother. And they call me Jane anyway. And I remember when they got to know about this little one coming along they said 'Oh, we don't want to think of it as a stepsister or brother'. and I think it was Charlotte who said 'Let's leave the step out of it. I don't like that. It's either sister or brother'. And I thought that was rather sweet and so we've kept it like that.

Interviewer: And do you get involved in, sort of, parenting issues? The day-to-day stuff?

Jane: No, if they're discussing things informally – about school or boys or friends or what's been going on – then I'll listen and probably put my point of view across if it's just a very informal chat. But if it's something about making a decision about what one of them should do or not do, whether they can do something, then I leave

	that entirely up to David because I don't feel as if that should be my role. ...
Jane:	Well, discipline ... he would do it probably on my behalf because he knows that I would feel uncomfortable doing that ... It shouldn't come from me or I wouldn't feel happy about it coming from me because I would feel that I was disciplining them, and I don't want to be in that role.
Interviewer:	So how do you see your role?
Jane:	As a friend really. Hopefully I'm more like a friend. Somebody to have a good time with and who's around to talk to and to share in whatever they're doing but not be a surrogate mother, they've got a mother.

Lesley, who had a natural daughter, Ellie, aged 13, from her first marriage, two natural sons, Dean, 7, and Joe, 5, from her current marriage, and two non-resident stepsons, Pete, 18, and Gus, 16, echoed some of the same issues as Jane, though her experiences had been somewhat more complex.

Lesley:	Now that's quite interesting, now Pete and Gus are older, there's not the bickering with Ellie, Pete and Gus like there used to be. There used to be a lot of bickering. And it was hard, sometimes very hard to accept. Now Ellie, Pete and Gus get on extremely well and are quite close; Pete favours Dean, and Gus favours Joe. ... But really, I've had quite a hard relationship with them 'cos when they first came they wouldn't accept me; they wouldn't sort of do anything I asked them to do. And bear in mind I've got Ellie having to abide by house rules, then Dean and Joe and they sort of come in and, you know, house rules went out the window for the weekend. And then Ellie was saying 'I'm not allowed to get away with that. Why do they?' This is where the problems start, isn't it? But as they've got older, things have got a lot easier. And it's really nice, because they're like adult. ...
Interviewer:	And how do you see yourself in relation to them, I mean do you see yourself as a stepmother?
Lesley:	No, not really. No. When they were little maybe, but not now. Because they're so sort of grown up. Um, no, they just call me Lesley and that's fine by me. ... because they've got their own mother.

Only one of the non-resident stepmothers interviewed, Gwen, reported playing an active part in disciplining her stepchildren, though she too distanced herself from taking on a mothering role. When she married her husband Seb, 12 years before the interview, his children, Chris and Alan, had been 9 and 7. Gwen's affair with Seb had led to Seb's marriage ending, in the process causing much conflict and ill-feeling on all sides. Gwen now had two natural sons of her own, Andy, 11, and Lyn, 9. Early on in her relationship with Seb, Gwen had had difficulty accepting Chris's and Alan's behaviour towards her, only later seeing much of it as 'normal'. In discussing her attitudes towards disciplining her stepchildren, Gwen said:

> But um, no I never felt awkward that I couldn't say anything. In fact I probably was too – from their point of view – I was probably too over the top. Because I did correct them. And I did feel that they'd always been made to feel welcome in our home but these poor, these two poor kids had to be faced with me and all whatever went on and being told about me at home, which obviously wasn't going to be good. And then, and yet we had, we had so much of them, so I always thought 'Well you can't have it both ways, I'm sorry about all that's happened, but we have all come to an agreement and I do have the children.' ... It was a huge life change to me. I was in my early twenties, I'd had nothing to do with children really. ... And then when we took them out they moaned and groaned and grumbled all the time, but as I say I only realized when I'd had my own that that's what they do. ... You can see it from their point of view. And think how difficult it must have been. And I never tried to be over gushy. I never wanted to replace their mother; I just was – and perhaps I could have been a bit more ... affectionate towards them; I never wanted to overdo it because I didn't want them to feel that I was trying to replace their mother in any way, so going up to bed and saying goodnight it was, they sort of said goodnight to me in a sort of half-hearted way, and then Seb put them to bed.

From her comments, it was apparent there had been a good deal of resentment on all sides over what had happened. Even now, her relationship with Alan was quite shallow.

> They were very young, I mean Chris has come through it all better than Alan, really. Even now at 20 he's – quite resentful. Even though his mother's now remarried and quite happy. ... Chris visits, rings,

Alan does occasionally, keeps in touch but only sort of – only, not particularly because he feels close to us, he just doesn't want to completely lose touch, but gets on with his own life really. ... So he doesn't particularly – he has a problem, he always has had a problem with me basically.

Like Jane above, the non-resident stepmothers in the sample were resistant to using the terms 'stepmother' and 'stepchildren' to characterise their relationships, both in the interview and in other contexts. They also consistently reported that their stepchildren called them by their given names rather than by familial ones (Doodson and Morley, 2006). Thus as the quotes above suggest, these stepmothers were quite careful not to be seen as usurping the mother's role in their stepchildren's lives. They tended to keep their distance from 'parental' decisions and presented themselves as not unduly interfering (Weaver and Coleman, 2005).

Family networks

In other ways though, these stepmothers asserted the importance of 'family' in their accounts of their relationships with their stepchildren. For example, they recognised the importance for their husbands/partners of maintaining relationships with their children, even if at times this did create additional stress in their own lives. As with some of the resident stepmothers, some of these non-resident stepmothers played a significant role in negotiating contact arrangements, especially when relationships between the natural parents continued to be fraught. Moreover there was a strong recognition of the power of kinship in the ways they described the relationships that had developed between their stepchildren and their own natural children from their current partnerships, that is, their stepchildren's half-siblings. Of the seven non-resident stepmothers in the sample, five had children who were half-siblings to their stepchildren. As suggested in the material from Lesley and Jane above, these relationships were seen as having great significance for all the children and as being highly integrative within the stepfamily.

I mean as I say Chris and Alan used to come over and they thought it was lovely having these two, the babies, to look after and cuddle and so they have been brought up with them. ... Because Chris and Alan actually held them as babes in arms, there's always been a closeness between the four boys. And my two adore them. And really they keep the contact not because of their dad, because of their brothers.

(Gwen – see above)

I had Denise very quickly, so especially Linda, she sort of doted on her. She was a proper little mother at twelve, you know. ... It brought them closer, yes.

> (Andrea, mother of Denise and Matt, stepmother of
> Linda and Pearl)

[Pete's and Gus's regular weekend visits] stopped, because obviously they're sort of getting older, want to do their own thing, and we've just recently started it again because they were saying that they missed Dean and Joe.

> (Lesley – see above)

In summary, there was a degree of 'familial distancing' in the ways these stepmothers characterised their relationships with their non-resident stepchildren. It was not that their stepchildren were understood to lie right outside the realm of 'family'; it was more that these relationships were 'indirectly' family. They were usually seen as mediated ones, consequent upon the their partnership with the stepchildren's father, augmented by their mutual connection through any half-siblings. Generally, though with some variation, these stepmothers expressed a degree of warmth and fondness to their stepchildren, despite the difficulties and frustrations there may have been in their relationships. In the main, they gave the sense of wanting to be involved in their lives, while also recognising that their involvement was likely to be somewhat peripheral, precisely because the relationship was a mediated one. As indicated above, the respondents also emphasised the need for tolerance and acceptance in the management of these relationships. They understood that structurally they were not easy relationships for any of those involved, with irritations developing readily. Remaining flexible and somewhat distanced were seen as ways of helping to make them work.

Later-life stepchildren

In the final section of this chapter we turn to examine the degree of family connection expressed in stepmother/stepchild relationships that develop after the 'children' involved have became adults. In other words, we are focussing on relationships in which the children were at least 18 at the time their father's new partnership formed, which for ease we will call 'later-life stepchildren'. Traditionally these have not really been considered as stepmother/stepchild relationships, principally because they do not involve co-residence or other obvious forms of dependence. This though makes them of interest from a kinship perspective, with a key issue being the extent to which these ties ever come to be defined as 'family' ones. In total, there were 15 respondents in our sample who reported that their fathers had repartnered after the respondents were adults. There were also four respondents who had become stepmothers to adult children through partnering their fathers, one of whom, Sue, was also one of the 15 respondents who had become a stepchild in adulthood.

It was rare for any of these respondents to use stepfamily or kinship terminology in referring to their stepmothers or stepchildren. In general they did not feel that such language was appropriate except when they needed to explain their relationships to others. As might be expected, the dominant perspective expressed in the interviews was that these people were their father's new partners, or their partner's adult children, rather than being family members in their own right. Clearly there was some variation in this, influenced by a number of factors including the degree of compatibility and liking there was between them and relationships with grandchildren. Age issues also influenced the development of stepmother/adult stepchild relationships. In four of the 19 cases in the study, the age difference between stepmother and later-life stepchild was relatively small – between three and 12 years – so that any ideas of 'mothering' were particularly inappropriate in their consequent relationships.

The following quotes from the interviews with later-life stepchildren capture the dominant spirit. They illustrate the general acceptance there was of the other person's position as their father's partner even when there was little positive affect, but also indicate an absence of any real sense of kinship or 'family' involvement.

> At first no, we absolutely hated each other, but now, yeah, we get on fine. ... We hated each other! I think probably it was a lot of jealousy, I don't know if she was jealous of me because Dad used to spend a lot of time with me or what, I think probably a lot to do with it was age, but now it doesn't make any difference at all to me but, we get on fine now.
>
> (Joanne, 43, whose father remarried when she was 19)

> Carol [stepmother] is really nice and she's very pleasant and all that lot, but I mean we're not close, and it's you know, it's a nice relationship. I'm happy they're together and things like that.
>
> (Jocelyn, 21, whose father remarried when she was 19)

Nowadays I get on well with her. I don't like her particularly, I can still say she's not the type of person that in any other circumstance I would form a relationship or friendship with. But we get on well enough. ... She's not my cup of tea, but Dad obviously likes her, so.

(Natalie, 31, whose father remarried when she was 25)

Interviewer:	And do you have a lot to do with Pat [stepmother]?
Mike:	Wouldn't say a lot. But yes, get on very well with Pat. I think they're very suited. ... I always hear about them [Pat's children from her previous marriage] ... I don't say I've got a really buddy-buddy relationship with all of them, but ... it's a nice family, they're a very close family as well and they like to accept people in.

(Mike, 40, whose father repartnered when Mike was in his late 20s)

As discussed in the previous section, sometimes other kin – in particular half-siblings and stepgrandchildren – can act as a 'bridge' between stepmothers and their stepchildren, adding a different dimension of shared kinship focus to their relationships. As might be expected given the ages of those involved, the number of half-siblings for the later-life stepchild subset of the sample was small, involving only three of the stepchildren and one of the stepmothers. In one of these cases there was no contact with the father or the half-sibling. In two of the other three cases, the relationship between the half-siblings did not seem to be particularly strong, perhaps because of the comparatively large age difference between them. The family connection with the half-siblings was recognised, but the respondents' involvement with them was somewhat limited. In turn, while the half-sibling relationships imbued the stepmother/later-life stepchild relationship with a sense of family relevance, the kinship connection remained quite distanced.

The one exception here involved Sarah, a respondent whose half-brothers were close in age to her own children – mid-teens at the time of the interview. As the following extracts from her interview details, Sarah's 'family' connection with her stepmother (and her half-brothers) developed more strongly following her father's sudden death ten years prior to the interview:

As soon as my father died, ten years ago, I became next or whatever to my brothers – took on some responsibility for them, if you like ... Ellie [stepmother] and I got on quite well but actually I didn't spend that much time with them, although we all had babies together. ... But when we did, then we were more like sisters than mother. ... So what we decided was that we would make her our family so it was done. Not like we sat down and thought about it but we did do it because we liked her. We all got on with her anyway and we were slowly dragging her in, with the children. ... And then what would happen was that we would arrange things for the children, because also the children became incredibly close. ... I mean, they [Sarah's half-brothers] have a relationship with me but it's not half as good as the one that they've got with my kids because actually they're peers ... They're half-uncles, but they are like cousins. They are like immediate cousins. And they look alike, I mean, you know, the family thing is there and they are very similar.

The significance of Sarah's half-brothers in cementing the relationship between her and her stepmother is evident here. More commonly, it is the presence of (step) grandchildren that foster a family connection between stepmothers and the later-life stepchildren. In those cases where there were positive relationships between the father, the stepmother and the later-life (step)child, the stepmother was generally recognised as an honorary grandmother and given some form of grandparental kinship title, such as 'Granny Sue' or 'Nana Elizabeth'. However, as we shall discuss more fully in Chapter 7, for this to happen, it seemed important that the stepmother be involved with the grandchildren from when they were quite young and for them to be 'active' as grandparents. If they were not of significance in their grandchildren's lives, then more commonly they continued to be seen as a (grand)father's partner rather than as part of the broader kinship network.

Conclusion

This chapter has focussed on stepmothers' relationships with their step-children, concentrating particularly on resident stepmothering. We have argued that the conventional gendered division of labour makes this relationship particularly complex. In particular, the responsibility that mothers – resident stepmothers as well as natural mothers – normally have for establishing family order means that their involvement with their stepchildren is typically more intense and more complex than that of any of the other step-parent/stepchild dyads. Because of the nature of childcare activities, it is likely to entail comparatively more involve-ment with the stepchildren. As we discussed, the processes inherent in generating and maintaining the desired family order routinely requires a level of direct managing, cajoling and disciplining them that stepfathers can generally avoid.

However, the large majority of stepmothers are not resident stepmothers. Some of these non-resident stepmothers have little to do with their stepchildren, while others only have contact for relatively short periods during access visits. This alters the dynamics of the relationship significantly. In particular, such stepmothers rarely define themselves as responsible for parenting or overseeing stepchildren's development. Some may be quite highly involved with them during visits, but equally many take a back seat and define access time more as 'father/child' time than 'family' time. The patterning of the interaction between stepmother and stepchildren will also be influenced by the age of the children, and by the presence of any of the stepmother's own children in the household, be they half-siblings or stepsiblings. Tensions can at times develop with the stepchildren's natural mother over the arrangements made for access visits and the stepchildren may at times be found irritating. In general though, relationships between non-resident stepmothers and stepchildren do not usually generate very many difficulties. Especially when the stepchildren are older, the relationships tend more typically to be defined as cordial but as relatively limited in content.

In the next chapter, we shall consider stepfathering. Because the large majority of children with separated parents live with their mothers, the chapter will be concerned with resident stepfather/stepchild relationships. Drawing on relevant material from our own study, we will examine these relationships from the perspectives of both stepfathers and the stepchildren.

6
Stepfathering Stepchildren

In this chapter we turn to analyse the character of stepfather–stepchild relationships. In line with the main theme of the book, we will be concerned principally with the boundaries of family and the ways stepfathers are – and are not – incorporated into people's understandings of family connection. As suggested in Chapter 5, stepfather–stepchild relationships tend to be somewhat less involved and consequently somewhat more straightforward than those that stepmothers have with their stepchildren. However, as with all stepfamily relationships, there is variation in the patterns that emerge. Among the factors influencing the character of these ties are the ages of the stepchildren at the time the new union is formed, whether the stepfather and stepchildren live in the same household, and the relationship each stepchild has with their natural father. In what follows, we will draw once again on the interview material we collected to illustrate and explore some of the different ways in which stepfather relationships are constructed. As with the previous chapter, this cannot be done in isolation; relationships between stepfathers and their stepchildren are embedded in wider family formations that influence the patterning of the constituent ties.

In this chapter we will be predominantly concerned with resident stepfather–stepchild relationships, examining their patterning both when the stepchildren are young and when they become adult. From a demographic and a policy angle, this is of course the most important mode of stepfathering. There are far more resident stepfathers than resident stepmothers, principally because children tend to stay with their mothers after parental separation or divorce. Of course, not all stepfathers live with their stepchildren. A small minority of dependent stepchildren live with their natural father (and possibly a stepmother) rather than their mother and a stepfather. Other stepchildren will have lived for a period of their childhood with a stepfather (and in some instances, more than one) but no longer do so because they are now adults and live independently. We will not here be considering relationships between stepchildren and stepfathers who live with dependent children's non-resident mothers, largely because like the non-resident stepmothers considered in the previous chapter, these people usually lie outside the realm of recognised kinship (though at a later stage some may be incorporated as 'honorary' grandparents – see Chapter 7). Our focus throughout will be on analysing the differing degrees to which resident stepfathers are understood to be integrated into the realm of family. To start, we shall return briefly to the case illustrations discussed in Chapter 3.

In these case illustrations, five stepfather relationships were discussed, in all of which the stepfather had lived with the stepchild(ren) in question. They were: Steve's relationship with Christine, where we have both his and her accounts; Mark's relationship with his stepfather, Tom; Sandie's relationship with her stepfather Andy; Alan's relationships with Louise's children, Ellen and Mark; and finally, Reb's and Alex's relationships with their stepfather Simon, Sandie's husband. In the first three, we interviewed one (or more) of the people directly involved in the relationship in question. With the last two the information we collected was provided by the intermediary mother/partner, Sandie and Louise respectively, although Sandie's daughter, Reb, was also present for a part of Sandie's interview.

The most straightforward of these cases were the ones that involved Sandie. Both her natural father and her children's natural father effectively played no further part in their children's lives after their separations from the children's mothers. Her stepfather, Andy, and her children's stepfather, Simon, had both become fully integrated into their stepchildren's lives, in every respect being regarded as their father figures and replacing their natural fathers as members of their families. In both these cases, children were born in the new partnership, that is, half-siblings to the stepchildren in question, in the process strengthening the sense of family connection that already existed. In turn too, both these stepfathers were recognised as full grandfathers in the lives of their stepchildren's children. Thus, according to the accounts we were given, across both generations of this family, there was full incorporation of the stepfathers into each family's routines, with both being treated unproblematically as fully the children's fathers by all involved.

The case of Mark was in many ways similar. The key difference was that though Mark had lived with his mother and his stepfather Tom since he was an infant, his natural father also played a part in his life, visiting him fortnightly throughout his childhood. As Mark made clear in the interview, he found aspects of this arrangement quite difficult. Indeed he said he would in many ways have preferred it if his family life had been simpler and more like those Sandie described. He felt that Tom had done everything that could be expected of a father. Moreover Mark's own sense of family clearly prioritised his mother, his stepfather and his two half-siblings as family. This had left him with a degree of conflict over his loyalties to Tom and his natural father, Michael, that he attempted to resolve through downplaying his family connection to Michael as one of 'friendship'.

The interviews with Steve and Christine revealed a somewhat different picture of family connection and solidarity. Christine's natural father played a smaller part in her life than Michael did in Mark's, yet it was evident from both interviews that there were limits to Steve's involvement as a father in his stepchildren's lives. One key factor here was that Christine, and her brothers David and Ben, were significantly older when their mother married Steve. They had clear memories of a different family arrangement. Indeed Christine felt that with Steve's marriage to her mother a new set of family practices had been imposed on her and her brothers without any of them being given much voice in the decisions. The dynamics of the family also made evident differences in Steve's relationship with Nick, his natural son (and her half-brother). Steve clearly demonstrated a stronger love and commitment to Nick than was expressed in his relationships with Christine and his stepsons. The boundaries within the family were also made manifest in the ways Christine and her full brothers colluded with Sally, their mother, to resolve some of their issues they had with Steve. In all these ways, Steve can be recognised as more marginal to Christine's 'core' family grouping than Tom, Simon and Andy were within their stepchildren's construction of family.

Finally, consider Alan's relationships with his stepchildren Ellen and Mark, as reported by their mother, Louise. Her account is likely to contain its own biases, but nonetheless the differences between his involvement as a stepfather and the other examples we have so far considered are apparent. According to Louise, Alan's relationships with her children were both limited and at times conflictual. As we discussed in detail in Chapters 3 and 4, there were strong tensions within this family network, partly as a result of its different members having competing senses of family connection. It would seem that Alan's response to this was to have comparatively little involvement with his stepchildren, leaving their active parenting to Louise. They shared a house but, from Louise's account, her children saw Alan more as her partner than as a father figure for them. That is, there was little sense of any family solidarity or communion being established in these relationships.

Clearly in these cases there were significant differences in the degree to which these stepfathers were incorporated into the stepchildren's family practices. Indeed, it is noticeable that resident stepfather involvement in their stepchildren's routines are framed quite differently to that of the resident stepmothers discussed in the last chapter. This is an issue we will discuss more fully below. Here it is sufficient to emphasise again the impact of gender divisions within domestic organisation in shaping step-parents' involvement in routine family activities. They consequently also influence how family-as-kinship is constructed and understood by all those involved.

As we develop these issues, we will draw on further examples from our study. In the course of the study, we interviewed ten people who were (or had been) stepfathers. We also interviewed 29 respondents who had (or once had) a stepfather, including those who had a parent remarry after they had become adult. In addition, we interviewed 18 mothers who, like Louise and Sandie, reported on stepfather–stepchild relationships they had experienced indirectly through their own remarriage or repartnership. However in this chapter we will draw only on those accounts we were given by stepfathers and stepchildren, although our interviews with repartnered mothers helped substantiate our analysis of the diverse family practices and boundaries constructed in resident stepfather families.

Resident stepfathers

As we saw in the previous chapter, it is difficult for resident stepmothers not to become quite fully integrated into their stepchildren's lives. The routine ways in which gender identity is constructed normally entails their carrying the major responsibility for household management. Consequently, they are usually quite highly involved in managing domestic order, including childcare for those stepchildren who live with them. Over time the family-as-household relevance of these activities frequently results in these stepmothers and stepchildren being incorporated into each other's construction of family-as-kinship. As already indicated, this tends to be rather less so with stepfathers (Fine, 1995). Or more accurately, some stepfathers become highly involved in their resident stepchildren's family lives, while others play a far smaller part, leaving most childcare issues to the child's mother. As a result, the sense of family generated in stepfather relationships varies widely.

As already suggested, patterns of resident stepfathers' parental involvement will be influenced by a number of demographic and structural factors: the age of the children when the stepfather joins the household; the level of continuing involvement of the non-resident father; and the length of time the stepfamily has been in existence. The personalities and interests of the stepfather also play a major part in this, but so too the patterns that develop will be consequent on the dynamics of the overall set of relationships that are involved. That is, to understand the present relationship a stepfather has with his stepchildren, it is important to recognise how the histories of these and the other relationships within the stepfamily network have developed across time. A sense of family connection needs to be understood as an emergent property of the family practices that become established.

Consider the account provided by one of the stepfathers in our sample. John, who three years before the interview had moved in with his partner, Sue, and her three children, then aged 15, 17 and 19. When he was asked how he would describe his relationship with his stepchildren, he replied,

> Well all three of them, I fix their cars – so you take a sort of fatherly role don't you? I'll lend them money if Sue hasn't got any to lend, but Sue will pay it back to me. But normally Sue would lend it first. So if they want something like that, they don't ask me directly. And often, if Lisa or Amy want something, they'll ask me directly but Dan wouldn't. He's always through Sue. OK. In terms of getting on with – Lisa is an extremely – she's quite an angel to get on with really. She's just one of those people who gets on with it, you know. Doesn't want any hassle – she's very sensitive, but she's sort of intelligent with it and you know if like you – if she did something that was wrong, she knows it's wrong, there's no point chasing her because it would just make her cry, so there's no point. Not that I do any discipline really, you know ...

Later on in the interview, John talked specifically about Dan, with whom he had a more difficult relationship than he had with Lisa:

John: I thought I'd better go out because I was getting tense, 'cos that's what Dan does, he says in your face. If Sue won't lend him money, or what she does is decline to start with, says 'No, we haven't got any' although they

	know she has, and he's like really giving her the verbal stuff you know.
Interviewer:	So he's quite hard on her then?
John:	Verbally, yes. I just let him get on with it. You know I sort of, I mean sometimes I get out of the way, 'cos you know Dan might want to talk about a more sensitive issue and so I think: 'Right he wants a bit of time. He needs to talk, just get out the way, you know'. But if I'm cooking dinner, or we're doing something – you know if there's a situation where you have the right to be there and it's just a pure confrontation thing, why should you go? I don't want to be seen to be backing out all the time. So I take the, support Sue, you know if she gets a bit stressed from it, you know. As soon as you give Dan his couple of quid it's – phew! – gone. Not another whisper, you know. He's quite interesting. I haven't really worked him out yet because when he talks, he talks quite seriously. To me it sounds aggressive, but that is, that is just who he is, the way he is. It's not aggressive, it just appears to be aggressive.
Interviewer:	But Sue takes that in her stride?
John:	Yeah. Yeah. I mean she's dealt with, she's had a lot of you know, Amy and Dan are very similar, in that respect. You know Amy gives a lot – she had a lot of verbal and stuff like that. We think the reason Lisa's different is that she's got a different relationship with [her father].

We have quoted at some length from the interview with John because it illustrates a number of important points about the development and patterning of stepfather relationships. John's involvement with his stepchildren was relatively recent, going back only some three years. Moreover the children were all already teenagers by that time. While their mother's relationship with their natural father had been conflictual, all three children had a continuing relationship with him. Thus there was little reason for – or indeed possibility of – John acting as a 'replacement' father. He lived with the children but was not in a position of 'in loco parentis'. While in the first extract he talked about taking a 'fatherly role', this involved no more than his helping them out with practical issues as appropriate. Indeed, as he went on to say, mainly he saw himself as being there to support Sue in her dealings with the children. His (essentially masculine) role was to help the children with the things men could do – fixing cars, helping them with computer issues, etc – and be there to provide supportive back-up (direct or more often indirect) for their mother when the children were making unreasonable demands or in other ways making her life difficult.

His 'fatherly role' did not stretch as far as being involved in disciplining the children – 'Not that I do any discipline really, you know'. This was understood to be rightfully Sue's responsibility. She was their mother. She was the one with the right to set the rules. He could discuss issues he had with the children's behaviour with her, usually outside their hearing, but she retained overarching responsibility. Equally, as with Steve's involvement with his stepchildren discussed in Chapter 3, the children were of an age where they would not be prepared to accept his attempting to dictate disciplinary matters. They too looked to their mother. As John indicates, this at times could lead to conflict between him and Dan especially. Depending on the contexts, his preferred responses to such conflict were either to walk away and calm down or to support Sue without becoming too directly involved, both of which can be seen as indicative of his outsider, 'non-parental' position in the household (Coleman et al., 2001).

The age of his stepchildren, their continuing relationship with their natural father and the short time with which he had lived with Sue were clearly important in shaping the nature of John's relationship with his stepchildren. Given these factors it is not surprising that his position within their family-as-kinship was marginal. Yet it is also apparent how much more limited his involvement as a stepfather was to the likely involvement of a stepmother in similar circumstances. Certainly he was able to avoid conflict more readily by walking away. But more importantly here, there are differences in the permitted scope for active parenting, or perhaps more accurately that required of stepmothers and stepfathers. Given the standard division of domestic labour within households, it is much easier for resident stepfathers like John to adopt a position of parental 'distancing' than it is for resident stepmothers who are more intricately bound up with the domestic management and relational ordering.

In discussing family boundaries in Chapter 4, we emphasised the extent to which cultural understandings of 'family' are tied in with our ideas of solidarity, connection and belonging. From a parental point of view, the notion of children 'belonging' to their parents is a powerful one, rooted in ideologies of blood connection as well as developmental biographies. Culturally conceptualisations of 'my child' or 'our children' are readily understood as expressive of parental love, rights and responsibilities. As discussed in Chapter 5, non-resident stepmothers frequently allude to these ideas of children belonging to their natural parents in saying that they try not to interfere in the way the children are brought up. Equally we saw how much more difficult it is for resident stepmothers to take this line as they are so involved in creating family order and managing the domestic and other behaviour of their stepchildren.

But resident stepfathers, like non-resident stepmothers, are usually freer to take on the more distanced involvement with their stepchildren that John had. Through their blood connection, their familial history and their pivotal role in establishing family order, the central parental tie within the newly formed stepfamily is understood by all to be that between mother and children. She is the one who is most highly involved with them, who makes the major decisions and who is seen as more fully responsible for their well-being. The stepfather enters into this existing parental relationship as the outsider, in essence connected to the children through his commitment to the mother. While most mothers want their new partners to be involved with their children, they want it to be in a way that is compatible with their (the mother's) understanding of the children's needs.

As a consequence, resident mothers and stepfathers typically negotiate, in Finch and Mason's (1993) sense, parental responsibilities around a dominant understanding that the children involved 'belong' more to their mother than to their stepfather (Coleman et al., 2001). It is she who has the greater right to determine what happens to them. In Vogt Yuan and Hamilton's (2006, p. 1208) terms, family life tends to be premised on a 'mother-as-manager' model 'with resident mothers [acting] as managers determining how involved a stepfather will be with a child'. Weaver and Coleman (2010) develop this idea further in one of the few studies specifically concerned with mothers in stepfather families. They examine the 'protective stances' that these mothers routinely adopt in managing their children's relationships with their stepfather. Their concern here was not with abuse, but more subtly with ensuring that their children were not 'being misunderstood, judged too harshly, or receiving inequitable treatment or "slights" from their stepfathers' (Weaver and Coleman, 2010, p. 313).

Such an understanding of mothering within stepfather families is evident in the interview with John. He recognises Sue's greater knowledge of *her* children, her better understanding of their needs and the long-term history of their (Sue and the children's) family practices. Over time, John indicated he was getting to appreciate the personalities of the children better, learning which responses worked and which did not.

As he said, Lisa was particularly easy: she's 'quite an angel to get on with really'. Dan on the other hand was still something of a puzzle: 'He's quite interesting. I haven't really worked him out yet'. Yet while over time he was engaged in reflexively reinterpreting his stepchildren's character, this could never equate to the largely tacit, almost intuitive, knowledge that Sue, as their mother, was accepted as having. From this perspective, her enduring commitment and solidarity was unquestioned, while his relationship with them remained far more contingent on his relationship with her.

This comparatively distanced 'parental' involvement is a relatively common feature of resident stepfather families in which there are dependent children, especially when the natural father still plays some part in the children's lives. It was captured well by another respondent, Terry, who said in his interview that he saw himself as 'the adjunct to the parent'. Terry's two stepdaughters were in their late twenties at the time of the interview but were 5 and 3 when Terry and their mother, Pam, first cohabited. In the interview Terry described how he was fully involved in the routines of the children's lives, sharing childcare activities in a range of ways. At the same time, he was aware that he did not have the same level of emotional involvement with them as their mother had.

> Interviewer: Did you get involved with the day-to-day parenting things?
>
> Terry: Oh yeah, yes. All the doing and the mechanics and all that, very much. It was a sort of equal thing. It was more the sort of confrontational, emotional, behavioural thing where I would say I was in the shadow of mum.

Elsewhere in the interview, Terry described how at times the girls would get frustrated that he always supported their mother and never seemed to express his own independent views:

> Terry: But I kind of thought that's what I was supposed to do, I think.
>
> Interviewer: The united front thing?
>
> Terry: Yeah. And also that I wasn't, in a sense, however much or little they might see him, they knew they had someone else who was their dad, and so I was kind of – I was there because I was with Pam, rather than having a

right, as it were, to say something to them through any other means. And I think that probably – I don't think anybody was telling me that, I think it was a self-censorship that I probably put that on myself. And therefore, I think, at times they were resentful. But I wouldn't just say what I felt if that was a different thing to what Pam felt they were doing or saying or how they should be. ... But it was always outside their hearing that I'd say something to Pam.

In his terms, Pam was the 'moving spirit' at the centre of the family, while the part he played was more peripheral.

This aspect of stepfathers seeing themselves as an 'adjunct to the parent' was significant in a number of stepfather families in which there are dependent children. In some regards though, it is also a structural feature of many natural families with dependent children. In these too, mothers are typically the ones most fully involved in childcare and are often seen as being at the centre of family life in a way that fathers are not. This is simply a reflection of the highly gendered divisions of responsibility that characterise many family practices, rather than being peculiar to stepfather families. Nonetheless there are evident differences in the ways that stepfathers describe their involvement with their stepchildren and in the ways they describe their relationships with their natural children. The case illustration of Steve given in Chapter 3 provides a clear example of this. As described there, he felt a degree of frustration at his marginality in his three stepchildren's lives, but felt a much deeper, and fully appropriate, involvement in his son Nick's life.

Of course there are some exceptions to this. In a small number of cases, stepfathers play a full, albeit still gendered, parenting role, as we saw in Chapter 3. The case illustration of Mark in that chapter was clearly one of these cases. While we do not have Tom's (Mark's step-father) perspective on this, Mark himself saw Tom as a very important figure in his life, a man for whom he had an abiding love, respect and trust. For Mark, Tom was his father. As we saw, his feelings towards his natural father, Michael, were more ambivalent. Mark was unusual among cases where stepfathers become the full father figures in the family in that his natural father continued to be active in his life. In most other cases, the natural father was essentially absent in the children's day-to-day lives. On the other hand, Mark's example was more typical in that he had lived with his stepfather from a very young age and had no memory of a different family form. On the basis of the study, this was a common feature of families where stepfathers came to be regarded, by themselves and others, as having full parental involvement.

Stepchildren's views

With the exception of Mark, we have so far focussed on the perspectives of stepfathers. We want now to consider stepchildren's perceptions of their relationships with their stepfathers. Here our concern is still with resident stepfamilies formed while the children were dependent. However the respondents in our study were of course all adults at the time of the research. Consequently the accounts they provided of their experiences of living with a stepfather are retrospective. This does not render them inaccurate, but it does mean that what they discussed in the interviews is informed by their knowledge of how their relationships have developed since childhood. Conversely, the major benefit of having adult respondents is precisely that they can provide information on how the relationships altered over time as they, the stepchildren, became independent.

As would be expected, the focus of the interviews with respondents who had lived with stepfathers as children concerned the degree to which their stepfathers had been active in parenting them and had – or had not – become members of their family-as-kinship. Many of their comments echoed those of the stepfathers we talked to, though in some regards the stepchildren reflected more overtly on the quality of the solidarity they felt existed in the relationship. Linked with this were different expectations of the role of stepfathers, itself partly dependent on the age of the children when the stepfamily was formed but equally influenced by the dominant models of stepfathering current at the time. What was also evident though was the importance of the stepchild's perceptions of the impact of the stepfather on family life when the stepfamily formed. Factors involved in this included the character and personality of their stepfathers; the extent to which established family practices were altered, either positively or negatively; and their understanding of the impact of the new partnership on their mother's happiness and life-style. While these perceptions evidently derived from the interactional dynamics within the stepfamily, what came over in the interviews was the perceived power of the stepfather's agency in the construction of their relationship with their stepchildren.

Such a perspective is hardly surprising. Any stepfather entering into an existing family household is bound to be influential in determining the role he plays within that family and the type of impact he has on the everyday, taken-for-granted worlds of the children involved. Established family practices are inevitably altered as a result of the incoming adult's presence in the family household and the need to accommodate to the assumptions and demands he makes about how family life should be ordered. While mothers generally act as a 'buffer' between their children and the stepfather – as, for example, Steve Richard's wife Sally did for Christine and her other children (see Chapter 3) – the dynamics of the family are necessarily altered. From the children's perspective, the evident element of change to which they need to adjust is the stepfather; it is his being, his character and personality, how he relates to them and their sets of existing relationships, that matter.

To express this differently, the accounts respondents gave of their relationships with their resident stepfathers were generally framed around the degree to which they felt their stepfathers had 'embraced' them as children. In cases where the children felt welcomed as part of the new partnership arrangements, where they felt the stepfather had a concern for them as people and, in Fine's (1995, p. 20) terms, showed them 'warmth', then the respondents reported essentially positive and valued relationships (Ganong et al., 1999). They liked the stepfather as a person and respected the part that he played in the new family (Michaels, 2006). In cases where there was apparent disregard for the children or indeed a greater sense of ambivalence experienced, then generally there was less warmth for the stepfather. In these cases any sense of family solidarity was limited. Of course, these relationships change over time as we will discuss more fully in Chapter 8.

In Chapter 3 we portrayed Christine's relationship with her stepfather, Steve, and Mark's relationship with his stepfather, Tom. Here we will draw on three of our other interviews with stepchildren to illustrate the emergence of stepfather relationships from stepchildren's perspectives and the types of factors that shape the quality of the relationships that develop. These interviews were with Denise, Gareth and Rich.

Denise was in her early 40s when we interviewed her. Her father had died when she was nine after a long illness. Her mother married her stepfather, Arnold, four years later though they had been a 'couple' for some time before that. In the interview Denise said that when her mother married Arnold, he tried to persuade her to send Denise and her two younger brothers to live with their grandparents. 'He wanted us to go and live with our grandparents, so that wasn't really a very good start, was it? ... And that's the way it continued.' Denise discussed the difficulties she had with her relationship with Arnold at various points in the interview. 'It's not hostile now, because I don't live in the same house, but it was hostile while I lived there.' She added,

> I still find it difficult to be tolerant of his ways, [but] to keep the peace you speak civilly to them, don't you? ... See we were really close with our mum all of us, and he couldn't cope with that. We didn't try and close him out, but he just didn't want to – he wanted Mum to himself, he made that plain from the start. And we wanted Mum to be Mum. And she tried to be both things and she used to kow-tow to him a lot, but gradually she didn't. She just used to stop taking it in the end, and she would just tell him straight that is not the way to be, but it was really difficult for us you know, all those years.

Denise described her relationship to her mother as very close, but said her mother's relationship with Arnold had been volatile. Denise had found Arnold's tempers and violence very hard to take, especially in contrast to her natural father's calm manner:

> That's why I didn't like him, because he was such a violent man. We were so used to my father who was so easy going ... It was always the threat there. Always a threat ... And as I said to you, I didn't dislike the man, it was just his violent behaviour and everything that I – I mean at nine, I would have been OK to I'm sure to have got on with someone, but because he was quite a violent man and his behaviour wasn't what I would call normal.

Some other respondents also found their stepfathers' attitudes and behaviour highly problematic. Mandy's stepfather had not been particularly rejecting of her or her sisters, but he had adopted a relatively traditional masculine role. He expected her mother, who before the marriage had run a small business successfully for ten years, to give up this work and devote herself to serving the household. Somewhat like Arnold, from Mandy's perspective he wanted her mother to focus more on his needs and less on her children's. Another respondent, Len, expressed a similar theme in describing how much more harshly he was treated by his stepfather than his half-brothers (his stepfather's natural sons). He graphically described feeling like 'a cuckoo' in the household and, from his stepfather's perspective, 'surplus to requirements'. Although he later came to understand better his stepfather's behaviour towards him, their relationship remained strained until his stepfather's death some 40 years later.

Gareth's relationship with his stepfather was stronger and more positive than those just discussed. Gareth was in his early 50s when we interviewed him. His parents divorced when he was 12 and his mother married Stanley two years later. Stanley had been married previously and had two sons a little younger than Gareth, Ray and Paul. Gareth also had three younger sisters. It was clear from the interview that Gareth had a great deal of respect for Stanley, saying 'Oh yes, he's great, Stanley … very fair, very straightforward … a man of principle … the sort of man that's gone now… total principles, honour'. While Gareth recalled having some difficulties adjusting to the new marriage, in the process giving Stanley 'a lot of stick', he also recognised how happy Stanley made his mother, especially given the tensions and rows of her marriage to Gareth's father. 'No, I mean when my mother married Stanley it was actually the first time that I heard her laughing again and it was fun again.'

At the same time, he also recognised that Stanley's relationship with his natural sons had always been different from his relationship with Gareth. Even now when both Gareth's mother and Stanley were in their 80s, the fact that theirs was a 'step' tie continued to be relevant to his understanding of his family network. Indeed, somewhat surprisingly Gareth still modified the father's day card he sent to Stanley. 'I mean, technically. "Happy stepfather" is what we put. Just write it in front, you know.' So despite the strong sense of (evidently mutual) affection he felt for Stanley, he could still say,

> Oh it's always there – yes there is that, it's almost like a fault line that runs through you, it's always, it's never on the same level. Always slightly different. Yes, there is that – there's always been that feeling. And with Ray and Paul, if they're on the scene there is this thing, they're his *real* boys, and I'm not his *real* boy. Real son – I'm somebody else's son who happens to – he's looking after. Yeah there is a definite um – I don't know what to call it really. Well there's a definite awareness that you are not of the same status, you see, as the sons. The immediate children.

The final interview we want to draw on here was with Rich who was 27 at the time. His father died when he was 11 and his mother had lived with Ron for the last 14 years. Rich's relationship with Ron was now a strong one. As with the other examples discussed here, there had been tensions when he lived at home, especially when he lived there during his time at university. Now they no longer live in the same household, the conflicts had ended. From his account Ron had played a relatively full 'father' role when Rich was younger, evidently supporting him in various ways and being active in disciplining him when necessary. Although he did not call him 'Dad', Rich said that that was how he generally referred to him. Similarly, according to Rich, at times Ron also referred to Rich as his son. The following passage captures the spirit of Rich's relationships with his mother and Ron.

Interviewer:	And your relationship with your mother, is that a very strong relationship would you say?
Rich:	Very, very, very, I'd say. Got a really close relationship. Yeah, really close. We get on really, really well. I love going home and seeing her. I went back for a weekend a week or so ago and just had a really great time.
Interviewer:	And it is going home, do you feel?
Rich:	Yeah, definitely going home. I really enjoy it. Ray enjoys it as well, he looks forward to seeing me. Apparently he was quite upset when I could only stay for a weekend. He thought I was going to stay a little bit longer, perhaps. Me and my mum we get on really well together. There's not very much I don't tell her.

Clearly Rich's relationship with his mother was the one prioritised here. Elsewhere in the interview he talked about how much she had supported him and how protective of her he felt. While undoubtedly important, his relationship with Ron was still secondary to this. Nonetheless he stated very clearly that he had an independent relationship with Ron, one which he thought would continue even if his mother and Ron separated. 'Yeah, definitely. I mean I just can't contemplate that. Well I just don't see it happening.' This reflects what seemed to frame Rich's overall understanding of his relationship with his stepfather. While he had an independent relationship with Ron, this was built upon Ron and his mother being so established and contented as a couple. Ron cared for Rich's mother and made her happy. Rich recognised this and without putting it into words, as a result, felt secure in these family relationships. In this sense Ron and Rich's relationship was so positive partly because of the support Ron had given him in later adolescence/early adulthood, but mainly because of the continuing commitment and love evident in the relationship between Ron and Rich's mother.

On being a stepfather

As the various examples discussed here indicate, the relationships that develop between stepfathers and stepchildren vary widely, sometimes within the same sibling set. Some of these ties involve a high degree of mutual solidarity and care. Where this was so, respondents often referenced the strength of the relationship by emphasising that in all key matters their stepfather was their 'dad'. In so doing they were deliberately disconnecting themselves from their natural father and recognising the significance of the part their stepfather had played in their lives. As we have discussed earlier, this pattern most commonly arises when a natural father either dies or effectively disappears from a child's life after marital separation, with the stepfather consequently taking on full and active fathering within the family. With time, the commitment shown is recognised as having all the attributes expected of natural fathering. To use the term we drew on earlier, in these cases the stepfather clearly 'embraced' a fathering role as well as the stepchild as an individual.

In distinct contrast to these relationships, a number of respondents, like Denise above, reported quite conflictual relationships with their stepfathers. In these cases, there was little indication of stepfathers 'embracing' a parental role or valuing their relationship with the child. From the stepchild's perspective, the stepfather provided little emotional or even practical support in their childhood. As a result they felt antagonism rather than solidarity with their stepfather, a response that usually continued to shape their adulthood relationship, especially if they also had concerns about the quality of the relationship between their mother and their stepfather. Other respondents felt little connection to their stepfather but were not as directly negative. Some of these respondents characterised their stepfathers as in some ways 'strange' or 'odd' or even 'difficult' as personalities, but over time had negotiated understandings and patterns of interaction – family practices – that rendered the relationships unproblematic. There was a sense of rubbing along together, even if there were no strong feelings of connection.

Other respondents were more positive, conveying a greater solidarity but at the same time recognising that their sense of familial connection was framed around understandings of step relationships. In general these respondents were not critical of their stepfathers; indeed a number were appreciative of the specific help their stepfathers had given them on different occasions, sometimes implying that this was more than could reasonably have been expected. The help most commonly reported was instrumental and practical – fixing cars, helping to decorate, assisting with college assignments, etc. At the same time as recognising support, these respondents were also conscious of the boundaries of their relationships, often conveying the impression that these relationships continued to be mediated through their mothers. In childhood, their stepfathers did not generally get involved in disciplinary or educational issues, and nearly always it was mothers whom they asked for money. Similarly in adulthood it tended to be mothers who were first approached for different forms of support rather than stepfathers.

As noted earlier, it could be argued that this is in line with normal gendered family practices. Mothers typically play a greater part in managing relationships, which often includes mediation within the family network. Fathers are commonly understood to be more adept with practical matters. However the accounts stepchildren gave of their relationships with their mothers and stepfathers seemed to indicate rather more than this. A degree of reservation was often portrayed about the stepfather relationship, with the strength of the tie to the mother accentuated. A number of respondents said that they tended not to talk to their stepfather about anything significant. Rather the relationship was kept at a cordial level. For example, Gina, who appeared to rely on her stepfather for regular help with house maintenance, said that at a personal level her relationship with him was relatively limited. She felt they did not really engage with each other at any meaningful level. Instead they both tended to communicate with and through her mother.

Indeed even in relationships that were characterised more positively, where there was a genuine liking and a respect, stepfathers were frequently discussed in ways that indicated a parental location that continued to be symbolically mediated through the mother. The case of Gareth and his stepfather Stanley discussed above is a case in point, as is Rich's relationship with his stepfather Ron. Gareth's account of his relationship with Stanley was especially interesting. Throughout the interview Gareth talked positively about Stanley both as a man and as a stepfather. As noted, he regarded him as a man of high principle, someone who could be relied on and who had a sound sense of judgement. He was clearly fond of his stepfather and regarded him as part of his kinship. However, at the same time, Gareth still discussed what he termed 'the fault line that runs through you'. This was captured in his feeling that Stanley loved his natural sons – his *real* sons – in a different way to his love for Gareth, and even more graphically in his continued practice of writing 'Happy *step*father' on his father's day card.

To conclude this section, we want to return to two issues mentioned earlier in our study, both consequent upon the impact of family network characteristics on individual ties. First, as discussed above, the stepchild's perception of the quality of the mother's relationship with the stepfather is an important factor influencing the strength of solidarity and connection between the stepchild and the stepfather. Where this latter relationship was recognised as having been supportive and beneficial, where the stepfather was seen as bringing the mother happiness, the stepchild typically reported having a positive relationship with the stepfather. It was not coincidental, for example, that Gareth talked about there being laughter in the house when his mother married Stanley. Other respondents similarly reported how well their stepfather had taken care of their mothers, had opened up new horizons for them or had otherwise continued to show them love and concern (Michaels, 2006). For a few respondents, this had not been the case and relationships with their stepfathers were, as a result, more problematic. Where a stepfather was thought to be too controlling, where there had been episodes of domestic violence or where he was otherwise seen as behaving inconsiderately towards the mother, respondents were, like Denise above, considerably more critical towards their stepfathers.

Second, we want to highlight the importance of generational time and process. Many stepchildren, like Denise, Gareth and Rich above, reported elements of conflict and antagonism in their relationships with their stepfathers when they shared a home. Even if there were continued reservations, in adulthood it was much easier to avoid conflict and remain cordial. Denise was clear in her dislike for her stepfather, but she still reported that keeping the peace and being civil was easier now that they no longer shared a home. A further factor that we will consider in more depth in the next chapter is the relationship stepfathers usually create with the stepchild's children. For the latter, the stepchild's mother and stepfather generally appear as a grandparental package. They have not known otherwise. Usually terminology reflects this, with the stepfather being given a form of grandparental title – 'Grandad John', if not straightforwardly 'Grandad'. As this happens and becomes taken-for-granted within the kinship network, so a kinship connection between step-parents and stepchildren itself becomes more fully established.

Later-life stepchildren

As we have stressed, the stepchildren referred to so far in this chapter were now adults. The information they gave us was based on their recollections of their experiences in childhood, together with their descriptions of the character of their relationships with their stepfathers in adulthood. In addition though, the sample contained a small number of respondents whose mothers had repartnered or remarried since the respondents had left home and become adult. While these respondents – who as in the last chapter we will term 'later-life stepchildren' – did not necessarily categorise their mothers' partners as stepfathers, it is worth considering these relationships briefly here.

From the accounts we were given, the factors shaping the connection and solidarity experienced with these stepfathers tended to mirror those given by respondents who were still dependent when the relationship started. In particular the three main issues discussed above were also influential in the development of these relationships. First, judgements made about the personal qualities of the stepfather clearly structured respondents' understandings of these ties. As above, some of the step-fathers were seen as positive and accepting, willing to make an effort to incorporate the adult stepchild and, where relevant, their partner and children, into the new relational network. Others were seen as more difficult and as more distant; from the stepchild's perception of 'family' they remained more peripheral.

However this evaluation of character was also strongly linked to judge-ments made about how good the partner relationship was proving to be for the mother. As above, some of these later-life stepchild respondents reflected on the benefits their mothers had gained from the relationship. Pat, for example, said,

> Oh yeah, brilliant together. I mean mum never went abroad with my dad because dad wouldn't go anywhere and they didn't have the money anyway. It's been very good. It's been good for each other, you know. … If something had happened to one of them, I think the other one would just roll up because they go to their clubs four or five times a week.

Echoing similar issues from a different perspective, Sophie reflected on how her stepfather had become the peace-keeper in the family, intervening positively in the series of conflicts that tended to emerge between her mother (who Sophie characterised as very difficult), her brother and herself. Conversely, where an adult stepchild felt that their mother was being mistreated by her partner, then divisions between the stepfather and the adult stepchild quickly emerged. Thus not only did Matt feel his stepfather had shown too little interest in and too little patience with his (Matt's) two young children when he first married Matt's mother, he was now also bitter that his stepfather appeared to be having an illicit relationship with another woman. From his perspective, whatever cordiality had been negotiated early in his mother's partnership had now been exhausted. He felt angry with his stepfather and had little sense of family connection.

The third issue to consider here concerns the involvement of later-life stepfathers as stepgrandfathers. In the case mentioned above Matt felt that his stepfather had made little effort to become involved in his children's lives. While acknowledging that his stepfather had little experience of young children, he still found his stepfather's attitude, to the disruption his young children caused when they visited, militated against the development of positive relationships. Conversely when later-life stepchildren's stepfathers behaved in child-centred ways towards their stepgrandchildren and embraced that role, then their position within the family network was consolidated. In reality the three factors we have discussed here tend to be associated. Unsurprisingly, later-life stepfathers who are liked, who are seen as having a positive impact on the mother's well-being and who embrace their new 'family' connections are incorporated more positively into generational kinship practices than those who do not.

Conclusion

In this chapter we have considered the relationships that develop between stepchildren and resident stepfathers. As with all stepfamily relationships, there is a good deal of variation how these are structured; they need to be seen as emergent, with their histories shaping the ways they are currently experienced. However, despite the variation there is, it is possible to specify some commonalities in their patterning. Importantly, there is an evident tension in the family position in which many resident stepfathers find themselves. As adults within the family/household, they are inevitably involved in parenting. However their involvement is usually far more limited than that of resident stepmothers. Given the gendered division of domestic labour that prevails, as men they are typically understood as having less responsibility for day-to-day aspects of childcare and family order. In addition though, ideologies of parenting mean that (natural) mothers' right to determine questions of their children's needs and conduct are prioritised over those of stepfathers.

As a consequence, in the context of parenting, most resident stepfathers were understood by all to be somewhat marginal or distanced, with mothers being the more central 'moving spirit'. As noted above, this was at times expressed quite graphically by the respondents – 'adjunct to the mother' or 'the sixth member of my family'. Their role often came to be understood as one of providing support for the mother rather than engaging directly with the children, especially over issues of discipline and order. Of course, the age of the children, both at the present time and at the time the stepfamily was formed, influenced this. However it was really only in cases where the stepfamily was formed when the children were very young and where the natural father played no significant part in their lives that stepfathers were accepted as occupying a fuller parenting role.

Sometimes relationships between resident stepfathers and stepchildren were difficult, even fraught, though this tended to be more so during adolescence. Occasionally a stepchild's dislike of a stepfather continued into adulthood, especially when the stepchild felt that their stepfather had shown little interest or concern for them. In adulthood too, stepfathers sometimes remained on the periphery of full family membership, but often there was also a greater appreciation of the role the stepfather had played both as mother's partner and more generally while the (step) child had been growing up. As we shall see in the next chapter though, it was when the stepchild had his or her own children that many stepfathers came to be fully incorporated into family.

7
Stepfamily Kinship

A key concern of this book has been with exploring the extent to which stepfamily relationships are understood by the participants as family ties. Based on the notion that 'family' membership is not simply a consequence of genealogical connection, important though conceptions of genealogy are to it, we have sought to understand the processes that lead to individuals positioning their relationships with particular others within the realm of family and kinship. In particular, we have been examining whether and when individuals who are part of one another's personal network as a result of a remarriage or repartnership develop a sufficient sense of mutual commitment and solidarity to be understood as family. Put simply, under what circumstances, if any, do these people come to be defined as 'family'?

So far, we have been focussing predominantly on step-parent/stepchild relationships, especially, though not solely, where there is or has been coresidence. We now want to consider a wider range of step relationships. Our reason for doing this is not simply because the patterning of these relationships is interesting in its own right, but also because an important feature of family and kinship ties lies in their interconnection. That is, family and kinship rarely involve just two individuals. Rather, particular family relationships are routinely embedded within a wider network of family ties. In part, the degree to which an individual is understood as being 'family' depends on the nature of the connections they have with those others who are also recognised as family. Certainly, to understand the nature of stepfamily kinship it is important to look beyond household relationships and consider the wider constellation of different stepfamily ties there are.

In principle, such an analysis could include a considerable range of people. Here though we are going to concentrate on just two forms of stepfamily ties, the two that involve those others who are genealogically closest to the step-parent. We begin the chapter by focussing on step-grandparental relationships. Our aim here is to analyse the kinship basis of these generational relationships and examine how the solidarities they entail compare with those characteristic of ties between natural grandparents and grandchildren. After this, we will examine stepsibling relationships, again evaluating the diverse levels of family connection that are found in these ties.

Grandparents

Until quite recently, grandparental relationships have not received much attention from sociologists, especially in Britain. In part this reflected the dominant concern within family sociology on 'family-as-household' issues rather than 'family-as-kinship' ones. However since the 1990s a growing body of research has explored the role of grandparents in children's lives, highlighting the emotional and material significance of grandparent/grandchild relationships (for example, Attias-Donfut and Segalen, 2002; Cherlin and Furstenberg, 1992; Dench and Ogg, 2002; Ferguson et al., 2004; Kemp, 2004; Mason, May and Clarke, 2007). From the different studies there have been, it is clear that grandparental relationships vary quite widely. This is hardly surprising, given the diversity there is in the circumstances of different grandparents as well as in the circumstances of their adult children and grandchildren. Moreover these relationships are not static; they inevitably change over time as the generations age and their situations alter.

Importantly too, as we have emphasised elsewhere in this book, grandparental relationships, like other kin ties, are part of a kinship network and consequently influenced by the character of the relationships sustained by intermediary kin. Thus the relationships between grandparents and parents are normally crucial in shaping grandparent–grandchild ties. When grandparents and parents are more involved in each other's lives, it is likely that grandparents and grandchildren will also have active relationships with each other. Conversely, where there is a weak relationship between the second and third generation, the tie between the first and third is also likely to be less close. As discussed below, this becomes particularly relevant when parents separate or divorce. In these instances the character of non-resident grandparent–grandchild relationships is likely to be affected by any tension which develops between the resident parent, on the one hand, and the non-resident parent and his/her parents, on the other (Ferguson et al., 2004).

At this stage, it is helpful to clarify terminology, as specifying exactly which grandparents are being referred to is often confusing in families where there has been divorce and remarriage. Following the practice developed in the previous chapters, we wish first to distinguish between *resident* and *non-resident natural grandparents*. To be clear here, this distinction does not relate to whether grandchildren ever lived with their grandparents. Rather, the term 'resident natural grandparents' refers to the natural grandparents of grandchildren who live or, if now adult, lived during their childhood with the relevant intermediary adult child/parent. We use the term 'non-resident natural grandparents' to refer to the natural grandparents of children who do not, or did not, live with the intermediate adult child/parent during their childhood. Finally there are *stepgrandparents* who, as we will discuss more fully below, can result from remarriage or repartnering within either the parental or the grandparental generations. Of course, some grandparents fill more than one of these positions, either to sets of grandchildren in different households or to children living in the same household.

Natural grandparents

While the main focus of this section is on stepgrandparents, it is first worthwhile considering the character of natural grandparental ties. As noted above, there is considerable variation in grandparental relationships, depending in part on the circumstances of the different generations (Dench and Ogg, 2002; Clarke, Evandrou and Warr, 2005). Some grandparents, and grandmothers especially, take quite a 'traditional' role, with 'family' being highly pertinent in their lives. They are in regular contact with their children and grandchildren, provide a range of practical and emotional support and in a variety of ways express close as well as enduring solidarity. Other relationships between natural grandparents and grandchildren are somewhat less involved. Geographical distance can play a part in this. But also important are notions of generational independence and the dangers of 'interfering' (Mason, May and Clarke, 2007). In other words, in some families/relationships there is an acceptance that there can be appropriate solidarity without commitment being expressed through high degrees of contact, information flow or practical services. Finally a small minority of grandparents have very limited involvement with their grandchildren, sometimes as a result of conflict between the first and second generations, sometimes because of divorce and separation and at other times because the grandparents choose lifestyles in which intergenerational involvement is a low priority (Cherlin and Furstenberg, 1992).

Notwithstanding these latter cases though, what is generally most noticeable about grandparental relationships is the extent to which a sense of solidarity and commitment is seen as central to them. While circumstances, feelings and family culture enter into the expression of this commitment, its existence is largely unquestioned, instead being taken as a natural feature of family life. Indeed, the idea of grandparents 'being there' for their children and grandchildren seems quite fundamental to cultural understandings of the grandparental role, though, as above, exactly what 'being there' entails is generally ill-defined and open to negotiation (Ferguson et al., 2004). Nonetheless, the routine practical, material and emotional intergenerational exchanges that emerge within different families serve to cement the sense of connection and shared identity there is between the generations. Reflected in the symbolism of shared 'blood', natural grandparents are thus normatively accepted as having a diffuse and enduring commitment to their grandchildren and both a right and an obligation to be involved in their lives (Schneider, 1968).

In principle, these same beliefs apply to all natural grandparents. By the fact of their biological link, they are seen as appropriately having an interest in their grandchildren, with 'interest' here signifying both a 'concern for' and a 'stake in' their grandchildren. While this is normally uncontentious, the rise in divorce rates over the last two generations has had a significant effect on this otherwise taken-for-granted reality, as to a lesser extent has the rise of non-married motherhood and the incidence of cohabitation. For many non-resident natural grandparents – that is, those whose grandchild(ren) do not live with their son or daughter – there is less certainty that a continuing relationship with their grandchild(ren) will be sustained (Ferguson et al., 2004). In most, though not all, of these cases, the relationship between these grandparents and their grandchildren is mediated by the relationship the non-resident parent has with the child(ren).

In those cases where the intermediary non-resident parent continues to be involved with his or her children, it is also usual for the grandparents to maintain their relationship with their grandchildren. Where the son or daughter has repartnered, grandparental involvement is likely to follow from the routine organisation of intergenerational family life in similar ways to resident grandparent–grandchild relationships. However because the parent in question happens not to be as fully involved at a day-to-day level as resident parents, interaction between the first and third generation is likely to be less frequent and requires greater co-ordination. Similar patterns arise with non-resident parents who have not repartnered, with some non-resident fathers using their mothers – the children's grandmothers – to help with childcare during access visits (cf. Burgoyne and Clark, 1984).

In cases where the non-resident parent – usually the father – has lost effective contact with their children, the children also frequently end up having little contact with their grandparents on that parent's side. However this does appear to have been a more common consequence of parental separation a generation ago than it is now (Bradshaw et al., 1999). Given the greater social and policy emphasis there has been in recent years on non-resident fathers maintaining a role in their children's lives because this is understood to be in the children's interests (Smart and Neale, 1999), the kinship links with genealogically close relatives on the father's side are also more likely to remain active in some measure.

Stepgrandparents

As noted earlier, stepgrandparents can be consequent on either a natural grandparent repartnering or on a parent repartnering. We shall refer to the latter stepgrandparents as Type 1 stepgrandparents. These are the parents of your step-parent. We shall refer to stepgrandparents who are the partners of a natural grandparent, that is, parent's step-parent, as Type 2 stepgrandparents. (Ganong and Coleman, 2004, p. 177, sub-divide Type 2 stepgrandparents into two further categories based on the time when the grandparental partnership was formed, but the division here into Type 1 and Type 2 stepgrandparents will suffice for our purposes.) We will discuss each of these separately, starting off with Type 1 stepgrandparents, drawing on a range of material from our research interviews to illustrate our analysis.

Type 1 stepgrandparents

As with other relationships, there is diversity in the relationships maintained between Type 1 stepgrandchildren and stepgrandparents. Some are very close, being seen as equivalent in kinship terms to natural grandparents. However this is not the dominant pattern. In the majority of cases, stepgrandchildren and stepgrandparents appear to be of limited consequence in each other's lives. While there is generally recognition of a mediated kin tie – these people are the parents of either their mother's or father's partner, or conversely the children of their child's partner – they are not thereby seen as members of one's own kin universe. In general the evidence from our study as well as elsewhere suggests there is little sense

Table 7.1   Type 1 stepgrandparents and stepgrandchildren

Respondents who were	
Stepgrandmothers	2
Stepgrandfathers	1
Stepgranddaughters	12
Stepgrandsons	4
Mothers of stepgrandchildren	18
Fathers of stepgrandchildren	4
Stepmothers of stepgrandchildren	16
Stepfathers of stepgrandchildren	6
Total number of respondents providing data on Type 1 stepgrandparent/ stepgrandchildren relationships	52

Note: Some respondents occupied more than one of these positions

of connection and little involvement except through the intermediary second generation (Coleman, Ganong and Cable, 1997; Thompson, 1999). Usually, they remain on the boundaries of each other's kinship.

While in what follows we will draw on our respondents' accounts of relationships between Type 1 stepgrandparents and stepgrandchildren, it needs noting that not all our information came from those directly involved in these relationships, that is, those who were stepgrandparents or stepgrandchildren. We also collected accounts of these relationships from the intermediate parents and step-parents. Table 7.1 provides information about the set of respondents who discussed these Type 1 stepgrandparental relationships. As can be seen, while there were a number of stepgrandchildren in the sample, there were few stepgrandparents. We make each respondent's genealogical position within the stepgrandparent/stepgrandchild relationship clear in the examples we give.

Three case examples

Natalie

Natalie, who was 31 at the time of the interviews, was 16 when her mother died. Her father, Paul, had married Moira when Natalie was in her mid-twenties (see Diagram 7.1). Natalie's relationship with Moira was cordial but not warm. It was evident from the interview that Natalie's relationship with Moira's mother, Jean, was of quite limited significance. She defined her as Moira's mother rather than as a grandparent, and saw her only occasionally. 'I never go and visit her, but she

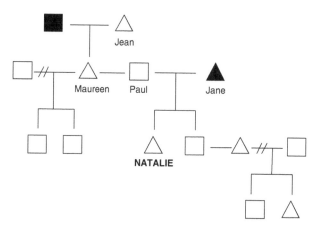

Diagram 7.1   Natalie

goes to stay with my parents quite frequently, so I see her at Christmas or if I go up to visit and she's there. She's OK, kiss her and say hello, kiss her and say goodbye.' It was clear from Natalie's description that she did not see Jean as part of her own kinship, defining their relationship as incidental and contingent on her father's relationship with Moira.

Emma

Emma, whose experiences of being a stepmother were raised in Chapter 5, provided information on her children's and stepchildren's stepgrandparents (see Diagram 7.2). Emma, 36 at the time of the interview, had three children, Adam, 11; Bob, 8; and Jimmy, 4, from her first marriage to Simon. She and Simon separated three years before the interview, soon after which she started cohabiting with Nick. Nick had previously been married to Tammy. He and Tammy co-parent their two children, Alan, 8, and John, 6, on alternate weeks. Emma's parents had separated when Emma was young. Her father had died when she was in her early twenties. Her mother had remarried and now lived some 10 miles away but according to Emma had relatively little to do with Emma's children, and had no relationship at all with her stepgrandchildren, Alan and John. In grandparental terms, Nick's parents, Mary and Ray, were very different. They helped Nick a good deal when he first started co-parenting after his separation from Tammy and continued to be actively involved. Like Alan and John, Adam, Bob and Jimmy, their stepgrandchildren, now also called them 'Nan' and 'Grandad'. However their relationship with these children remained different from their relationship with Alan and

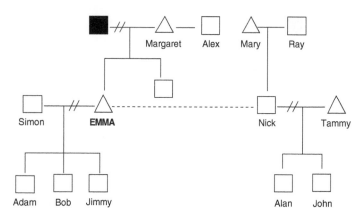

Diagram 7.2   Emma

John. While, according to Emma, Mary and Ray made a clear effort to be 'fair' to all the children when they were together, in reality Alan and John were 'special'. They were the ones Mary and Ray came to see; they were the ones to be taken out to the pantomime, an adventure park or on other trips. While there are obvious difficulties of managing five young children at once, this was indicative of the different attachments which Mary and Ray had to the children. Such differences in treatment were understood and accepted, even though Emma's own children at times feel left out.

Maureen

Maureen was in her 60s and had been widowed for 10 years. She had three sons, Graham, 36, and twins, Donald and Alan, 33. Graham was also interviewed as part of this study. Graham married Veronica two years ago. They have an infant son, Charles. Veronica had 2 children from a previous marriage, Claire, 11, and James, 7, who lived with Graham and Veronica (see Diagram 7.3). These children had no contact with their natural father and Graham planned to adopt them. Alan was not married and had no children. Maureen's third son, Donald, married Steffi and now lived in London with her and her two daughters from a previous marriage. Maureen disapproved of this marriage and since the wedding had had no contact with Donald or his family. She knew his stepdaughters were now in their late teens, but had never met them and claimed not to know their names. Maureen herself had been in a committed 'living-apart-together' relationship with Michael for six years.

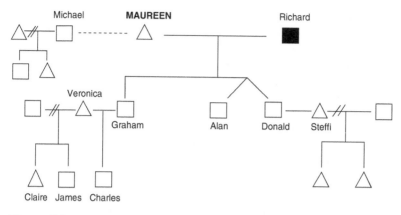

Diagram 7.3 Maureen

Though she spent each weekend with Michael, she had no significant involvement with his children; nor was Michael involved to any significant fashion in the lives of her children.

Maureen, who lived some 50 miles from Graham, visited him and his family most weekends on her way to stay with her partner, Michael, who lived some 10 miles from Graham and his family. According to both Maureen and Graham, Maureen had a wide range of interests and led an independent life. She said that while Charles, her baby grandson, was 'gorgeous' and she 'loved him to bits', she had felt no strong desire to be a grandmother and had 'got things going on in my life ... you know I'm not wrapped up in my family'. In discussing her relationship with her stepgrandchildren, Claire and James, she said 'Well I like them, yeah. And I think they like me. Yes, we all get on alright together'. It was clear from the interview that Maureen's feelings towards Charles were much stronger than her feelings towards Claire and James. Nonetheless she also believed very strongly that they should all be treated the same: 'I would never differentiate. You couldn't do that.' In his interview, Graham also emphasised how fair his mother was towards the three children in the family.

A sense of kinship?

As these examples indicate, the specific circumstances in which different stepgrandparental relationships develop structure their patterning (Attias-Donfut and Segalen, 2002). However, the extent to which the stepgrandparents are involved in the family/child's life at a young age appears to be of particular importance. Numerous factors can bear on this, including the age of the children when the stepfamily was formed, which parent they live with and the proximity of the stepgrand-parents. The 'demography' of grandparenting may also have an impact on stepgrandparental relationships. For example, the number of natural grandchildren the stepgrandparents have, whether any of these grand-children live in the same household as the stepgrandchildren and the role the stepgrandchildren's natural grandparents play in their lives can all influence the ways that stepgrandparental relationships develop. Overall though, it is the quality of the relationships sustained between the different members of the stepfamily that seems to have the most impact on the character of stepgrandparent/stepgrandchild ties. The key relational constellations here are between the stepgrandparent(s), their child and their child's partner, and between the stepchild, his or her natural parent and the step-parent (Ganong et al., 1998; Schmeeckle et al., 2006).

The most extreme example above of this was Maureen's relationships with her son, Donald, and his partner Steffi. Their absence of involve-ment also meant that there was no relationship between Maureen and Steffi's daughters from her previous marriage. Equally though, the limited contact Emma had with her mother and stepfather resulted in there being virtually no recognition of a relationship between Emma's step-children and her mother. Both these cases are somewhat extreme in that both are consequent on significant difficulties in the grandparent/parent relationship. Natalie's relationship with her stepgrandparent, Jean, was more typical. There was no marked conflict between the generations here, though as mentioned in Chapter 5, Natalie was not especially fond of her stepmother, Moira. Nonetheless the relationship between Natalie and Jean was of little significance. As Natalie said, there were no problems on the occasions when they met. They even greeted each other with a conventional, if rather meaningless, kiss. But equally there was no solidarity between them and no sense of shared heritage. They remained two individuals brought together through their connections to their father and daughter respectively.

Natalie's relationship with Jean was very similar to Mark Burton's relationship with his stepgrandmother, Barbara. As will be recalled from the discussions in Chapters 3 and 5, Mark had very strong stepgrand-parental relationships with his stepfather's parents (see later in this chapter), but a rather insignificant relationship with his stepmother's mother. Like Natalie and Jean, they met on occasion, usually family ceremonies of one sort or another, but, according to Mark, did not feel any sense of personal solidarity. In this, Mark's relationship with Barbara was influenced by the patterning of his relationships with his father and stepmother. His relative lack of involvement in their domestic lives resulted in his having little contact with Barbara.

Despite the individual differences there are within such relationships, Natalie's and Mark's relationships with their respective stepmothers reflect the generality of Type 1 stepgrandparental relationships. Before analysing this in more depth, it is worth highlighting a key aspect of Natalie's relationship with her stepgrandmother, Jean, that has wider implications. Natalie's father had married her stepmother, Moira, when Natalie was 25. Natalie had by then left her father's home and was living independently. Her ensuing relationship with Moira's mother, Jean, was characteristic of those stepgrandparental relationships which were formed after the stepgrandchild had become adult. Typically these relationships are defined by those involved as incidental. In other words, when a parent repartnered after the child had left home, cordial though the ensuing relationships with that partner's parents may be, they are not normally conceived of as falling within a grandparent–grandchild remit. These are people related to the parent's/child's new partner, but no fuller commitment follows from this. Indeed in general this also applies if the stepgrandchild was older than his or her early teens when the step relationship started, as was the case with Mark.

In contrast, when a child is still dependent at the time a parent forms a new partnership, the relationship between the new partner's parents and the stepgrandchild may come to be framed in a more 'family relevant' way. Even here though there is considerable variation, in part shaped by issues of residence and the patterns of involvement that emerge between the stepgrandparent(s) and the members of the child's stepfamily household. Indeed just as it is generally necessary for the stepgrandchild to be a child in age for any sense of family connection to emerge, so too the child usually needs to be part of the step-parent's household if the stepgrandparents are to be seen as in any way comparable to natural grandparents (Cherlin and Furstenberg, 1994). But again, even in these circumstances, it does not necessarily follow that the ensuing relationship develops in this way. Nonetheless, where the child and step-parent do share a home, there is a greater likelihood of the stepgrandparent/stepgrandchild tie being structured in ways analogous to natural grandparental solidarities.

On reflection, it is hardly surprising that young children not living in the same household as their step-parent develop comparatively little family connection with that step-parent's parents, especially if there are no half-siblings living in the household. Even if the child visits the household frequently, the family practices that typically emerge in these circumstances tend to militate against the development of strong bonds between stepgrandparents and the stepgrandchildren. Indeed, generally they do not even meet that frequently. Mainly this is because contact between the step-parent and his or her parents is generally organised so as to avoid overlap with any periods the children are spending with their non-resident parent. In other words, the time a non-resident parent has with their children is usually set aside for servicing and sustaining the parent–child relationship. If family ties outside the household are to be involved during these contact periods, precedence would normally be given to the natural grandparents (or other relatives) on the non-resident parent's side rather than to the stepgrandparents (or other stepkin).

Resident stepgrandchildren

As a consequence, only a subset of Type 1 stepgrandparent/stepgrandchild ties are really considered pertinent to the kinship domain: those cases where the stepchild is young and living in the household with their step-parent at the time the stepfamily was formed. However, even within these parameters, stepgrandparents and stepgrandchildren are generally aware of difference; only rarely do they define their relationship as wholly equivalent to natural grandparenthood. Indeed in our sample, instances of Type 1 stepgrandparent/stepgrandchild ties being construed in this way arose only when a step-parent had taken on significant parental responsibility for infants or young children, often combined with the birth of half-siblings/natural grandchildren. Where these two conditions were met, the distinction between being a stepgrandparent and a natural grandparent tended to carry less relevance within the context of that family's routine kinship practices. To different extents the grandparents became grandparental figures for all the children in the household.

The most obvious example of this was Mark Baldwin's relationship with his stepfather's parents, Grandma and Grandpa (see Chapter 3). Mark regarded them in the same way he regarded his natural grandparents. They had been important figures throughout his life and at the time of the interview he remained very close to them. Indeed, as reported in Chapter 3, Grandpa had rung him to make arrangements to go out during the interview itself. Mark's commitment and sense of kinship to them can be understood as a direct consequence of their being so fully integrated into the routine 'Wellington' family practices constructed by Mark, his mother, stepfather and half-siblings. As we have indicated though, among our respondents, Mark's relationship with his stepgrandparents Grandpa and Grandma was exceptional. In other cases there was recognition of a grandparental relationship, but this was tempered more by a sense of difference between natural and step connections. The case of Maureen's relationships with Claire, James and Charles discussed earlier in this chapter was a good example of this, as was the case reported by Emma about of the way Mary and Ray treated their grandchildren and stepgrandchildren. The relationship between Sandie Noonan's daughter, Reb, and her stepgrandfather Stan, discussed in Chapter 3, also illustrates how stepgrandparents who are more fully integrated into the routine of their child's (the step-parent's) family and domestic life come to be more clearly identified as occupying a 'grandparental' position.

Differences in the commitment and solidarity expressed in natural and step grandparental relationships seem to generate few difficulties. The idea that natural grandparents and grandchildren have a closer, more significant relationship than stepgrandparents and stepgrandchildren is accepted as normal and appropriate. Certainly in our interviews there was little evidence that these different commitments caused much family stress or tension. Such differences were not seen as problematic; they reflected cultural expectations about natural grandparents' involvement with and interest in their grandchildren that did not apply to stepgrandparents.

At the same time though there was also normative acceptance that children, as children, should be treated 'fairly'. This generally did not lead to many concerns when grandparents had natural grandchildren in one household and stepgrandchildren in another. However, questions of fairness became more of a concern when grandparents had natural and step grandchildren in the same household, though often it was unclear exactly what constituted 'fairness' or how this should be managed. According to the respondents' accounts, some grandparents tried to make a conscious effort to *treat* all their 'grandchildren' similarly, though it was usually recognised that they *felt* differently about their natural grandchildren. Maureen, above, captured this well when she explicitly said that she 'would never differentiate. You couldn't do that', yet clearly felt a stronger attachment to Charles, her natural grandchild, than to her stepgrandchildren, Claire and James.

Other grandparents were reported more openly as treating natural grandchildren differently from their stepgrandchildren, but this was found acceptable by the respondents, sometimes being justified in terms of the role the stepgrandchildren's other (natural) grandparents were playing in their lives. This in turn was often linked to the continuing involvement of the non-resident parent in the children's lives. To put this the other way around, when a resident step-parent takes on a full parenting role, that step-parent's parents are more likely to be involved in the stepchild(ren)'s lives as active grandparents than when this is not the case. As illustrated in the case examples of Emma and Maureen above, this is in part a result of their routine involvement in the 'doing' of their son's or daughter's family and their desire to support their child in this project – the construction of what Burgoyne and Clark (1984) termed an 'ordinary family life'. Additionally though, as again evident in the examples of Emma and Maureen, where the stepgrandparents also have natural grandchildren in the household – perhaps especially half-siblings to the stepgrandchildren – then through their routine integration as grandparents in the family's practices, these grandparents are more likely to construct bonds with their stepgrandchildren that are framed by all involved as 'grandparental'.

At the heart of these issues around grandparental fairness lay a tension between two basic principles, both of which are evident in the examples given earlier. On the one hand, there was the notion that children in a household should be treated equivalently. When they visited they should be welcomed in the same way and get the same treats; so too there should be a balance in the set of gifts they received at Christmas, birthdays and other such occasions. On the other hand, there was the pull of 'blood': a recognition of belonging and similarity; of the diffuse enduring solidarity of 'nature' (Schneider, 1968) which could not be recreated so fully in the purely 'social' tie of step relationships. This was more than just a question of the time in which the relationships had been active. It was a matter of kinship and of belonging. Being a natural grandparent meant a level of connection, interest and emotional attachment that could not easily be forged with other children who were not part of one's 'blood'.

Type 2 stepgrandparents

As identified earlier, there is another route into stepgrandparenthood. This is when a natural grandparent has remarried or otherwise repartnered. We are referring to these relationships as Type 2 stepgrandparental relationships. In our sample we had a number of respondents who were involved in this type of stepgrandparental tie, directly or indirectly, from different generational positions – see Table 7.2.

As with the other grandparental ties we have discussed, there is significant diversity in the patterning of Type 2 stepgrandparental relationships.

Table 7.2 Type 2 Stepgrandparents and stepgrandchildren

Respondents who were	
Stepgrandmothers	6
Stepgrandfathers	6
Stepgranddaughters	5
Stepgrandsons	2
Mothers of stepgrandchildren	20
Fathers of stepgrandchildren	8
Total number of respondents providing data on Type 2 stepgrandparent/ stepgrandchildren relationships	41

Note: Some respondents occupied more than one of these positions

Three general patterns stand out though. First, there are those Type 2 stepgrandparental relationships which are extremely limited in terms of contact and involvement. Generally these are a consequence of a poor relationship existing between the parent and grandparent following the divorce in the first generation. In particular, when fathers had little contact with their children after separation, usually neither they nor their new partners (the Type 2 stepgrandparents at issue here) were active in their grandchildren's lives. Their separation had resulted in the effective ending of their parenting relationship, and consequently they were uninvolved as grandparents. In turn, their new partner was also inconsequential in these grandchildren's lives. At times, especially where there had been little geographical mobility, there may be some knowledge about these grandparents, and even occasional chance meetings, but neither the natural grandparent nor the stepgrandparent were in any sense active grandparents.

Second, there were a small number of other potential Type 2 stepgrandparental ties in which the relationship was not really defined in grandparental terms. In the main, these arose when a grandparent had remarried or repartnered relatively recently. Here the issue was not a matter of conflict, but more of time for integration into the family network. Indeed generally, as with Type 1 stepgrandparents, if the grandparental repartnering had occurred after the grandchild(ren) were quite young, the relationship tended not to be defined as really a grandparental one. Instead they tended to be framed in partnership rather than grandparental terms. They were a grandparent's partner or spouse rather than being a grandparent in their own right.

In the remaining pattern of Type 2 stepgrandparental relationships – the most common of the three – there was a much fuller recognition of a grandparental bond. These mainly involved remarriages (or repartnerships) that had occurred when the parental generation were still dependent children. The Type 2 stepgrandparent, in other words, had been a step-parent to the parent in question since that parent had been a child. Most markedly, where a stepgrandparent had been a resident step-parent during the parent's own childhood, in effect he or she usually formed part of a grandparental 'package' with the natural grandparent, and were treated more fully as if they were natural grandparents. Even if the step-parent/stepchild relationship had proved problematic in earlier life phases, these step-parents were normally – though not always – assigned the status of honorary natural grandparents, especially from the perspective of the grandchildren. Indeed in some cases the grandchildren were not even very aware that a step relationship existed, especially if the other natural grandparent (that is, their parent's non-resident parent) played no part in their lives. From the stepgrandchild's perspective, the grandparent and stepgrandparent acted as grandparents do: generally visiting together, giving gifts jointly and routinely being referred to in grandparental terms.

Within the sample there was a slight tendency for Type 2 stepgrandparents to be known by a combination of grandparental terminology and name – 'Grandad John' or 'Nana Mary' – rather than by grandparental terminology alone. This seemed at times to reflect a subtle marker of difference between natural and stepgrandparental ties, though it may be emerging as a more common means of differentiating grandparents generally in an era of greater kinship complexity.

Overall, recognition of the kinship relevance of Type 2 stepgrandparents was more routine than with Type 1 stepgrandparents. In part, this is a consequence of time and the extent to which the stepgrandparent had become embedded in the family network. Boundary issues that were likely to have played a significant role in configuring notions of kinship in earlier family phases were now less relevant. Moreover in the third category of Type 2 stepgrandparents, the stepgrandparent was a constant fixture within the familial landscape of the stepgrandchild, and one that had been there throughout their lives. As above, they were likely to be seen as part of the taken-for-granted grandparental 'package'. Over time these same processes will in all likelihood apply to current stepfathers and stepmothers. Even when there are relatively strong boundary issues around kinship recognition between a step-parent and a stepchild, these issues will become less relevant to their routine relationship as the stepchild reaches adulthood, as was discussed in Chapters

5 and 6. This becomes even more the case with the birth of the third generation. In most cases, though not all, the presence of the child is liable to provide a focus for grandparental family practices that readily incorporate the stepgrandparent.

Stepsiblings

The second category of stepkin we want to focus on in this chapter is stepsiblings. As we have noted previously, our sample consisted of individuals with a wide range of stepfamily involvement. In this section we will focus most heavily on those accounts we collected from respondents who were themselves stepsiblings. However we have also paid heed to the accounts provided by other respondents with experience of stepsiblings ties, in particular parents of children who were stepsiblings. In all, there were 23 respondents in the sample who reported having stepsiblings, and a further 19 whose children had stepsiblings. As a consequence of focussing principally on stepsiblings' own accounts of their relationships, the emphasis in this section is on the character of stepsibling relationships in adulthood rather than childhood. This is appropriate given our focus in this chapter is on stepfamily kinship solidarities. As an aside, it is perhaps also worth emphasising that we are concerned here with *stepsiblings*, not *half-siblings* (that is, those siblings with a natural parent in common). We collected various accounts of relationships between half-siblings, but of themselves these are not pertinent to our focus here.

As we have been arguing throughout this book, each stepfamily has its individual circumstances and history which shape how different relationships within the stepfamily constellation develop. This is certainly true of stepsibling relationships which differ widely in the ways they unfold. Some exist in name only, with knowledge of the existence of stepsiblings but no contact at all. Other ties involve a degree of contact but little solidarity while still others may be much more active. In this, stepsibling relationships as a category are noticeably different from sibling ties. By and large, though with exceptions, sibling ties are characterised by a marked degree of continuity across the life course. That is, these relationships are sustained. The relationships may not be very active, though certainly some are. Nonetheless they endure even where they are relatively low in exchange content, sometimes effectively becoming more central as those involved reach later life (Allan, 1977; Chambers et al., 2009).

This is not the case with stepsibling relationships considered collectively. While the solidarity of siblings can be traced back to their shared upbringing and their common parentage, both of which signify the siblings' joint heritage, stepsiblings only rarely have any such sense of common heritage. To put this a little differently, the social and cultural mechanisms that foster solidarity between siblings are far less likely to apply to stepsiblings. By definition stepsiblings have different sets of parents to one another. Most spend a good deal, if not all, of their formative years in different households, with the majority never living together. They may not even meet that frequently during access visits as these may be arranged to occur at times when the stepsiblings are visiting their own non-resident parent, as discussed above with regard grandparental contact. Moreover, a significant number of stepsiblings are already in late adolescence or adulthood when they first become stepsiblings. Thus the largely unexceptional and taken-for-granted shared histories of childhood experiences that provides the bedrock of continuing solidarity between siblings is noticeably absent from most stepsibling ties. Consider the following three case examples:

Sophie

Sophie was in her early thirties at the time of the interview. She lived alone but had a long-term boyfriend. Her parents had finally divorced when she was in her early teens after what Sophie characterised as a relatively tempestuous marriage. Two years later her father, John, started cohabiting with Harriet, a woman who had two daughters from her previous marriage. John and Harriet's relationship ended some ten years later. Since then John has lived with Anne who had grown-up daughters, Rachel and Liz, from her previous relationship. John and Anne had

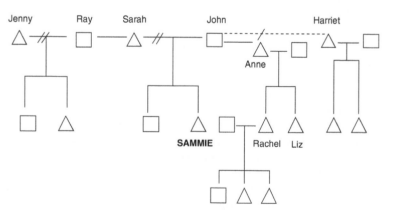

Diagram 7.4 Sophie

married a year before the interview. Sophie's mother Sarah had married Ray when Sophie was at university. Ray had a son and daughter from his earlier marriage, who were also in their early 30s. Thus, as shown in Diagram 7.4, Sophie had three stepsisters and a stepbrother from her parents' current relationships and had had two stepsisters from her father's previous long-term relationship. Her relationships with these different stepsiblings varied considerably.

Sophie reported never having had much of a relationship with Harriet or her two daughters, despite their being of a similar age to Sophie. Once the sisters had left home, Sophie had seen them only rarely when she had been visiting her father. There had been no contact at all with Harriet or either of her daughters after John and Harriet's relationship had ended. Similarly, while Sophie had a strong and positive relationship with her stepfather Ray, she had no relationship with Ray's daughter. According to Sophie, this was because this daughter had had very little contact with Ray since his divorce from her mother, Jenny. Sophie had a more active relationship with Ray's son, though they were not close. They were in occasional contact with each other about family issues through email and Christmas cards but otherwise met only on family occasions involving Ray.

Unlike her tie with Harriet, Sophie had a very positive relationship with Anne: 'Oh, she's lovely, she's far too good for [my father]!' She was also more involved with Anne's daughters, Rachel and Liz, than she had been with Harriet's daughters. Both Rachel and Liz lived close to their mother and were often there when Sophie visited. From Sophie's perspective, John had become quite fully integrated into their lives. She particularly liked Rachel, who was married with three children, but had more difficulty with Liz. She saw Liz as immature and lacking social skills, and as being too demanding of John's good will. 'Maybe there's a bit of sibling, source of sibling rivalry going on here ... . and I was perhaps losing time with my father because he was busy running around [sorting out Liz's problems] or whatever ... So you sort of have to bear with her a bit. Whereas Rachel's lovely.'

Gina

Gina was 27 at the time of the interview. As shown in Diagram 7.5, she had a two-year-old son but now had little contact with the baby's father. Her own mother and father had separated when Gina was 10. Both had remarried when Gina was 14. Her mother, Mary, had married Jim who had also been married previously and had two children who were now in their early thirties. They had lived with their mother after their parents'

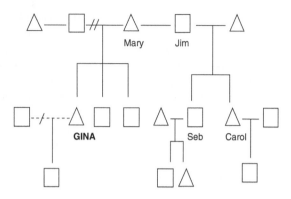

Diagram 7.5   Gina

separation. Gina had lived with her mother and Jim until she left home in her late teens. She described a strong bond with her father though they saw each other only every two or three months. When her baby was born she moved back to live with her mother and Jim for a short while but had recently moved into her own flat a short distance from their house. Gina was close to her mother and relied on her in numerous ways: 'I don't know what I would do without her'. She liked Jim and thought he was very good for her mother. Gina also described numerous ways in which he had been supportive of her (that is, Gina).

Gina reported having not seen Jim's daughter, Carol, for years, saying the main reason for this was that Jim and Carol were not close and did not see each other very often. Gina did see Jim's son, Seb, and his family more frequently, meeting them principally when they visited Jim and Mary. She said she did not have an independent relationship with Seb, but 'if they came to see Jim and I'm around then it's OK'. From Gina's account, such meetings were clearly coincidental rather than organised. She would not go to her mother's and Jim's home just because Seb and his family were visiting. Her relationship with Seb was cordial but of relatively little consequence.

Ruth

Ruth was 43 at the time of the interview. She was single and had no children (see Diagram 7.6). Her parents had separated when she was five, with custody being awarded to her father, Rob. From the age of 7 she lived with him and his new partner, Pam. Until recently she had had little to do with her natural mother who had been quite abusive to her as a child. Pam, an American citizen, had also been married previously

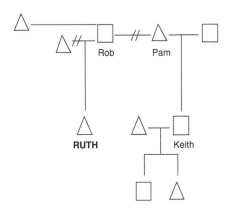

Diagram 7.6 Ruth

and had a son, Keith, who was three years younger than Ruth. Neither Pam nor Keith had any relationship with Keith's father after their separation. Thus from the age of 7, Ruth had lived with her father, Pam and Keith, spending a part of her childhood with them in the US. Pam and Rob had separated about 15 years before the interview took place, with Rob having remarried again.

As briefly discussed in Chapter 5, Ruth made it clear throughout the interview that she thought of Pam as her mother, and still did so even though she now had some contact with her natural mother. She said they spoke on the phone 'all the time'. Similarly she regarded Keith as a brother. She remembered her relationship with Pam had been difficult in the early years, but said that Pam had always treated Keith and her the same. She also said that Pam's parents and Rob's parents had never differentiated between them. Thus although they were technically a stepfamily, this was not how Ruth experienced it. For her, they were just a family. Keith was – and is – her brother. She is aunt to his children. In other words, while Ruth may not see Keith very frequently, she is fully incorporated into his, as well as Pam's, family networks. From her account, they share an enduring solidarity and a common kinship.

Variability and connection

Even in these three examples there is wide variability in stepsibling solidarity. Ruth's relationship with Keith was in all regards equivalent to a sibling tie. She may not now see much of Keith, but her commitment to him was as sustained and broad-ranging as that commonly occurring between natural siblings. In this, it was of course relevant that Ruth and Keith had been brought up in the same household from an early age and that both Ruth's natural mother and Keith's natural father played little part in their childhood. Their new family was one in which issues of differential or permeable family boundaries were of little relevance, so that the tie between Ruth and Keith could evolve through much the same processes as natural sibling bonds develop.

Notwithstanding the degree of diversity within each set, the stepsibling connections developed by Gina and Sophie were clearly quite different from this. Gina's stepsibling ties are the more straightforward. By her own account, she effectively has no relationship with Carol. They never lived together; Carol was adult and independent when the relationship between their parents started; and most importantly, Carol has comparatively little contact with her father, Jim, Gina's stepfather. Most of these factors also apply to Seb, Jim's other child. The main difference is that Seb is in much more regular contact with his father, so that he and Gina also have a relationship. This though is a 'coincidental' relationship. It arises because of their common connection to Jim rather than through any deliberate agency on their part. It is a cordial relationship but not one that contains its own solidarity.

Gina's relationship with Seb represents a common form of stepsibling relationship. In an earlier publication, one of this book's authors coined the phrase 'structured chance' to characterise the processes through which some kinship ties remained active (Allan, 1979). These were relationships in which those involved rarely made deliberate arrangements to meet, but who nonetheless remained connected as a result of established patterns of familial organisation. The most common of these are joint involvement in different forms of family ceremony (weddings, funerals, celebrations like Christmas or major birthdays), and (largely) unplanned and coincidental meetings while visiting intermediary kin. This captures well the interactional basis of Gina's relationship with Seb. While it was cordial, it was one that existed only because of their mutual though independent involvement with the parental couple.

Sophie's relationships with some of her stepsiblings were very similar, though her case illustrates the impact of a somewhat broader set of issues. First, Sophie's set of stepsibling relationships demonstrate well the importance of relational histories as well as circumstance. In particular, the antagonistic history of Ray's separation and divorce from his first wife shaped his lack of involvement with his daughter. Sophie consequently never had much opportunity to build a relationship with this stepsister, though she had some, albeit perfunctory, involvement with

Ray's son. In essence neither of the stepsiblings was ever anything but a peripheral figure within Sophie's personal network. Such accounts of stepsibling relationships where contact between the step-parent and his (or sometimes her) children had ceased were quite regularly reported in the study.

Sophie's relationships with Harriet's children were also shaped by 'external' circumstances, though in addition issues of compatibility and liking played their part. Essentially Sophie had had rather little to do with these two stepsiblings. It was apparent that, unlike Sophie and Ray, Harriet and Sophie had never established a good bond, with the consequence that Sophie had not become actively involved in her father's new household. Indeed, once she was adult, Sophie and her father generally chose to meet in more public places, like pubs or restaurants, rather than at his home. This avoided involvement with Harriet but also meant that Sophie had little contact with Harriet's daughters. As noted above, in the absence of independently established relationships, Sophie had no involvement at all with her stepsiblings (or their mother) after Harriet and her father separated.

Sophie much preferred her father's new partner, Anne, to Harriet. She not only felt Anne was better for her father but also found her a much easier personality. The result was that she now visited her father at home far more frequently, thereby further developing her relationship with Anne. In the process, she had come to know Anne's daughters, in large part because they were close to Anne, both emotionally and geographically. Any time she went to see her father she was likely to see them too. In this way Sophie was much more embedded in Anne's family network than she had been in Harriet's or was in Ray's. Importantly, while neither Rachel nor Liz was seen as a sibling by Sophie, her greater embeddedness meant that she did perceive them in more family-relevant ways than any of her other stepsiblings.

Analytically the issue of embeddedness is important for understanding the character of stepsibling ties generally, just as it is for understanding the relationships between natural siblings. As indicated earlier, sibling ties are typically enduring and involve a diffuse solidarity that is by its nature hard to specify with any precision. Siblings may or may not like each other; they may or may not spend much time together. Their relationships can entail highly varied patterns of exchange and reciprocity. Nonetheless most, though not all, sibling relationships are active at some level and involve a relatively strong sense of family connection. In part, this is a consequence of shared childhood experiences. It is also a manifestation of the symbolism of family as shared blood. In addition though, it is also the result of sibling ties being routinely embedded in a wider network of family relationships. Mundane though this is, such mutual embeddedness in a family network acts to reinforce a sense of commonality.

In other words, the solidarity existing between siblings cannot be understood as just a relationship between two individuals in the way that solidarity between two friends might be. What also colours the patterning of sibling relationships is the impact of the other family relationships in which they are mutually involved (Schmeeckle et al., 2006). Parents in particular are important in this especially in acting as intermediaries, passing news backwards and forwards between the different siblings, co-ordinating visits, keeping them abreast of other family events and the like. Family ceremonies and informal gatherings also serve to connect the siblings, together with their children and partners, as members of a wider collective that share a common identity as family. Overall, such mundane family activities and network involvement constitute important mechanisms through which sibling relationships are sustained, acting alongside whatever personal – that is, individual – connection exists between particular sibling pairs.

The circumstances of stepsibling connection are generally noticeably different. Only rarely are they embedded in family networks to anything like the same degree. The example of Ruth and Keith given above is, of course, here an exception. To begin with, as discussed above, Ruth and Keith did share childhood experiences. They were brought up for the most part in the same household and had parents in common. Effectively neither Ruth's mother nor Keith's father played much part in their lives, leaving Pam and Rob as their shared parents for all practical purposes. Equally though, Ruth and Keith have been embedded in the same family networks throughout their lives. Even though Pam and Rob eventually divorced, in every regard aside from birth, Ruth and Keith experienced much the same family. Across nearly all their life course, they have been treated by all, including each other, in the same way as full siblings are.

As we have argued, this degree of mutual embeddedness in family networks is comparatively unusual among stepsiblings. For most, in adulthood as well as childhood, the routine organisation of family life serves to demarcate rather than integrate their family membership. Obviously for some, there is no overlap because they have no, or else a very limited, relationship with the non-resident parent. The stepsiblings are never involved in each other's family networks. Even in those cases where there is a continuing relationship with the parent and their new partner, family difference between the stepsiblings is implicitly sustained through everyday family practices. For example, while talk between parents and their (adult) children will, as above, embrace discussion of events in other family members' lives, the activities of stepsiblings are unlikely to be central within these. Major news, like new births or job change, may well be passed on, but more mundane chat about stepsiblings usually plays only a small part in their conversations. Similarly when people talk with their other kin – grandparents, siblings, cousins or whatever – news of stepsiblings' activities rarely figures due to the absence of any shared kinship connection.

Importantly, the same logic routinely applies to visits. Whereas parents may arrange for adult siblings to meet at the parents' home, especially if one sibling is visiting from a distance, this is far less common with stepsiblings. Indeed generally, a parent and step-parent couple may well try and keep such visits separate, not for the sake of separation itself, but rather to ensure that those visiting have appropriate time and space. As a result, unless they live locally, the stepsiblings may meet each other only quite rarely, as was the case with Gina and Seb, for example. There is usually a similar segregation of wider kin interactions and visits, with grandparental contact providing an obvious example. As discussed in the first part of this chapter, the grandchildren who are involved when a grandparent visits are much more likely to be natural grandchildren than stepgrandchildren, in adulthood as well as childhood. The outcome of such patterns is that shared kinship involvement between stepsiblings generally continues to be limited. There may be greater involvement of these kin at family ceremonies of different types, but these typically entail cordiality rather than a deeper engagement. Moreover, family festivals like Christmas may be organised so that involvement with the different sets of kin occur on different days – Christmas Day for one set, for example, and Boxing Day for the other.

In such ways as these, the boundaries between stepsiblings in adulthood as well as childhood tend to remain relatively well marked. When adult stepsiblings interact – and of course not all do – their relationships are likely to be cordial, but only rarely will they perceive each other as part of their family. They typically remain embedded in different family networks. Their relationships are based upon family connection, but that connection is indirect and not cemented through the range of family and kinship practices that effectively support natural sibling ties. Within our sample, there were certainly cases where stepsibling relationships were important within people's personal networks – including one case where a stepsister had even been chosen as a birthing partner – and other cases where there was a strong element of family embeddedness. But such cases were rare. The stepsibling relationships outlined in the example of Sophie above are more typical of the range of solidarities that usually develop between stepsiblings, especially among stepsiblings who had not shared a household in childhood. In terms of family unity, markers of difference – implicit and explicit – are generally more evident than markers of similarity.

Conclusion

In this chapter we have been concerned with the extent to which stepkin regard each other as members of their own kinship. In particular we have examined the character of stepgrandparent and stepsibling relationships. We have argued that the social organisation of family practices within stepfamilies generally makes it unlikely that stepkin will think of each other as family. It is much more likely that they will see their connection as based upon overlapping family networks, but this of itself does not usually generate any strong sense of shared family commitment. Relationships are usually cordial, but in many cases they are of little consequence. They are understood as incidental and mediated through the separate connection each of them has to the repartnered couple.

This was evident in our discussion of most Type 1 stepgrandparental relationships, especially where the intermediate step-parent was non-resident. To differing degrees these people were known, but the relationships were generally understood to be dependent on circumstances rather than deliberate agency. In the main any interaction there was occurred at family ceremonials or when both happened to be visiting the parental home at the same time. Thus in contrast to natural grandparenthood, these ties were not normally seen as particularly significant or solidaristic. Within the study, there was generally limited interest, minimal recognition of commonality and little personal commitment evident in the ways respondents described these relationships. Similarly most stepsibling ties were seen in a similar light. There was some knowledge, but for most little shared involvement.

However some of these stepkin relationships were much more important than this, usually as a result of a history of significant interaction during childhood. As a result, some Type 1 stepgrandparents and some stepsiblings became far more actively involved with the stepfamily through their routine visits. These people were fully integrated into the routine family practices that developed within the stepfamily. In this sense, they became a more evident part of the family. Similarly the majority of

Type 2 stepgrandparents were integrated into their stepgrandchildren's family routines. In particular, those who had been a resident step-parent when the intermediary parent was a child were normally accepted as part of the grandparental package along with the natural grandparent. Overall though such a sense of commitment and common heritage was absent with most other stepkin. Rather than being rooted in the realm of kinship, most of these ties were seen as essentially peripheral to family, defined as kin of a parent's or child's partner rather than kin of one's own (Simpson, 1998).

8
Conclusion: Change and Continuity

Families are what families do

A key theme of recent family sociology, including this book, is that family life is diverse. Moreover this diversity is itself multifaceted. One consequence of this is that any discussion of '*the* family' reifies the practices that different families generate at different times. In this regard, families are always changing, sometimes slowly, sometimes more radically. As the personal and life course positions of a family's members – however defined – alter, so the patterning of the emergent interactions and the consequent relationships involved change. But equally, as Hareven's (1982) conceptualisation of change highlights, change also occurs historically and not just at the individual or life course level. That is, as different social and economic conditions develop, across time the resultant practices that different families collectively construct generate a new sense of what is acceptable and normal within family life. In this regard, the greater tolerance of diversity now found in the construction of family life reflects a historic shift in understandings of the boundaries between private and public spheres.

But while change is inherent in family life, so too is continuity. At times in our everyday family routines, we are aware of change – young children go to school; older children leave home; marriages and partnerships go through difficult periods, sometimes resulting in separation. But most of the time our family relationships continue today much as they did yesterday, often appearing to become quite highly routinised. So too, even though we are aware that family patterns have altered across the generations, the things we do in families remain essentially similar. In Medick's (1976, p. 295) terms, families continue to 'produce, reproduce and consume', even though the ways they do these things alter in line with changes in the broader social and economic formation. In particular, at an everyday level gender and generational relations appear to have a degree of constancy, even though we can recognise that parental and partnership practices are different from the past.

Indeed paradoxical though it sometimes seems, change and continuity coexist within family life, with some elements more or less radically changing during specific periods while at that same time other elements have a greater constancy. Importantly in the present historic era, the shifts in family life that are occurring do not reflect a move from one type of family form – say the nuclear family – to some other given form. Rather the changes happening encapsulate an increasing diversity in which no particular mode of family is normatively prioritised to a high degree. The nuclear family still exists, though itself is less tightly specified than in the past, but so do lone-parent families, stepfamilies, gay and lesbian families and the like. And of course, within any particular classificatory mode, there is also diversity, with, for example, different lone-parent families or different stepfamilies managing their routines and relationships, that is, their family practices, differently (Crow, 2002, 2008).

As Elizabeth Beck-Gernsheim (2002, p. 8) expresses it, 'The answer to the question "What next after the family?" is thus quite simple: the family!'. Returning to Medick (1976), analytically what matters is how families, whatever their form, construct and modify the processes of production, reproduction and consumption. In this regard families are what families do. And of course they do many things. They perform paid and unpaid labour, they prepare and consume food, they provide each other with love, care and support, they create a shared home life, they socialise in both senses of the term (i.e. socialisation and sociability) and so forth. Of course they do not do all these things as a collective; to differing degrees individuals within families do these things as individuals acting as family members, frequently following generational and gendered scripts. Families also row, fight, fall out, fail to provide support, hurt and disappoint each other; indeed as we have become increasingly aware some family members damage and abuse other family members, systematically or otherwise.

The recognition of increasing diversity in both family form and family practices is thus central for understanding the patterning of contemporary family life. It also highlights the need to recognise two important features of contemporary stepfamilies. The first is that while at times they face quite distinct dilemmas and issues to first-time families, there are also many issues and dilemmas, joys and satisfactions that they experience in common. That is, at one level stepfamilies need to be understood as just families doing what families do. They have a particular demographic form that carries consequences, just as lone-parent, nuclear and other family forms do. But, as with all families, they are mainly occupied in routinely conducting the diverse and generally mundane business that is 'family'. Moreover, as we have pointed out in Chapter 1, stepfamilies are no longer unusual. Indeed, in an interesting disjuncture from normative convention, Michaels (2006, p. 53) argues that 'there is a trend occurring in America in which step-families are becoming the typical American family'. Whether or not this is so, it is certainly the case that in terms of 'family-as-kinship' many of us now have involvement of some sort in stepfamilies.

Second, as we have illustrated in the different case illustrations drawn on in previous chapters, it is just as important to recognise the diversity there is within stepfamily relationships as to recognise it across family forms. There is no given way of being a stepfamily any more than there is a given way of being a nuclear family. The different individual, biographical, familial, social and economic contexts in which stepfamilies 'do' their family shape the family practices which emerge. This is so, of course, both in terms of how stepfamilies construct their ways of being households and how they construct their ways of being kinships. To echo the point above, stepfamilies are just families. This is where Morgan's (1996, 2011) concept of family practices is so useful. The different experiences and agencies of stepfamily members result in diverse ways of organising and conducting family life, just as they do in other family forms. There is no simple uniformity about this. Just as the demographic constitution of families in general has become more flexible, so too the family practices emergent in different stepfamilies similarly reflect diversity.

And equally, the family practices that different stepfamilies generate themselves alter across time. Though at a day-to-day level they may be experienced as routine and unchanging, fluidity is inherent within them. This is most apparent in periods of family fusion and fission – cohabitation, marriage, separation, divorce and child birth for example – but in all families ways of doing family are emergent; routinely renegotiated – generally implicitly but sometimes explicitly – by those involved as their circumstances alter. New patterns of interaction – new family practices – emerge which gradually reframe people's understandings of their family relationships.

Although this perspective has clearly informed the analysis we have presented, we have so far not explicitly focussed on issues of time for understanding stepfamily ties. In this concluding chapter, we will consider how time influences people's experiences of stepfamily relationships, focussing on the dynamics of family and kin connection, solidarity and schism inside and outside the stepfamily household. In doing this, we will quite deliberately revisit a number of the issues that have been key to the analysis we have developed. We will focus on four themes pertinent to stepfamily time, change and continuity: family development; 'special' time; conflict and time; and processes of negotiation. We will conclude by considering shifts in stepfamily kinship across time.

Fresh starts?

From Burgoyne and Clark's (1984) study of remarriage in the 1970s it is possible to distinguish three broad ways in which people in stepfamilies related to their pasts. The first possibility – and by far the commonest in their study – revolved around the idea of making a 'fresh start' through the pursuit of an 'ordinary' family life that left the past behind. The second option involved stepfamilies in which the children were approaching independence. Here there was less a denial or rejection of the past than a temporary toleration of its legacy. The third alternative, which Burgoyne and Clark (1984, p. 193) referred to as the 'progressive' stepfamily, was a more positive celebration of the past in which the boundaries around the stepfamily household were creatively redrawn so as to accommodate the continuation – in suitably modified form – of what are now non-household familial relationships.

When Burgoyne and Clark's research was undertaken, making a 'fresh start' was the obvious route for many newly-formed stepfamilies to take. At the time there were strong normative and institutional pressures upon parents to safeguard what were then understood to be the interests of their children by facilitating the recreation of a nuclear family unit. This entailed the 'replacement' of the 'absent' parent (nearly always the father) through the step-parent taking on a full parenting role in the newly constituted family. Thus the standard expectation was that the non-resident parent would play little or no part in their children's lives once the parents' separated. Indeed there was often encouragement for the step-parent to legally adopt the children involved.

The cultural context has changed significantly in the intervening period. Legislation in the late 1980s and 1990s altered the balance of post-divorce relationships by emphasising the importance for children of maintaining links with their natural parents who no longer lived with them (Smart and Neale, 1999; Ribbens McCarthy, Edwards and

Gillies, 2003). Such a reworking of priorities and the associated move away from 'clean break' divorces can be recognised as making it more difficult for stepfamilies to achieve a 'fresh start' which leaves past problems behind. While for the adults involved there are undoubtedly a number of dilemmas inherent in the emergent 'divorce-extended family' model (Stacey, 1998, p. 61), the dominant understanding of children's best interests now mirrors Gorell Barnes et al.'s (1998, p. 271) view that the pursuit of a 'fresh start' can 'exacerbate the difficulties of the non-resident parent in retaining a caring parental role and also provoke more severe loyalty conflicts in children'.

Mirroring Burgoyne and Clark's (1984) findings, respondents in our own research identified different ways of attempting to organise step-family life in relation to the past. As might be expected in the light of the above comments about the past norm of the 'fresh start', older respondents who had been children in stepfamilies when they were younger reported that they had had little contact with their non-resident parent. From their accounts, it seemed evident that one or both of their parents had decided to make a 'clean break' and to have little or nothing further to do with their previous partner. Usually this happened as a result of separation rather than remarriage, though quite frequently remarriage and the creation of a stepfamily was accompanied by geographical mobility which exacerbated the rift. In a small number of cases the desire to make a 'fresh start' resulted in step-parents putting pressure on the natural parent to make alternative arrangements for the care of the child(ren). Recall here the cases of Denise and Len referred to in Chapter 6. Denise's new stepfather had made very evident his desire that Denise and her brothers should live with their grandparents. Even more graphically, Len, who had been sent to live with his maternal grandparents for the first ten years of his life after his mother repartnered, said, 'My mother and stepfather, they couldn't think for me at all. No way ... No, I was surplus to requirements, most of the time I felt'.

However, the notion of stepfamilies actively making a 'fresh start' was largely absent in our interviews with respondents *currently* living in step-families in which there were young children. For these families, the whole idea of making a 'clean break' with the past was far less prominent. Within contemporary families there is far greater acceptance that non-resident parents have a right to remain actively involved in their children's lives and that this is of benefit to the children concerned. Thus, even in cases where in reality the non-resident parent had little or no contact with the child(ren), the step-parent – usually the stepfather – was at pains to empha-sise that they were a step-parent, not a parent. They quite consciously highlighted the distinction and, even when they were undertaking a lot of 'fathering' tasks, were clear that they were not attempting to replace the natural parent in the child's life. For example, Jeremy, a stepfather of two teenage girls, said,

> I've never suggested that they call me 'dad' although I've never objected when they have. But I don't think it's my place to say 'Look, I'm your dad now' or 'You've got two dads' because I am not their dad. David is.

As we discussed in Chapter 6, the few exceptions to this involved cases where the stepfamily had been formed when the child(ren) had never had any contact with the absent natural parent and/or had been too young to remember any differently. Even in these cases, there was generally agreement that the child should know about their circumstances and not grow up thinking that the step-parent was their natural parent. This contrasted noticeably with the case of one of our older respondents who was only told late in life – in his 50s – that the person he thought of as his natural father was in fact his stepfather, an extreme case of a 'fresh start' through the presentation of a stepfamily as a natural family.

Yet, while there was little evidence of the past being discarded and 'fresh starts' being enacted in contemporary stepfamilies in the sample, this did not mean that these families fully embraced a 'progressive' stepfamily model (Burgoyne and Clark, 1984). Indeed it was clear that many of the adults involved would *for themselves* have liked to have made much more of a fresh start. However, they recognised that this was not feasible, or at least not until the children were older. In other words, there was some degree of tension here between the rights and needs of children and non-resident parents, on the one hand, and the preferences of the couple as a couple, on the other. As a result, the relationships in these families were complex and varied, and at times fraught with difficulty. In line with other research (Simpson, 1998; Smart and Neale, 1999; Ribbens McCarthy, Edwards and Gillies, 2003), many of the parents and step-parents interviewed indicated how much simpler life would be if they did not have to bother with the practical and emotional heritage of previous partnerships. To quote Jeremy again,

> I think that the stepfather can't expect to take over from the father because they've still got a father. I mean sometimes I do wish that they didn't have one – have contact I mean – because it would be easier for us to – we wouldn't have to consider anyone else then.

Because you do have to consider someone else all the time. He's in the frame, even if he's not very active sometimes.

It will be recalled that similar sentiments were expressed by, for example, Louise Buchanan with regard Layla's grandparents in the case illustration presented in Chapter 3 and by Carla and others in Chapter 5. Remember too the striking comments made by Mark Burton, in another of the case illustrations included in Chapter 3. Mark, who had been a stepchild in one of the more clear-cut 'progressive' stepfamilies in our sample, had had frequent and regular contact with his natural father, Michael, throughout his life. Yet, as reported in Chapter 3, at the end of his interview, he remarked with a degree of passion:

> I think you've got to pick one side of the family for being family, you can't have two families I don't think. You've got one group of a family, and the other group are going to be friends ... You've got to put your flag in the – on this level you've got to put your flag in the ground one side.

Overall, managing these networks of extended family relationships was rarely straightforward for any of those involved. They were dependent on goodwill and co-operation which, given their histories, had often come to be in short supply, and so were consequently vulnerable to tension, discord and fragmentation.

Special time

In all families there are times when family solidarity is expressed – and displayed (Finch, 2007) – most clearly. These are occasions in which the family celebrates some special achievement or particular event. They may, like birthdays or Christmas, be rituals of some form or another or they may be more idiosyncratic – a job promotion or examination success, for example. In many regards, stepfamilies are no different. They too construct their own rituals for celebrating events which are, on whatever grounds, seen as particularly noteworthy. At the same time though, stepfamilies *are* different, a point that has been emphasised by numerous researchers. In particular, as discussed at length in Chapter 4, stepfamilies differ because the boundaries of the family are less clear-cut; different loyalties exist and it is sometimes less easy to define the limits of family membership. In some instances family displays are actually displays of division. For example, Freisthler, Svare and Harrison-Jay

(2003) discuss the regrets some stepchildren feel at never having all those they love most in the same place at the same time. Similarly in stepfamilies where relationships have been sustained with the non-resident parent, there is often a tension experienced between 'normal' family celebration and the need to be 'fair' and create an appropriate degree of balance in the involvement of both the natural parents. However there may be little agreement as to what counts as 'fair' or 'balanced' in specific circumstances (Ribbens McCarthy, Edwards and Gillies, 2003).

For many of our respondents with young children, Christmas was a key period in which the complexities of stepfamily life became manifest. Resident parents often bemoaned the need to negotiate and manage Christmas across households, rather than simply being able to do what they wanted. For them, having to orchestrate arrangements and accommodate the wishes of the non-resident parent served, in classic fashion, to highlight the permeability of their family boundaries at a time which was commonly supposed to signify family cohesion. For some this was not a problem. The non-resident parent either played no part in their lives, or else arrangements around Christmas had become routinised in a manner that appeared to suit all involved. For others though, complex arrangements were constructed, with the child spending Christmas Day with one parent/kin group and Boxing Day with the other parent/kin group, sometimes alternating which day was spent where on an annual basis. For some, Christmas had become particularly poignant, in particular when a child went to stay for the whole Christmas period with a geographically distant non-resident parent, leaving the resident parent with a sense of Christmas as incomplete. For example Deb, who was interviewed shortly before Christmas, said that her four children and four stepchildren, were all spending Christmas with their other parents. As Deb said, 'We haven't [got them]. We just found out a couple of weeks ago that we're not actually having them for Christmas. We're gutted.' Interestingly, children's birthdays did not usually seem to generate the same types of issue for our respondents. Indeed the problems that arose at birthdays tended to concern absent, rather than involved, non-resident parents. Not having a birthday recognised through a present or even a card could be upsetting for a child, however unrealistic such a yearning might be.

Access time with the non-resident parent can also represent 'special time' within stepfamilies. In some stepfamilies, this was time which the couple could use to cultivate their own relationship. For the majority though, it was a time of some disruption, as noted above. At the heart of this 'special time' lay the 'special' treatment of children by their non-resident parent. From the latter's perspective, they were usually attempting to ensure that their children enjoyed the limited time they had with them, on occasion exacerbated by the 'McDonalds syndrome' of using commercial provision as a place to interact. Often they wanted to 'spoil' their children a little to make up for all the times they were not there. From the resident parent's (and step-parent's) perspective, though, such 'spoiling' or 'special time' could undermine the family and household order they were attempting to establish. Certainly some respondents complained, at times strongly, that the non-resident parent acted irresponsible. They were free to make it 'party time' when the children were with them, but did not have to concern themselves with the ramifications of such treats or with broader issues of discipline. Nor, from the resident parent's viewpoint, did they have to handle any emotional disruption access visits generated. They could give the child a good time and play the good parent, but then pass her or him back to the resident parent without concern for any aftermath. As Cathy said of her ex-husband,

> I get annoyed when they go over there at weekends. It's a ... well, they're not exactly allowed to do what they like but it is much more relaxed. I don't think their father sees it as him being responsible for them. I get cross because Charlotte will ring here to ask 'Can I do such-and-such?' and I think 'Well, he is your dad. It could be up to him, ask him'. And I get annoyed and I think that there are things that he doesn't ... I mean, he doesn't seem to think that he's responsible for bringing them up as well. He doesn't think about what they should be allowed to do or not allowed to do. But he doesn't think like that. He's just got them for the weekend and it's more like he's an auntie or an uncle – so that annoys me, but then lots of things do [laughs].

Time and conflict

Literature on stepfamilies often highlights the potential conflicts that arise as a result of their greater complexity and the uncertainty there is over what the appropriate 'rules' governing them are. The fluid character of stepfamilies produces a complex situation in which there are competing interests and conflicting expectations. However it is important to recognise that conflict – and, for that matter, harmony – in relationships has a time dimension (Cherlin & Furstenberg, 1994; Stewart, 2005b).

In some relationships conflict is endemic; the relationship starts badly, for whatever reason, and changes little, often despite the efforts of others to fashion a peace. In most cases though, relationship trajectories are more variable.

Consequently it is hazardous to venture generalisations about stepfamily dynamics; any effort to specify a standard timescale governing the development of stepfamily relationships is bound to be suspect (Coleman, Ganong and Fine, 2000; Afifi, 2008). As with all family ties, relationships may be characterised by conflict and tension in some phases, but by greater rapport and affinity at other times. Certainly the interviews with our respondents contained a good deal of evidence of the character of particular stepfamily relationships changing over time. A similar message comes from Baxter, Braithwaite and Nicholson's (1999) research on the 'turning points' of stepfamily development. Their focus was on the extent to which stepfamily members reported 'feeling like a family' during the initial four years of being a stepfamily. They found considerable fluctuation in the trajectories taken by different families, with no single pattern being dominant. In our research, similar processes were reported, sometimes over a much longer period.

As might be expected, conflict between a step-parent and stepchild(ren) was sometimes evident when stepfamily households were first formed, particularly when stepchildren were approaching adolescence. This could take a number of forms from sullenness to active attempts at sabotage. As stepfamily guidance literature often emphasises, children are likely to experience conflicts of loyalty when the new household is formed. Moreover, there is no reason to assume that they will like the newcomers just because the adults are attracted to one another. As we have reported in earlier chapters, a number of our respondents discussed the difficulties they had experienced – or caused – when a stepfamily was first formed. The most graphic example of this was provided by Lousie Buchanan whose circumstances were discussed in Chapter 3. As might be recalled, Louise recounted how her daughter Ellen had 'welcomed' her stepfather and her stepsister, Layla, into the family by cutting the buttons off her stepfather's suits and poisoning Layla's goldfish with bleach. As Louise remarked somewhat sardonically in the interview, the transition into a new family had not been as easy as she had originally imagined it would be! Yet, expressions of conflict early in stepfamily formation tended not to be dwelt on by our respondents unless it continued longer-term. In general, such conflict appeared to be expected as part of the construction of the new family and was usually handled with a degree of patience and understanding.

Adolescence was a period in which strains appeared to become particularly evident in stepfamilies, especially in stepfamilies which had been relatively recently formed (Felker et al., 2002). It was at this time of emergent independence that the stepchild could most readily assert an unwillingness to follow the 'house rules' and so undermine the construction of a family life based upon notions of unity and co-operation. Moreover where significant conflict arose, it tended to have an impact on all household relationships, generating a degree of tension that could not easily be ignored. On the other hand, later adolescence also tended to reduce any conflict between the resident and non-resident parents because there was less need for mediation. As the child became more independent, so he or she could make their own arrangements for travel and access visiting without these impinging on the other members of the stepfamily to the degree they did when the child was younger.

As significantly, the tension discussed above characterising some relationships between step-parents and stepchildren in later adolescence often diminished when the child became adult. Once out of the household and more independent, the tensions of daily living and adult control dissipated and allowed less intense, and more tolerant, relationships to develop. As discussed in Chapters 5 and 6, at times relationships that had been conflictual in the early phase of the step relationship continued to be viewed in a somewhat critical light in adulthood, though managing these relationships civilly became much easier. But equally, for a small number of stepchildren in the study, adulthood brought with it a shift in their perceptions of their step-parents. They now understood the step-parent's perspective better, were aware of the tensions their adolescent behaviour had generated and were more appreciative of the part the step-parent had played in their lives. Only rarely was overt antagonism between step-parent and stepchild evident in adulthood. As discussed in Chapter 6, this in the main arose as a result of a now adult child perceiving that his or her stepfather was mistreating their mother or otherwise being unfair to her.

Negotiation and the construction of relationships

As discussed in Chapter 2, it has become common for the analysis of family relationships in the context of fluidity and change to be interpreted as one of construction, agency and negotiation. Yet, our respondents' accounts indicate that there are limits to how far negotiation, as normally understood, can be used to explain modification and change in particular stepfamily relationships over time. The concept of 'negotiation' is, of course, a thorny one, open to various interpretations. As Finch and Mason (1993, p. 65) emphasise, 'there is a range of ways in which people can and do negotiate with relatives, and these often contain both implicit and explicit elements'. Equally though, it can be argued that in some situations a focus on 'negotiation' does not capture fully the processes by which stepkin relationships are constructed. In particular, even allowing for the breadth with which Finch and Mason conceptualise the idea of negotiation, there seems to be little scope for active negotiation in situations were one or more of the parties are excluded or exclude themselves, as is the case with 'absent' natural parents who play no further part in their children's lives. Moreover some relationships do not allow negotiation of any sort, with issues being treated as non-negotiable rather than open to debate. In other instances, there may be 'token negotiation' (Dempsey, 1997, p. 203) in which the exercise of their advantage by the more powerful people involved makes the word somewhat euphemistic. It can be argued that Finch and Mason's (1993) categories of 'clear intentions' and 'non-decisions' incorporate these possibilities. But they nonetheless leave some people feeling so marginalised from the process of relationship construction that the concept of 'negotiation' becomes descriptively and analytically questionable.

Often though, especially where there were young children involved in the stepfamily, respondents did identify processes of more explicit negotiation, frequently quite lengthy and complex ones. These referred to both negotiations with others in the stepfamily household and with people outside the household, in particular non-resident stepchildren, non-resident parents and occasionally more distant kin like grandparents. The form these negotiations took varied quite significantly, as Finch and Mason's (1993) analysis suggests, often not being definitive or conclusive. In many ways, they were a continuing aspect of family life, each negotiation being part of an ongoing series responsive to the changes occurring within the family milieus as children became older and as the circumstances of others in the kinship network altered (Baxter, Braithwaite and Nicholson, 1999). With a degree of goodwill and affinity, the processes could be managed, but where there was discord and acrimony such negotiation frequently came to be strongly resented, as we discussed in Chapter 5.

Moreover, 'negotiation' was not always regarded as an appropriate way to resolve the tensions of stepfamilies. Finch and Mason's approach highlights the way in which family members arrive (via different routes) at 'a common understanding' (1993, p. 60), but sometimes it is necessary to make a choice between alternatives rather than to seek a solution which is understandable (let alone acceptable) to everybody. Some people saw it as important to start off as they intended to go on, rather than allowing arrangements to develop in a more negotiated way, though often such views were at least partially rescinded in the light of experience. In other circumstances uneasy compromises existed over arrangements, for example where conflict was avoided only by keeping different elements of stepfamily networks apart, or by following the 'when in Rome' principle to determine the rules applying to children who spent time in different households. Such an uneasy compromise was not regarded as a successful 'negotiation' by those parents whose former partners were seen as undermining their efforts to provide their children with consistency through having different family orders or through treating access visits as 'party time'.

The point we want to emphasise is that the accounts of how stepfamily life developed which respondents presented contained much else besides evident 'negotiation'. In particular, at times the idea of negotiation seemed too closely aligned to notions of 'rationality', 'interest' and 'strategy' to capture adequately the emotions involved in the changing relationships. Outcomes emerged out of processes of adjustment in which anger, jealousy, frustration, hate, love, guilt, loyalty and altruism figured alongside more calculating states of mind. But as Harris (1990, p. 59) notes of family relationships more widely, 'jealousy, hatred and rivalry are just as much affective relationships as those of amity'.

Other processes were also at work. As indicated above, time itself altered people's understandings of their stepfamily relationships. As people experienced living in a stepfamily, so their expectations altered and became matched to the realities of their lives. Lousie Buchanan, whose circumstances were discussed in Chapter 3, provided a classic example of someone who started off wanting to create an integrated family but who found the different biographies and connections of those involved made this far harder than she had ever imagined. She consequently came to accept a different vision of how her family would be. Similarly Steve Richards, also discussed in Chapter 3, eventually accepted his role was not simply that of his stepchildren's 'father' as he had assumed it would be. He was, like Terry whose case was discussed in Chapter 6, always more peripheral within the stepfamily than he had desired. Recall too the account provided by Gwen in Chapter 5. In the interview she said how she had initially defined one of her key tasks as that of teaching her stepchildren better manners. Not only had she had limited success in this mission, causing a degree of tension in the process, but also once she had her own children she came to realise how unrealistic she had been: 'All this time I thought they were these weird kids, and mine were just the same!'.

Without always being quite so explicit, other respondents also emphasised how over time their attitudes had altered. Indeed, in general our respondents were highly reflexive about their experiences, and it would seem not just as a consequence of being interviewed. Being in a stepfamily was understood to be problematic and thus, in line with the spirit of the age, warranting reflexivity about the relationships entailed. In other words, being part of a stepfamily appeared to encourage a level of 'relationship monitoring' which in turn led, usually gradually, to modifications in the ways relationships were understood. As might be expected, women in the sample were more reflexive about these relationships than men, in line with their greater involvement in the management of domestic relationships. Nonetheless many of the male respondents indicated in their responses that they too engaged in reflexive monitoring of their stepfamily ties. Such reflexivity did not always result in positive reconstructions. New understandings of relationships could also emerge from, and contribute to, deteriorating situations. The point though is that active negotiation was not inevitably involved; relationships altered over time as a result of their own dynamic.

The structure of stepkinship

A major concern of this book has been with stepfamily kinship, and in particular the degree to which people connected through stepkinship come to regard each other as 'family'. The main message, unsurprisingly, has been 'It depends!'. In particular, it depends on context and circumstance, but most importantly it depends on the character of the relationships that develop between those involved. As we have stressed throughout, stepkinship is emergent, constructed by those involved through their interactions (and the interactions of others), and consequently liable to change as the situation and patterns of involvement of the different individuals concerned alter over time. To express this slightly differently, they are framed by – and constituent of – the family practices engaged in by the stepfamily grouping, with family practices themselves altering as time passes and new circumstances arise. Certainly the histories of these relationships are important for understanding their present. But their histories do not set their present; they influence them but do not determine them. While continuity is to be expected, change is always a possibility.

Accepting this, for analytical simplicity we can divide stepkin into three broad categories. The first of these consists of stepkin relationships that are effectively relationships in name only, lacking any interactional content. Typically these are relationships which result from an absent parent's new (or consequent) partnership following separation from the other (natural) parent. Thus an individual whose father – or, occasionally, mother – plays no part in his or her life is extremely unlikely to have any relationship with that parent's later partner. Little, if anything, will be known about these people or about any of their family connections. Thus they lie outside the realm of 'family' from the perspective of the stepchild.

The second category of stepkin relationship involves what can be termed 'mediated' relationships. In these cases, there is a relationship but it has limited content and is principally defined as contingent on the existence of the partnership that creates the step tie. Thus an individual may acknowledge the existence of, say, stepsiblings or stepgrandparents and interact with them in a piecemeal fashion. However the ties themselves are understood simply to be the result of their shared connection to the stepcouple whose relationship provides the rationale for their interactions. So, in these cases, stepsiblings or stepgrandparents may be met when both happen to be visiting the stepcouple or collectively celebrating some event in the latter's lives. But the tie is rarely if ever activated independently of the couple. It is not seen as existing for its own sake but only as a result of the connections both happen to have to the individuals in the stepcouple. These relationships will be recognised as consequent on family connection but will not in any strong sense be defined as 'family' by those in the stepkin relationship.

One way of expressing this is to think of family rituals, especially birthdays. These are times when, to draw on Finch's (2007) concept, families are 'displayed'. Birthday celebrations often involve bringing together those people who are most clearly recognised as 'family', sometimes with friends and other such non-family, sometimes not. For example when a stepfather has a birthday celebration, those involved could easily include his natural children, his parents and his stepchildren – those who are recognised by him and others as his family, whether as 'family-as-household' or 'family-as-kinship'. However it does not follow that those stepkin involved in the celebration (i.e. stepchildren, stepsiblings and stepgrandparents) also regard each other as family. Indeed for those stepkin relationships fitting into this second 'mediated' category, this is unlikely to be the case. Rather the birthday celebration will be an instance of the sort of contingent interaction that characterises the understanding they have of the basis of their relationships with these stepkin. It is possible that over time relationships in this second category will change and come to be recognised as more evidently family ones, but in most instances, this appears not to happen. It is more likely that these ties will continue to be seen as contingent and incidental.

It is normally only the third category of stepkin relationships which are defined by those involved to be 'family'. As we saw in Chapter 7, this category is relatively uncommon, generally including only kin of a step-parent who has taken on a full parental role in a young stepchild's upbringing. In these cases, the kin of the step-parent are much more likely than in other stepfamily circumstances to be incorporated into the stepchild's life. As a result they are also more likely to recognise each other as family. Drawing on birthday celebrations again as a mode of family display in which family membership is made apparent, it is much more likely that these stepkin will be part of the stepchild's own birthday celebrations than it is with the second category of stepkin relationships just considered. Unlike those in the second category, these stepkin, perhaps most typically though not only the step-parent's parents, will be incorporated into family routines, involved in different family practices and generally be defined by all as self-evidently 'family relevant'.

Importantly, this sense of family connection between such stepkin as stepgrandparents, stepaunts and stepsiblings is dependent not solely on the character of individual relationships and their histories, but also on the character of the wider set of relationships within the family/ stepfamily network. That is, the recognition of shared family member-ship is generated through those in the (step)family network collectively coming to share this perception and treating one another as family. As we have indicated, the starting point in these cases is generally the full parenting role taken on by the step-parent. As this happens, so others in the step-parent's kinship come to be more fully integrated into the step-child's life. The case of Mark Burton presented in Chapter 3 illustrates these processes extremely well.

In conclusion, there is no simple uniformity in patterns of wider stepkinship. However, as suggested in this section, we can categorise different levels of family involvement. Within each category there often seem to be strong continuities. Once set, the patterns that are gener-ated continue to frame the nature of the relationships. Much seems to depend on the extent to which people are incorporated into relatively active family networks from an early stage. Without this, the relevance of the stepkin connection is usually limited. Such continuity in stepkin relationships though highlights the constructed character of family ties generally, and of stepfamily relationships more specifically. It is through mundane family interactions and shared family practices that a sense of family is generated. Without that mundane sharing of family-relevant experiences, stepkin relationships generally remain somewhat peripheral within people's constructions of family; with it, the potential for new, 'progressive' forms of family remains on the agenda.

Appendix
Research Methods

Our research study consisted of interviews with 80 respondents, conducted between 1998 and 2000. Initially we sought to contact people in stepfamilies through circulating questionnaires to households in three different electoral wards in southern Hampshire with different socio-economic characteristics. These questionnaires were intended both to inform us of which households contained people in stepfamilies and to indicate willingness to be interviewed. Unfortunately this strategy proved to be largely unproductive. One problem was the low response rate to our initial questionnaires. Having selected appropriate localities for the study, we circulated questionnaires to households in the first area. Few responded, and many that did, wrote to tell us that neither they nor any of their kin were members of stepfamilies. As a result, we modified our procedures. First, we framed our initial approach to households in the form of a letter. Second, rather than asking people to respond to us by post, we said that we would call at the households shortly after the letter arrived. While this approach was more successful, it still resulted in few positive responses. Apart from difficulties of finding people in, it was evident that some of those we had written to did not welcome personal callers.

Other stepfamily researchers in the UK have also reported having difficulties obtaining samples of stepfamily respondents, including Burgoyne and Clark (1984), Bornat and her colleagues (1999) and Ribbens McCarthy, Edwards and Gillies (2003), notwithstanding growth over time in the number and social acceptability of stepfamilies. At this stage, we had conducted pilot interviews with people with experience of stepfamilies through snowballing techniques using third parties as intermediaries. This had proved a much more effective method of obtaining respondents. As it appeared we might be unable to generate a sample in time using our intended procedures, we made the decision to incorporate snowballing techniques within our main study.

At the same time we further modified our approach to households in our selected localities. Instead of personally calling at people's home, we approached them by telephone. While this meant we could send letters only to people listed in the telephone directory, it proved to be a far more successful strategy. While the majority of people were initially reluctant to participate, engaging them on the telephone enabled their kin circumstances to be explored more fully. As a result, we were often able to establish that they did have kinship experiences pertinent to our study and, simultaneously, allay any concerns they had about being interviewed.

Ultimately, we achieved a sample of 64 respondents through this combination of electoral register approaches and snowballing, 34 through the letters and phone calls to people living in the selected areas and 30 through snowballing procedures. As part of our initial design, we had planned to interview others in our respondents' family networks in order to examine how different people within the same network understood their stepfamily relationships. This also proved to be more problematic than we had recognised. At the end of many of the interviews, it was difficult to ask respondents who had disclosed quite detailed and personal information to us whether we could approach the people they had been discussing. Partly this was a matter of confidentiality, but it also implied a questioning of the accuracy of the accounts they had provided which, in the context of the interview, often seemed inappropriate. However we were able to conduct a further 16 interviews. Five of those interviewed as a result of the letters we sent introduced us to a further seven respondents who had a kin (or stepkin) connection to them, while seven of those initially snowballed introduced us a further nine of their kin. (In addition two siblings both lived in our selected areas and agreed independently to be interviewed in response to our letter.)

Consequently our sample comprised 80 respondents, 30 of whom were 'linked' to one another. The 30 respondents who had a kinship link to at least one other respondent in the sample comprised members of 13 separate kin groupings. There were 11 dyads – 5 married or cohabiting couples; 3 parent/child or step-parent/stepchild dyads; and 3 sibling, sibling-in-law or half-sibling dyads. There were also 2 sets of four 'linked' respondents, involving different constellations of family (and ex-family) ties.

Our intention was to generate a sample of respondents which reflected a range of socio-economic circumstances. In broad terms we were successful in this. We were less successful in obtaining an equal spread between male and female respondents. Family and kinship issues tended to be defined as more 'women's business'. In common with other studies, men often 'passed us on' to their partners, either when answering the telephone or at the interview stage (Ribbens Mcarthy, Edwards and Gillies, 2003). In 10 cases (5 couples) wives/husbands/partners were both interviewed. The sample did not include any Asian or black respondents; it also included only two respondents who reported being in gay relationships. Table A.1 provides demographic information on our respondents.

Table A.1   Age, gender and marital status of all respondents

Age	Male		Female	
	Married/ cohabiting	Divorced/ single	Married/ cohabiting	Divorced/ single
16–30	3	5	6	7
31–40	5	1	18	2
41–50	2	0	13	1
51–80	6	2	6	3

We were also concerned to achieve a sample of respondents with experience of different positions within stepfamily networks – stepfathers, stepmothers, stepchildren, stepgrandparents, etc. Initially we wanted to achieve a sample stratified by these different positions. In practice, this proved extremely difficult, partly because of the sampling difficulties mentioned above, but more interestingly because of the complexity of contemporary family networks. Some respondents could be identified clearly as, say, a mother in a stepfamily or a stepgrandparent.

Many though had multiple step roles. They were, for example, not just a step-father, but also a stepchild and a stepuncle. The sample thus contained people with a wider range of stepfamily experience than we had initially presumed, an outcome which clearly benefited our analysis.

Given the demographic changes there have been in family life, and particular partnership formation, in recent years, it has become more difficult than it was to decide when a 'stepfamily' is formed. In the past, the key determinant was usually remarriage. The rise of committed long-term cohabitation has altered this. (See the discussion in Stewart, 2007.) In this study we included respondents who were cohabiting provided this was seen as a relationship based on long-term commitment. In practice this was not a difficult issue to resolve as only those who were in a committed relationship defined themselves as members of stepfamilies.

The interviews

The interviews lasted between 60 and 90 minutes. All but seven of the interviews were tape-recorded and then transcribed in full. In seven cases respondents pre-ferred that the interview was not tape-recorded. Notes were taken during these interviews and then written-up as fully as possible immediately afterwards. As noted in Chapter 1, the interviews began with the collection of genealogical data through means of genogram techniques (McGoldrick and Gerson, 1985; McGoldrick, Gerson and Petry, 2008). The genogram was mapped as the respondents discussed their kin relationships, and used to structure the rest of the interview. The advantages of this technique have already been described in Chapter 1. Here it is enough to note that they provided a visual focus for the respondents and the interviewer. They appeared to ease the process of interview-ing for the respondents and through comparison enabled them to convey more readily the characteristics and subtleties of their various kin relationships.

Bibliography

Afifi, T. (2003). '"Feeling Caught" in Stepfamilies: Managing Boundary Turbulence through Appropriate Communication Privacy Rules'. *Journal of Social and Personal Relationships, 20,* 729–55.

Afifi, T. (2008). 'Communication in Stepfamilies: Stressors and Resilience'. In J. Pryor (Ed.), *The International Handbook* of Stepfamilies (pp. 299–320). Hoboken, NJ: John Wiley and Sons.

Allan, G. (1977). 'Sibling Solidarity'. *Journal of Marriage and the Family, 39,* 177–84.

Allan, G. (1979). *A Sociology of Friendship and Kinship.* London: Allen and Unwin.

Allan, G. (1998). 'Friendship and the Private Sphere'. In R. G. Adams and G. Allan (Eds), *Placing Friendship in Context* (pp. 71–91). Cambridge, UK: Cambridge University Press.

Allan, G. and Crow, G. (1989). *Home and Family: Constructing the Domestic Sphere.* Basingstoke: Macmillan.

Allan, G. and Crow, G. (2001). *Families, Households and Society.* Basingstoke: Palgrave Macmillan.

Allan, G., Hawker, S. and Crow, G. (2003). 'Britain's Changing Families'. In M. Coleman and L. Ganong (Eds), *Handbook of Contemporary Families* (pp. 302–16). Thousand Oaks, CA: Sage.

Atkin, B. (2008). 'Legal Structures and Re-Formed Families: The New Zealand Example'. In J. Pryor (Ed.), *The International Handbook of Stepfamilies* (pp. 522–44). Hoboken, NJ: John Wiley and Sons.

Attias-Donfut, C. and Segalen, M. (2002). 'The Construction of Grandparenthood'. *Current Sociology, 50,* 281–94.

Bainham, A. (1999). 'Parentage, Parenthood and Parental Responsibility'. In A. Bainham, S. Sclater and M. Richards (Eds), *What is a Parent? A Socio-Legal Analysis* (pp. 25–46). Oxford: Hart.

Baxter, L. A., Braithwaite, D. and Nicholson, J. (1999). 'Turning Points in the Development of Blended Families'. *Journal of Social and Personal Relationships, 16,* 291–313.

Becher, H. (2008). *Family Practices in South Asian Muslim Families: Parenting in a Multi-Faith Britain.* Basingstoke: Palgrave Macmillan.

Beck, U. and Beck-Gernsheim, E. (1995). *The Normal Chaos of Love.* Cambridge, UK: Polity Press.

Beck-Gernsheim, E. (2002). *Reinventing the Family: In Search of New Lifestyles.* Cambridge: Polity Press.

Berrington, A. (2001). 'Entry into Parenthood and the Outcome of Cohabiting Partnership in Britain'. *Journal of Marriage and Family, 63,* 80.

Berrington, A., Stone, J. and Falkingham, J. (2009). 'The Changing Living Arrangements of Young Adults in the UK'. *Population Trends, 138,* 27–37.

Bornat, J., Dimmock, B., Jones, D. and Peace, S. (1999). 'Stepfamilies and Older People: Evaluating the Implication of Family Change for an Ageing Population'. *Ageing and Society, 19,* 239–61.

Bradshaw, J., Stimson, C., Skinner, C. and Williams, J. (1999). *Absent Fathers?* London: Routledge.

Braithwaite, D., Bach, B., Baxter, L. A., DiVerniero, R., Hammonds, J., Hosek, A., Willer, E. and Wolf, B. (2010). 'Constructing Family: A Typology of Voluntary Kin'. *Journal of Social and Personal Relationships, 27*, 388–407.

Braithwaite, D., Olson, L. N., Golish, T. D., Soukup, C. and Turman, P. (2001). '"Becoming a Family": Developmental Processes Represented in Blended Family Discourse'. *Journal of Applied Communication Research, 29*, 221–47.

Burgoyne, J. and Clark, D. (1984). *Making a Go of It*. London: Routledge and Kegan Paul.

Carling, A., Duncan, S. and Edwards, R. (2002). *Analysing Families: Morality and Rationality in Policy and Practice*. London: Routledge.

Chamberlayne, P., Bornat, J. and Wengraf, T. (2000). *The Turn to Biographical Methods in Social Science: Comparative Issues and Examples*. London: Routledge.

Chambers, P., Allan, G., Phillipson, C. and Ray, M. (2009). *Family Practices in Later Life*. Bristol: Policy Press.

Chandler, J., Williams, M., Maconachie, M., Collett, T. and Dodgeon, B. (2004). 'Living Alone: Its Place in Household Formation and Change'. *Sociological Research Online, 9*.

Cheal, D. (2002). *Sociology of Family Life*. Basingstoke: Palgrave Macmillan.

Cherlin, A. (1978). 'Remarriage as an Incomplete Institution'. *American Journal of Sociology, 84*, 634–50.

Cherlin, A. (2004). 'The Deinstitutionalization of American Marriage'. *Journal of Marriage and the Family, 66*, 848–61.

Cherlin, A. and Furstenberg, F. (1992). *The New American Grandparent*. Cambridge, MA: Harvard University Press.

Cherlin, A. and Furstenberg, F. (1994). 'Stepfamilies in the United States: A Reconsideration'. *American Review of Sociology, 20*, 359–81.

Church, E. (1999). 'Who are the People in your Family? Stepmothers' Diverse Notions of Kinship'. *Journal of Divorce and Remarriage, 31*, 83–105.

Clarke, L., Evandrou, M. and Warr, P. (2005). 'Family and Economic Roles'. In A. Walker (Ed.), *Understanding Quality of Life in Old Age* (pp. 64–83). Maidenhead, UK: Open University Press.

Cohen, A. (1985). *The Symbolic Construction of Community*. London: Tavistock.

Coleman, M., Fine, M., Ganong, L., Downs, K. and Pauk, N. (2001). 'When You're not the Brady Bunch: Identifying Perceived Conflicts and Resolution Strategies in Stepfamilies'. *Personal Relationships, 8*, 55–73.

Coleman, M. and Ganong, L. (1990). 'Remarriage and Stepfamily Research in the 1980s: Increased Interest in an Old Family Form'. *Journal of Marriage and the Family, 52*, 925–40.

Coleman, M., Ganong, L. and Cable, S. M. (1997). 'Beliefs about Women's Intergenerational Family Obligations to Provide Support before and after Divorce and Remarriage'. *Journal of Marriage and the Family, 59*, 165–76.

Coleman, M., Ganong, L. and Fine, M. (2000). 'Reinvestigating Remarriage: Another Decade of Progress'. *Journal of Marriage and the Family, 62*, 1288–307.

Coleman, M., Troilo, J. and Jamison, T. (2008). 'The Diversity of Stepmothers'. In J. Pryor (Ed.), *The International Handbook of Stepfamilies* (pp. 369–93). Hoboken, NJ: John Wiley and Sons.

Crompton, R. (2006). *Employment and the Family: The Reconfiguration of Work and Family Life in Contemporary Societies*. Cambridge: Cambridge University Press.

Crow, G. (2002). *Social Solidarities*. Buckingham: Open University Press.

Crow, G. (2008). 'Thinking about Families and Communities over Time'. In R. Edwards (Ed.), *Researching Families and Communities: Social and Generational Change* (pp. 11–24). London: Routledge.

Davidoff, L. and Hall, C. (1987). *Family Fortunes: Men and Women of the English Middle Class 1780–1850*. London: Hutchinson.

Dempsey, K. (1997). *Inequalities in Marriage: Australia and Beyond*. Melbourne: Oxford University Press.

Dench, G. and Ogg, J. (2002). *Grandparenting in Britain*. London: Institute of Community Studies.

Doodson, L. and Morley, D. (2006). 'Understanding the Roles of Non-Residential Stepmothers'. *Journal of Divorce and Remarriage, 45*, 109–30.

Duncombe, J. and Marsden, D. (1993). 'Love and Intimacy: The Gender Division of Emotion and "Emotion Work"'. *Sociology, 27*, 21–41.

Duran-Aydintug, C. (1993). 'Relationships with Former In-Laws: Normative Guidelines and Actual Behavior'. *Journal of Divorce and Remarriage, 19*, 69–81.

Edwards, R., Gillies, V. and R. McCarthy, J. (1999). 'Biological Parents and Social Families: Legal Discourses and Everyday Understandings of the Position of Step-Parents'. *International Journal of Law, Policy and the Family, 13*, 78–105.

Fast, I. and Cain, A. C. (1966). 'The Stepparent Role: Potential for Disturbances in Family Functioning'. *American Journal of Orthopsychiatry, 36*, 485–91.

Felker, J. A., Fromme, D. K., Arnaut, G. L. and Stoll, B. M. (2002). 'A Qualitative Analysis of Stepfamilies: The Stepparent'. *Journal of Divorce and Remarriage, 38*, 125–42.

Ferguson, N., Douglas, G., Lowe, N., Murch, M. and Robinson, M. (2004). *Grandparenting in Divorced Families*. Brtistol: Policy Press.

Finch, J. (2007). 'Displaying Families'. *Sociology, 41*, 65–81.

Finch, J. (1989). *Family Obligations and Social Change*. Cambridge: Polity Press.

Finch, J. and Mason, J. (1993). *Negotiating Family Responsibilities*. London: Routledge.

Fine, M. A. (1995). 'The Clarity and Content of the Stepparent Role: A Review of the Literature'. *Journal of Divorce and Remarriage, 24*, 19–34.

Firth, R., Hubert, J. and Forge, A. (1970). *Families and Their Relatives*. London: Routledge.

Fischer, T., De Graaf, P. and Kalmijn, M. (2005). 'Friendly and Antagonistic Contact between Former Spouses after Divorce'. *Journal of Family Issues, 26*, 1131–63.

Freisthler, B., Svare, G. M. and Harrison-Jay, S. (2003). 'It was the Best of Times, it was the Worst of Times: Young Adult Stepchildren Talk about Growing up in a Stepfamily'. *Journal of Divorce and Remarriage, 38*, 83–102.

Furstenberg, F. (1980). 'Reflections on Remarriage'. *Journal of Family Issues, 1*, 443–53.

Ganong, L. and Coleman, M. (2004). *Stepfamily Relationships: Development, Dynamics and Interventions*. New York: Kluwer Academic/Plenum Publishers.

Ganong, L., Coleman, M., Fine, M. and Martin, P. (1999). 'Stepparents' Affinity-Seeking and Affinity-Maintaining Strategies with Stepchildren'. *Journal of Family Issues, 20*, 299–327.

Ganong, L., Coleman, M., McDaniel, A. K. and Killian, T. (1998). 'Attitudes Regarding Obligations to Assist an Older Parent or Stepparent Following Later-Life Remarriage'. *Journal of Marriage and the Family, 60,* 595–610.

Giddens, A. (1992). *The Transformation of Intimacy.* Cambridge, UK: Polity Press.

Giles-Sims, J. (1984). 'The Stepparent Role: Expectations, Behavior and Sanctions'. *Journal of Family Issues, 5,* 116–30.

González-López, M. (2002). 'A Portrait of Western Families: New Models of Intimate Relationships and the Timing of Life Events'. In A. Carling, S. Duncan and R. Edwards (Eds), *Analysing Families: Morality and Rationality in Policy and Practice* (pp. 21–47). London: Routledge.

Gorrell Barnes, G., Thompson, P., Daniel, G. and Burchardt, N. (1998). *Growing Up in Stepfamilies.* Oxford: Clarendon Press.

Grint, K. (2005). *The Sociology of Work.* Cambridge: Polity.

Hareven, T. (1982). *Family Time and Industrial Time.* Cambridge: Cambridge University Press.

Harris, C. C. (1990). *Kinship.* Milton Keynes: Open University Press.

Heath, S. and Cleaver, E. (2003). *Young, Free and Single? Twenty-Somethings and Household Change.* Basingstoke, UK: Palgrave Macmillan.

Henry, P. J. and McCue, J. (2009). 'The Experience of Nonresidential Stepmothers'. *Journal of Divorce and Remarriage, 50,* 185–205.

Holdsworth, C. and Morgan, D. H. J. (2005). *Transitions in Context: Leaving Home, Independence and Adulthood.* Maidenhead: Open University Press.

Hughes, C. (1991). *Stepparents: Wicked or Wonderful?* Aldershot: Avebury.

Jacobson, D. (1995). 'Incomplete Institution or Culture Shock: Institutional and Processual Models of Stepfamily Instability'. *Journal of Divorce and Remarriage, 24,* 3–18.

Jamieson, L. (1998). *Intimacy.* Cambridge, UK: Polity Press.

Jamieson, L. (1999). 'Intimacy Transformed? A Critical Look at the "Pure Relationship"'. *Sociology, 33,* 477–94.

Jamieson, L. (2005). 'Boundaries of Intimacy'. In L. McKie and S. Cunningham-Burley (Eds), *Families in Society: Boundaries and Relationships* (pp. 189–206). Bristol: Policy Press.

Jamieson, L., Anderson, M., McCrone, D., Bechhofer, F., Stewart, R. and Yaojun, L. (2002). 'Cohabitation and Commitment: Partnership Plans of Young Men and Women'. *Sociological Review, 50,* 356–77.

Jones, G. (2009). *Youth.* Cambridge: Polity Press.

Kemp, C. L. (2004). '"Grand" Expectations: The Experiences of Grandparents and Adult Grandchildren'. *Canadian Journal of Sociology, 29,* 499–525.

Lewis, J. (2001). *The End of Marriage: Individualism and Intimate Relations.* Cheltenham, UK: Edward Elgar.

Lewis, J. and Kiernan, K. (1996). 'The Boundaries between Marriage, Nonmarriage, and Parenthood: Changes in Behavior and Policy in Postwar Britain'. *Journal of Family History, 21,* 372–87.

MacDonald, W. and DeMaris, A. (1996). 'Parenting Stepchildren and Biological Children'. *Journal of Family Issues, 17,* 5–25.

Malia, S. (2005). 'Balancing Family Members' Interests Regarding Stepparent Rights and Obligations: A Social Policy Challenge'. *Family Relations, 54,* 298–319.

Manning, W. D. and Smock, P. J. (2005). 'Measuring and Modeling Cohabitation: New Perspectives from Qualitative Data'. *Journal of Marriage and Family, 67*, 989–1002.

Mansfield, P. and Collard, J. (1988). *The Beginning of the Rest of Your Life?* Basingstoke: Macmillan.

Mason, J., May, V. and Clarke, L. (2007). 'Ambivalence and the Paradoxes of Grandparenting'. *Sociological Review, 55*, 687–706.

Mason, M. A., Harrison-Jay, S., Svare, G. M. and Wolfinger, N. H. (2002). 'Stepparents: De Facto Parents or Legal Strangers?' *Journal of Family Issues, 23*, 507–22.

McGoldrick, M. and Gerson, R. (1985). *Genograms in Family Assessment*. London: Norton and Co.

McGoldrick, M., Gerson, R. and Petry, S. (2008). *Genograms: Assessment and Intervention*. (vols 3) New York: W. W. Norton and Co.

McKie, L. and Cunningham-Burley, S. (2005). *Families in Society: Boundaries and Relationships*. Bristol: Policy Press.

McKie, L., Cunningham-Burley, S. and McKendrick, J. (2005). 'Families and Relationships: Boundaries and Bridges'. In L. McKie and S. Cunningham-Burley (Eds), *Families in Society: Boundaries and Relationships* (pp. 3–18), Bristol: Policy Press.

Medick, H. (1976). 'The Proto-Industrial Family Economy: The Structural Function of Household and Family during the Transition from Peasant Society to Industrial Capitalism'. *Social History, 1*, 291–315.

Michaels, M. L. (2006). 'Factors that Contribute to Stepfamily Success: A Qualitative Analysis'. *Journal of Divorce and Remarriage, 44*, 53–66.

Minuchin, S. (1977). *Families and Family Therapy*. London: Routledge.

Morgan, D. H. J. (1985). *The Family, Politics and Social Theory*. London: Routledge and Kegan Paul.

Morgan, D. H. J. (1996). *Family Connections*. Cambridge, UK: Polity Press.

Morgan, D. H. J. (1999). 'Risk and Family Practices: Accounting for Change and Fluidity in Family Life'. In E. Silva and C. Smart (Eds), *The New Family?* (pp. 13–30). London: Sage.

Morgan, D. H. J. (2002). 'Sociological Perspectives on the Family'. In A. Carling, S. Duncan and R. Edwards (Eds), *Analysing Families: Morality and Rationality in Policy and Practice* (pp. 147–64). London: Routledge.

Morgan, D. H. J. (2011). *Rethinking Family Practices*. Basingstoke: Palgrave Macmillan.

Nelson, M. (2006). 'Single Mothers "Do" Family'. *Journal of Marriage and the Family, 68*, 781–95.

ONS (2005). *Stepfamilies*. Focus on Families [Online]. Available: http://www.statistics.gov.uk/downloads/theme_compendia/fof2005/families.pdf.

ONS (2009). *Household Projections to 2031, England* [Online]. Available: http://www.communities.gov.uk/documents/statistics/pdf/1172133.pdf.

Orchard, A. L. and Solberg, K. B. (1999). 'Expectations of the Stepmother's Role'. *Journal of Divorce and Remarriage, 31*, 107–23.

Parkin, R. and Stone, L. (2004). *Kinship and Family: An Anthropological Reader*. Oxford: Blackwell.

Parsons, T. (1943). 'The Kinship System of the Contemporary United States'. *American Anthropologist, 45*, 22–38.

Parsons, T. and Bales, R. (1955). *Family: Socialization and Interaction Process.* Glencoe, Ill.: The Free Press.

Pryor, J. (2008). *The International Handbook of Stepfamilies.* Hoboken, NJ: John Wiley and Sons.

Ribbens McCarthy, J., Edwards, R. and Gillies, V. (2003). *Making Families: Moral Tales of Parenting and Step-parenting.* Durham, UK: Sociologypress.

Robinson, M. and Smith, D. (1993). *Step-by-Step: Focus on Stepfamilies.* Hemel Hempstead: Harvester Wheatsheaf.

Sassler, S. (2004). 'The Process of Entering into Cohabiting Unions'. *Journal of Marriage and Family, 66,* 491–505.

Schmeeckle, M., Giarrusso, R., Feng, D. and Bengtson, V. L. (2006). 'What Makes Someone Family? Adult Children's Perceptions of Current and Former Stepparents'. *Journal of Marriage and the Family, 68,* 595–610.

Schneider, D. (1968). *American Kinship: A Cultural Account.* Englewood Cliffs, NJ: Prentice-Hall.

Seymour, J. (2007). 'Treating the Hotel Like a Home: The Contribution of Studying the Single Location Home/Workplace'. *Sociology, 41,* 1097–114.

Silva, E. and Smart, C. (1999a). *The New Family?* London: Sage.

Silva, E. and Smart, C. (1999b). 'The "New" Practices and Politics of Family Life'. In E. Silva and C. Smart (Eds). *The New Family?* (pp. 1–12). London: Sage.

Simpson, B. (1994). 'Bringing the Unclear Family into Focus: Divorce and Re-Marriage in Contemporary Britain'. *Man, 29,* 831–51.

Simpson, B. (1998). *Changing Families.* Oxford: Berg Oxford: Berg.

Smart, C. and Neale, B. (1999). *Family Fragments.* Cambridge: Polity.

Smart, C. (2007). *Personal Life.* Cambridge: Polity.

Stacey, J. (1998). *Brave New Families: Stories of Domestic Upheaval in Late Twentieth Century America.* Berkeley, CA: University of California Press.

Stewart, S. (2005a). 'Boundary Ambiguity in Stepfamilies'. *Journal of Family Issues, 26,* 1002–29.

Stewart, S. (2005b). 'How the Birth of a Child Affects Involvement with Stepchildren'. *Journal of Marriage and the Family, 67,* 461–73.

Stewart, S. (2007). *Brave New Stepfamilies: Diverse Paths Toward Stepfamily Living.* Thousand Oaks, CA: Sage.

Teachman, J. and Tedrow, L. (2008). 'The Demography of Stepfamilies in the United States'. In J. Pryor (Ed.). *The International Handbook of Stepfamilies* (pp. 3–29). Hoboken, NJ: John Wiley and Sons.

Thompson, P. (1999). 'The Role of Grandparents when Parents Part or Die: Some Reflections on the Mythical Decline of the Extended Family'. *Ageing and Society, 19,* 471–503.

Van Eeden-Moorefield, B. and Pasley, K. (2008). 'A Longitudinal Examination of Marital Processes Leading to Instability in Remarriages and Stepfamilies'. In J.Pryor (Ed.), *The International Handbook of Stepfamilies: Policy and Practice in Legal, Research, and Clinical Environments* (pp. 231–49). Hoboken, NJ: Wiley & Sons.

Visher, E. B. and Visher, J. S. (1978). 'Major Areas of Difficulty for Stepparent Couples'. *American Journal of Family Therapy, 6,* 70–80.

Vogt Yuan, A. and Hamilton, H. (2006). 'Stepfather Involvement and Adolescent Well-Being: Do Mothers and Non-Residential Fathers Matter?' *Journal of Family Issues, 27,* 1191–213.

Walker, K. N. and Messinger, L. (1979). 'Remarriage after Divorce: Dissolution and Reconstruction of Family Boundaries'. *Family Process*, 185–92.

Walzer, S. (2004). 'Encountering Oppositions: A Review of Scholarship about Motherhood'. In M. Coleman and L. Ganong (Eds), *Handbook of Contemporary Families: Considering the Past, Contemplating the Future* (pp. 209–23). Thousand Oaks: Sage.

Weaver, S. and Coleman, M. (2005). 'A Mothering but not a Mother Role: A Grounded Theory Study of the Nonresidential Stepmother Role'. *Journal of Social and Personal Relationships, 22*, 477–97.

Weaver, S. and Coleman, M. (2010). 'Caught in the Middle: Mothers in Stepfamilies'. *Journal of Social and Personal Relationships, 27*, 305–26.

Weeks, J., Heaphy, B. and Donovan, C. (2002). *Same Sex Intimacies: Families of Choice and Other Life Experiments*. London: Routledge.

Weston, K. (1991). *Families We Choose: Lesbians, Gays, Kinship*. New York: Columbia University Press.

Whitchurch, G. and Constantine, L. (1993). 'Systems Theory'. In P. Boss, W. Doherty, R. LaRossa, W. Schumm and S. Steinmetz (Eds), *Sourcebook of Family Theories and Methods: A Contextual Approach* (pp. 325–52). New York: Plenum.

Widmer, E. and Jallinoja, R. (2008). *Beyond the Nuclear Family: Families in Configurational Perspective*. Berne: Peter Lang.

Williams, F. (2004). *Rethinking Families*. London: Calouste Gulbenkin Foundation.

Wood, J. (1993). 'Engendered Relations: Interaction, Caring, Power and Responsibility in Intimacy'. In S. Duck (Ed.), *Social Context and Relationships* (pp. 26–54). Newbury Park: Sage.

Index